One Lifetime Is Not Enough

One Lifetime Is Not Enough

*

Zsa Zsa Gabor
assisted by, edited by, and put into proper English by
Wendy Leigh

Delacorte Press

Published by
Delacorte Press
Bantam Doubleday Dell Publishing Group, Inc.
666 Fifth Avenue
New York, New York 10103

Library of Congress Cataloging in Publication Data

Gabor, Zsa Zsa.
One lifetime is not enough/Zsa Zsa Gabor; assisted by, edited by, and put into proper English by Wendy Leigh.
p. cm.
ISBN 0-385-29882-X : $21.00
1. Gabor, Zsa Zsa 2. Entertainers—United States—Biography.
I. Leigh, Wendy, 1950– . II. Title.
PN2287.G33A3 1991
791'.092—dc20
[B] 91-19021
CIP

Interior design by Nancy Field

Manufactured in the United States of America

Published simultaneously in Canada

December 1991

10 9 8 7 6 5 4 3 2 1

RRH

Dedication

To my wonderful mother, Jolie—the most brilliant and wonderful mother anyone could have. To the memory of my father, Vilmos—who all my husbands tried to surpass but never could. To the memory of my second mother, Elizabeth Keleman—who was a complete contrast to Mother and who taught me how to be down-to-earth. To my wonderful daughter, Francesca. To my beautiful sisters, Magda and Eva. And to my husband, Frederick—only we know how we feel about each other.

ONE LIFETIME IS NOT ENOUGH

Prologue

*

El Segundo City Jail, Los Angeles, California, July 28, 1990. 2:00 A.M.

I awake from a dreamless sleep and plunge straight into a nightmare. A fist is smashing relentlessly into the walls of my eight-foot-by-ten-foot cell. The screams of a drunken man in the next cell echo around the room. Then the obscenities begin—obscenities directed at me—Zsa Zsa Gabor, Princess von Anhalt, Duchess of Saxony.

Terrified, I try to block out the noise, the words, and their explicit meaning by pressing my hands tightly against my ears. As I do so, I realize that, for the first time since I am a child, I—who normally sleep naked except for diamond earrings—am not wearing them.

In my dazed state I remember that jewelry is not allowed in jail. Bitterly, I tell myself that my jailers, my fellow prisoners, and the press—usually so favorable to me but now circling the prison like vultures—must have laughed heartily at the sight of the legendary Zsa Zsa Gabor bereft of all her diamonds.

The noise has stopped now and the drunken prisoner has been taken away. But I am cold in my flannel nightgown and can no longer sleep so I toss and turn in my iron cot. I close my eyes and, for a time (from the viewpoint of those who despise me), contemplate the legend of Zsa Zsa Gabor that my enemies have constructed—the legend of the glittering Hungarian heartbreaker (whom they accuse of being older than Methuselah yet still pretending to be seventeen), loved by some of the most illustrious men of our time, married to nine husbands, divorced from eight, in their view, a money-obsessed, diamond-encrusted, featherbrained bitch, who loves men, hates women, goes around slapping policemen, and believes she is a million miles above the law.

Little do my detractors (including Paul Kramer, the policeman I supposedly slapped, and Charles Rubin, the judge who sentenced me to prison) know that I would sacrifice every single diamond I own (or have ever owned, including the forty-carat diamond I once gave back to a millionaire who wanted to marry me) for the life of one of my animals. Little do they know how much I love and respect America and that I would give up everything for the good of my adopted country. That I'm not a spoiled movie star, but a hardworking actress who has made over seventy-five films, hundreds of television appearances, who loves her husband, her mother, her daughter, her sisters, and life itself.

Tears of self-pity begin to well up in my badly made-up eyes (I have used a blunt pencil for want of anything else). Choking back the tears, I sit up, square my shoulders, and talk to myself in the same way that my beloved mother would, had she (perish the thought) been in jail with me: "How can you cry, Zsa Zsa Gabor? You who have been through so much in life, who have escaped the Nazis, outwitted the Communists, defied millionaires and tycoons, captivated movie stars and moguls, and have remained fearless in the face of all manner of intimidation and danger.

"Remember that you are Hungarian, that the blood of Attila the Hun and Genghis Khan courses through your veins, that you belong to a proud nation, a nation of warriors and lovers, of passion and violence, intrigue, and imagination. Don't let this jail, this overblown drama, get the better of you. Remember that you are a Gabor and that, as a Gabor, you are born to survive."

At that moment, my uniquely Hungarian talent for melodrama and self-dramatization (as well as my American penchant for plain old positive thinking) saves me and I suddenly confront the truth. This jail sentence, this whole fracas, is just another episode in the continuing adventures of Zsa Zsa Gabor. I start laughing—laughing at the iron cot, at the prison bars surrounding me, at the coarse flannel nightgown I'm wearing—and, above all, at myself.

Budapest, Hungary, Somewhere in Time

*

MY name is Sari Zsa Zsa Gabor. I am twelve years old and, as a famous Hungarian writer once confided to my mother, destined to flout convention. I am in love and determined that my mother, Jolie, won't discover the truth. I am, as usual, optimistic because my mother is not at home but is currently being manicured at the Ritz Hotel, where once, to her delight, she saw Mrs. Simpson having her nails varnished and the Prince of Wales, the future king of England, kneeling to blow them dry for her afterward. Dazzled by this display of princely devotion, my mother promptly wrote to Buckingham Palace, informing the Prince that, on his return from Hungary, he should consider marrying her tiny daughter Zsa Zsa as soon as she came of age.

Although her hopes were severely dashed by an extremely courteous reply from Buckingham Palace, my mother's goals for me and my sisters were crystal clear. In Budapest, any girl—be she a princess or a beggar—was a pariah unless she married a rich man. Our family was already wealthy, so money was never an issue, but intelligence, power, and achievement definitely were. And my mother had no doubts whatsoever about us girls making the grade. We were born to be special, born to be queens and empresses, to marry the crème de la crème, to personify perfection.

I, however, have very different plans—plans that I intend to put into action that very day. For the object of my affections—a male who far surpassed the Prince of Wales, or anyone else (except my father, Vilmos, of course)—is about to be mine.

I hear footsteps outside the high grilled iron fence surrounding our mansion. Then the sound of the heavy bronze bell. I slip out of the library (where I often curl up under the polished grand piano and cuddle my German shepherd, Lady) and run to meet him. I get there before any of our seventeen servants. He reaches down from a great height and kisses me. And, although I am twelve years old and small, I kiss him back. He leaves without a word.

My mother arrives home, complete with perfectly manicured nails and twelve identical Lanvin dresses (all in different colors), which my love-crossed father has insisted on buying for her, and gasps at me in horror. My entire face is covered in coal. I confess. My great romance, the man who gave me my first kiss, the man who made my infantile heart beat far more quickly than decorum dictated is none other than the man (fourteen years my senior—I've always loved older men) who delivers the coal! Outraged, my mother pronounces, with fury in her voice, "This girl will come to a bad end." A born rebel, I make up my mind then and there to spend the rest of my life proving her wrong.

MY father, Vilmos, was a violent and passionate Hungarian, twenty years older than my mother and ardently in love with her. She, however, had sacrificed her dreams of a stage career to marry him, primarily because she had fallen in love after catching a glimpse of the diamond engagement ring that my father had brought to present to her older sister and decided she wanted to own it herself. Diamonds were a *leitmotif* in our family. My grandmother, Francesca Kende (a woman so elegant that as a child, when I had a fever, she would cure it by prescribing champagne for me) owned the Diamond House, a fashionable jewelry business with branches all over Europe.

For a while, my father ran his own Diamond House in Budapest, but grandmother wrested it back from him when she discovered that he was extending unlimited credit to all the most beautiful girls in Budapest. Grandmother—beautiful in her own right—was extremely chic and talented, and owned an elegant house on the banks of the Danube. But my father wasn't always welcome at Grandmother's house, especially after he had an argument with her during a formal dinner party and pulled off the entire tablecloth (complete with the most delicate porcelain, the most highly polished silver, and the most imposing of candelabra) off the table, flinging everything onto the crimson-and-gold Persian carpet, smashing the china into a thousand pieces. Her blue eyes flashing fire, Grandmother, her voice bristling with firmness, announced, "Never again can this wild man ever come to my house."

Father was, indeed, a wild man. He was what we, in Hungary, call a "big style man"—a gentleman. In my opinion, a gentleman is a man who always knows how to behave—knows when to be violent, when to be gentle, who can be a beast in the bedroom and a gentleman in a restaurant, who always underdresses, and never over- or undertips. Father was always immaculately dressed, changed his shirt three times a day, and even used to surreptitiously steal Mother's best French perfume (which always permeated the house whenever she was home) when the mood took him. Yet he was intensely masculine. Father was all man: passionate and powerful, with an unquenchable temper, insanely jealous, incredibly generous and extremely loving to me.

FROM the start, I was his favorite. My older sister, Magda, we called "the general." Magda was an intellectual, a gifted linguist, and, taking after my paternal grandmother, a natural redhead. My younger sister, Eva, was a born actress, at the age of five already imperiously demanding, "I need time for my beauty sleep," before smothering her arms and hands with rich dollops of cold cream. I was the tomboy, devoted to my dogs and my pet frog, Hans.

Father was bitterly disappointed that I had not been born a boy, but consoled himself by taking me to wrestling matches, prizefights, encouraging me to fence (eventually I was to became Junior Fencing Champion of Hungary), teaching me to play chess, while disgustedly muttering to himself, "She's so plain, I'll make a boy of her." Mother, however, did not agree. She knew all three of us were stars and just bided her time until the world acknowledged our star quality. In the meantime, we watched her in awe, overwhelmed by Mother's allure (an allure that won her a multitude of suitors, inflaming Father even further), her jewelry, the love letters she received from potential admirers (during one dinner actually swallowing a *billet doux* after Father demanded that she disclose the contents), her beauty, and her ability to charm everyone with whom shc camc into contact.

THE family led a life filled with grace and charm. There were vacations at our house on the shores of Lake Balaton, excursions in our Mercedes (the chicest model available—

gray with burgundy leather), parties glittering with beautiful women and dashing men, waltzing together under the flickering light of our crystal chandeliers.

Budapest was a wickedly glamorous city, vibrating with the sound of Gypsy music, infused with the scent of deep purple lilac, the pulsating heart of Hungary, a country whose people spoke a language all their own, the only non-Indo-European language, besides Finnish, in Europe. We belonged to the proud Magyar race, a non-European people possessed of a sizzlingly volatile temperament stemming from our long-ago links to an Asiatic past. We knew we were different and we were proud of it.

AT thirteen, as was the custom in our world, I was dispatched to school in Lausanne, Switzerland. Run by a certain Madame Subilia, the school's population consisted of a number of haughtily aristocratic English girls who found my wild Hungarian ways highly amusing until I won them over by writing naughty rhymes about our hated English teacher. From the start, I luxuriated in having an audience, in making people laugh, in binding them to me by all manner of spells.

That included men. As a baby, so family lore went, I only smiled when a male bent over my baby carriage, gurgling so animatedly that every man instantly wanted to adopt me. As a teenager, I preferred the company of boys to girls, focusing always on the most indifferent male and flirting with him until he became my slave. Even then, I was somewhat of a *femme fatale,* reading French novels secretly and imagining myself as the heroine, swept off my feet by a tall hero exuding machismo (but in actuality resembling my father, with whom I would always be in love), imprisoned in a palace, dressed in cerise silks and chartreuse satins, served by adoring attendants, while spending my days awaiting my lord's pleasure, eating only bonbons (yet not gaining any excess weight). Along the way, I spiced all that highly colored French romanticism with some of the more delicate passages from Father's pornographic books, which Eva and I had found in the library one day when he was out hunting.

After two years, I returned to Budapest, on my summer holiday, now an accomplished young lady, adept at painting (which I love and still enjoy), proficient at dancing, and (I was told) strikingly beautiful, a flirt who was patently ready for men, ready for love, perhaps even for marriage. First, though, my mother entered me into the Miss Hungary contest, which I won, only to be disqualified because I was too young. Distraught over my unjust defeat (and even more upset that she had lost the opportunity to escape from Father's increasingly unreasonable but often understandable jealousy, by claiming the first prize of a trip for us both to Cannes), my mother plunged momentarily into depression until Father consoled us both by sending us to Vienna for a few days, on a journey that altered the course of my entire life.

Everything, as always for me, happened with breathtaking speed: on our first night in Vienna, I was discovered, given a part in an operetta, *The Singing Dream,* had a flirtation with an older man, the German composer Willi Schmidt-Kentner, thus carrying on the pattern I had formulated at twelve by falling for a much older man. The Viennese press raved about my beauty, men threw themselves at my feet, and I reveled in my power. I knew, more than ever, that I wanted to be an actress.

My ambitions crystallized even more strongly one night when I saw the most incredibly beautiful human being I had ever seen in my entire life. She was leaving the Sacher Hotel, one of Vienna's most luxurious hotels. She wore a blue sequined dress, mirroring perfectly her azure blue eyes, a cluster of sparkling diamonds in her raven black hair, which was swept up into the chicest of styles. She was Hedy Lamarr, the Hollywood star, the epitome of sophistication and glamor. Intoxicated as I was by Vienna and my fleeting taste of fame, I fixed the brilliant image of Hedy in my mind forever, knowing somehow that I, Zsa Zsa, would one day equal and even surpass her.

DESPITE attending the Vienna Acting Academy, after three months in Vienna, the prospect of again returning to

Lausanne and Madame Subilia was extremely grim. I longed to escape, to be free, and to run away and go back to Vienna, to Willi, and to take my little Scottie dog, Mishka (at whom father would always scream in rage, "We have too many dogs at home, already—I don't want one more.") back with me. And although my motto in life is "Never complain, never explain," I spent my first week home sulking. Then I remembered Burhan Belge.

Burhan was press director of the foreign ministry of the government of Turkey and I had met him at Grandmother's house many times. He was in his mid-thirties and as animated as a patient in the throes of an appendix attack. Yet his air of sophistication, his dark handsomeness, and his air of mystery intrigued me. Deciding that he belonged in one of my French novels, I set about enchanting him—only to be enchanted *by* him. In his deep voice, Burhan announced, with only a hint of a laugh, "If you were only a little older, I'd buy you from your father for three pounds of coffee and make you one of my harem." My silk bonbon fantasy resurfaced and I listened, entranced, as Burhan gravely continued, "In Turkey, the pashas deigned to love a woman only if her waist size equaled the circumference of her head." That night, alone in my room, I solemnly measured the relevant areas and discovered that I had passed the test.

Now, back in Budapest again, succumbing to impulse (as was my style), I phoned His Excellency, arranged an assignation with him at the Ritz (during which he sipped Scotch and was unfailingly courteous to me), proposed marriage to him, whereupon a rather dazed Mr. Belge accepted. I was fifteen years old and bound for Turkey. The adventure had begun.

A**NKARA** electrified me, enthralled me with its winding streets, golden cupolas, exotic food, and erotic aura of Eastern promise. My new husband, however, was not so promising. Somber and taciturn, a famous man in his own country who was an award-winning author and the former Turkish ambassador to Budapest, he was weighed down by the responsibility of his lofty position. After only a few weeks, my mother's last words (whispered *sotto voce* so my new husband would not hear) as I left Budapest appeared almost prophetic: "Look, my darling, if you marry Burhan it does not have to be forever. You can always come back to me if you don't like him."

Any sadness at our parting had been slightly mitigated by the gift of a bloodred ruby and diamond necklace from both my parents. From Father alone came the gift of a ten-carat round diamond given along with the sentiment, spoken with a tremor in his voice, "My darling, you are so beautiful. You must never accept a smaller diamond from any man." Since then I have done my best to follow his advice.

*

*

*

ALTHOUGH my formal education had long ceased, Ankara became my finishing school and Burhan, the first of many husbands to educate me in the ways of the world. Burhan, as I had correctly sensed on our first meeting, was a man of mystery and power. A graduate of Heidelberg University and Cambridge University, he was a leader of Turkey's nationalist movement, the "Young Turks." Immediately I discovered that our house was a hotbed of conspiracy, revolution, and political intrigue, with dark suggestions that our phone might well be tapped, our letters censored, and our lives under surveillance.

Quickly, I made a new friend, Sir Percy Loraine, the British ambassador and ranking foreign diplomat in Turkey. He and his wife often invited us to their embassy parties, where their butler served us tea and Sir Percy talked of etiquette and protocol, priming me for my role as political wife and one of Ankara's leading hostesses. Soon, our guests included not only ambassadors and obscure foreign dignitaries but such luminaries as General de Gaulle. Some of Burhan's friends, however, were not as desirable as I would have liked.

In those days, before the war, like so many other misguided people, Burhan supported Hitler and Goering. Both my parents were anti-Nazi and I was not afraid to voice the sentiments I had learned from them—wherever and to whomever I wanted. At one official function at the German embassy presided over by Franz von Papen, Hitler's ambassador to Turkey, I boldly announced, "You Germans take all our good food and leave us only the leftovers." There was silence. My husband paled. Von Papen's only response was to smile sinisterly.

Even at fifteen, I wasn't intimidated by anyone or anything. Once, though, at the Russian embassy, I nearly went too far. Even though I was just learning the game, Ambassador Lev Mikhailovich Karakhan continued to play bridge with me. It had been reported to me that when the ambassador was asked why he continued to play bridge with the impudent Madame Belge, he had replied, "Because she has such a delicious décolletage."

That particular night at the embassy, we were served generous portions of beluga caviar, perfect pearls bursting with moisture. Gaily, I announced, "Caviar they have, but bread they don't have, because the Germans already took it from them." Stonily, Karakhan, my one-time admirer, looked at me and, with deliberation, said, "Madame Belge, there are some situations from which even your décolletage will not save you." I stared back, unafraid. Burhan, however, was not amused.

HE took me to London, where he had been invited by the British government to speak at the Royal Institute of International Affairs. There, we met Anthony Eden, who was most gracious to me. It was in London that Burhan (always a contemplative man), listening and understanding the words of Winston Churchill, saw the light, changed his mind about Hitler, and began to speak out bravely against him.

When Burhan lectured at the institute in Chatham House, H. G. Wells, the celebrated English author, was in the audience and invited us to go with him to visit playwright George Bernard Shaw. Shaw impressed me greatly—at a time when a segment of the English aristocracy was pro-Nazi—by denouncing Hitler and saying, "I can't stand the son of a bitch but my wife Charlotte is crazy about him."

Instantly, I put Shaw (with his gray hair, which I, to this day, love on a man) up on a pedestal. However, he soon tumbled down and became mortal when, over dinner, I felt his hand on my thigh and experienced a brief but distinctly Shavian pinch. Sex was suddenly in the air, with Wells shocking Burhan by saying that, on completing a good day's work, his favorite pastime was to have sex.

ALTHOUGH I had been Madame Belge for some months now, sex had not been a part of my marriage. First, I was completely ignorant of the facts of life. My mother, between fittings, balls, and visits to the furrier, had somehow forgotten to tell us the facts of life. Oddly enough, it was Eva, my younger sister, who, when we were babies, one day authoritatively informed me, "I know that a man will hurt you. After all, you are too little and the man is too big. So he can only hurt you."

I hadn't yet had the opportunity to discover whether my little know-it-all sister was right. Our honeymoon night had been spent on the Simplon Express, traveling from Budapest to Ankara. As I was preparing for my wedding night, I realized how far from home I was going and burst into tears. Hugging Mishka, my Scottie, close to me, I curled up in my berth and, with fear in my heart, waited for my husband.

Burhan arrived, took one look at me, with Mishka cradled in my arms, his leg pressed against the sheets of our bed, and bade me good night. Burhan, a devout Moslem, had been repelled by my closeness to a dog—an animal which, in the eyes of his religion, was unclean. As a result, my marriage remained unconsummated and now Madame Burhan Belge, I was nevertheless still a virgin.

I was also bored. My happiest times were when I was not with my august husband, but instead riding my beautiful white Arabian mare, Fatushka, or roaming around the mazelike streets of Ankara, exploring the two-thousand-year-old city, sometimes stopping and dreamily gazing up to a hill high above Ankara on which stood the great pink marble palace of the famed ruler of Turkey, the great demigod Kemal Atatürk. When the legendary hero was in residence, the lights of his palace gleamed brightly, casting a radiant glow over Ankara, and the people below slept peacefully.

As many of the women slept, they dreamed of Atatürk. Burhan, his voice bursting with cynicism, had once read to me from the national paper that, according to their survey, eighty-five percent of Turkish women dreamed of Atatürk. I could quite understand why, because the man whom they called the savior of Turkey was fashioned from the stuff that every woman's dreams were made of.

Atatürk was one of those rare men whom I believe the Lord sent to save their country. A masterly politician and fearless warrior, he was half man, half god, through his almost supernatural power transforming the entire country from feudal state into modern republic, abolishing slavery, polygamy, the turban and the veil, thus freeing women from servitude. Given the name "Gray Wolf" by his legions of followers, he was a man of sudden and terrifying moods, overwhelming, all-powerful.

Now in his early fifties, his sexual exploits were still the talk of Turkey. Legends abounded of his voracious appetites, his virility, his ability to exist on only four hours of sleep a night and to outdrink, outfight, and outlove rivals half his age. He was the conquering hero of his time, the subject of a million tales, with the eyes of his people always upon him, breathlessly tracking his golden path through boudoir and battlefield alike. At home I'd hear assorted whispers about his exploits: "Now he is in Istanbul." "Now he is in a whorehouse." "Now he is in London where he is ordering two dozen silk pajamas from Turnbull and Asser." His palace and his legend dominated Ankara utterly. Soon, too, it began to dominate me.

I'D seen him one night at a restaurant, with a black cloak swirled dramatically over his tuxedo, a man with gray hair, with strange, almost colorless green eyes, impeccably dressed, a man of many moods, a man whose civilized veneer disguised an implacable ruthlessness. At that moment, looking down at the tablecloth as protocol demanded, I remembered the tales I'd heard about him, how he discarded favorite mistresses by adopting them as his daughters, how he'd divorced a beloved wife after she harmlessly asked where he'd been one day, how he considered every woman to be his prey, following his desires with a passion so relentless that he had even once stolen one of Burhan's wives.

Burhan's face had darkened on Kemal Atatürk's entrance. In contrast, however, the face of his brother-in-law, Yakob Kadri, Turkish ambassador to Albania, who was with us that evening, lit up mischievously. Sensing Burhan's discomfort, he whispered to me, "Look at him, look at our Gray Wolf." Defying Burhan, defying convention, defying the beating of my heart and nakedly revealing the fire that had swept into my face, I looked up at the idol of all Turkey. And Atatürk looked back at me as if he had known me for a thousand years. Suddenly, everything seemed inevitable.

LAURENCE OLIVIER once said, "To oneself inside, one is always sixteen with red lips." Well, looking back at my entanglement with Kemal Atatürk, it is difficult for me not to view it with the eyes, and report it in the voice, of the fifteen-year-old I once was, a fifteen-year-old nurtured on French novels, half in love with her flamboyantly dominant father and ripe for romance and intrigue. A butterfly caught in a net woven with hands motivated by a mind far more cynical and wise than her own and whose goal was, for his own intricate reasons, to capture her. To put it simply: I was fifteen and yearning for romance. Atatürk was fifty-one and searching for a romantic accomplice. From the start, we were destined to be deeply compatible.

It began fairly routinely. Every Wednesday, I would go to the Riding Academy, then after my ride drink Turkish coffee in a small antique shop in the heart of old Ankara run by seven Armenian brothers. Fascinated, as always, by beautiful things, I'd wander around the store, trying on ornately bejeweled bracelets, examining engraved swords, and generally whiling a few hours away. This Wednesday, my visit to the shop began as usual with me sipping the rich Turkish coffee and gossiping with the young brothers. Then one of them produced the Hand of Fatima.

The hand was the most beautiful object I had ever seen in my life. Fashioned out of gold—with a diamond cuff—holding one perfect diamond, the truth was that the Hand of Fatima was a precious artifact from Istanbul's famed Museum Vieux Sérail. At the time, however, I didn't know that. All I knew was that Ahmed, one of the brothers, was whispering to me in his gutturally accented voice, "There is a man—a wonderful man—who wants you to have luck throughout your life. He wants nothing from you and he does not wish to harm you. All you have to do is take this silver key to an address I will give you, at four on any afternoon and open the door."

At another age, in another life, I might have been skeptical. Or afraid. But since childhood I have always been superstitious. Even today I am ruled by every superstition under the sun. I believe that if you put a hat on your bed, you will have bad luck forever. I believe that if a black cat crosses your path, you must walk, drive, or ride two steps backward. I believe that if a mirror breaks, you have to go to Paris, stand on the Pont Alexandre III, and throw the pieces over your shoulder into the Seine, or you will have bad luck for the rest of your life. Being superstitious is Hungarian Gypsy. I believe in fate, in good luck and in bad luck. And I always have.

I wanted the Hand of Fatima and I was determined to get it. My second husband, Conrad Hilton, a good judge of character, always maintained, "When you want something, you are like a woman wearing blinkers. Nothing will stop you." He was right. Nothing would stop me. Nothing would frighten me. I waited three days. Then I took the silver key and went to the address somewhere in the back streets of old Ankara.

*

*

I was throbbing with excitement as I opened the large oak door and found myself in a cobblestoned courtyard shaded by an ancient olive tree. The courtyard was filled with white doves. In front of me was a marble staircase with gilded iron banisters. Almost in a hypnotic trance, I went upstairs. And there, in a room in front of me, sat a man in an oversized carved-oak chair, his back to me, smoke from his hookah drifting high above him. Then he spoke, in a deep, beautifully modulated voice. "I knew you couldn't resist it. No woman can resist the combination of diamonds and luck."

Atatürk turned and faced me and I was struck forcibly by his strong resemblance to my father. Realizing that he had waited for me for three days, I knew that he must be angry and that he would want to make me feel the sting of his anger. I didn't have long to wait. "I knew you could be bought by the promise of good luck," he said contemptuously. But I didn't mind, knowing that his pride demanded that he belittle me to repay me for having made him wait.

His anger didn't frighten me. I was used to Father's anger and it excited me. Just as I was about to speak, Atatürk clapped his hands and, as he had orchestrated it, the dancing girls appeared, their multicolored veils floating suggestively in the coolness of the room. As they danced their slow, sensuous dance, wordlessly Atatürk motioned that I sit on the red velvet and copper-colored cushions next to him. Mesmerized, I complied. He offered me his pipe—and, unquestioningly, I took it. Then he passed me a gold-and-emerald-encrusted cup filled with *raki,* a potent drink made partly of anise. I sipped from the cup.

Until now, I have never before revealed what happened next, what happened when Atatürk dismissed the dancing girls and the two of us were alone. Sometimes I think it happened in a dream, sometimes that I was in an opium haze, or a stupor induced by the *raki.* All I know is that that day, Atatürk, the conqueror of Turkey, the idol of a million women and the envy of countless men, took my virginity.

*

*

*

AFTER that, we met regularly every Wednesday afternoon, once I had finished at the Riding Academy. We spent hours together in Atatürk's secret hideaway, locked in each other's arms, while he dazzled me with his sexual prowess and seduced me with his perversion. Atatürk was very wicked. He knew exactly how to please a young girl. On looking back, I think he probably knew how to please every woman, because he was a professional lover, a god, and a king.

I was petrified that Burhan would discover the truth, would find out exactly where I spent my Wednesday afternoons. But he didn't. He didn't discover my infidelity—an infidelity that far transcended sex. For unlike me, Atatürk was not a naive romantic. While I spent most of the time with him in a semi-awake state, a sleepwalker unable to see straight or to focus on reality, Atatürk's mind remained razor sharp.

He would question me ceaselessly about the parties Burhan held for the Young Turks every Tuesday, about the secret meetings held in our house, and about the true allegiance of the ambitious men who visited Burhan, their leader, to talk politics with him. As Atatürk must have known, these men talked quite freely in front of me, revealing their plans and their feelings about the man they called "The Savior of Turkey." And many of them hated him.

So it was that I, Zsa Zsa Gabor of Budapest, Hungary, a

coquettish fifteen-year-old who loved dogs, horses, and the admiration of all around her, held the fate of some of the most powerful men in Turkey in the palm of her delicate little hands. Yet, bewitched as I was by Atatürk, enthralled as I was by his might and grandeur, enraptured as I was by my first passion, a part of me remained alert, guarded, prompting me to offer him snippets of information that would not lead to the death of any of the men who had been guests in our house.

My romance with Atatürk lasted for six months and during that time he used me and I, in my own way, in return used him. I gave him information—harmless though it was. And he gave me lessons in love, in passion, and in intrigue. He also ruined for me every other man I would ever love, or try to love. In Turkey, Atatürk was a god. He was a god and he had loved me. For the rest of my life I would search for another god to eclipse him.

ATATÜRK died in Istanbul on November 10, 1938, at the age of fifty-two, of cirrhosis of the liver. All of Turkey mourned his passing and I felt numb and bereft. At his memorial service, Burhan gave the eulogy. I hid my grief and tried to be a good wife to him. But in my soul I knew that Atatürk's death meant the end of my life in Turkey. The magic had gone, so had the passion. All I had left was drab depression, and the opulence of our life in the *corps diplomatique* did nothing to change my feelings. I began to plan to change my life.

IN the New Year of 1941, my mother rang me in Ankara and, prophetic as always, informed me, "I think it is enough for you in Turkey. Come home." Europe was now being torn apart by war, but in Budapest my family was not yet involved in any upheaval. Mother and Father had divorced, the storminess of their marriage evolving into high passion and intense assignations once the decree had been issued. Eva was already in America, married to Dr. Eric Drimmer, Greta Garbo's doctor, and now being promoted as "the new Madeleine Carroll." Magda was involved with the Portuguese ambassador, a fortuitous stroke of luck that would eventually enable her to save both Mother and Father, although not our beloved grandmother and uncle, who were both slaughtered under mysterious circumstances by the Nazis or the Communists.

TELLING Burhan that I wanted to visit my mother, I left for Budapest. As soon as I got there, I began the fruitless task of begging Mother to leave her boyfriend and come to America with me. Refusing, she changed the subject and asked, "What will you do about your Turk?" With steely determination, I answered, "I will divorce him in America. I don't think it will be difficult because when he finds out I have run away, he will want a divorce. Besides, he has two mistresses and we never consummated the marriage either."

However loveless it had been, my marriage to Burhan had not been a waste of time. I was an Excellency's wife, I'd loved and been loved by Atatürk, and I'd become a woman. There was one further advantage—in the shape of a diplomatic passport—essential in escaping war-ravaged Europe. Initially, I appealed to the German embassy, in particular to a secretary I knew there, a German baron, gray-haired, imposing, and exactly my type.

He invited me for tea at his castle, tried to kiss me, got as far as undoing two buttons of my blouse, realized I wasn't going to sleep with him, and then sat down and started talking to me honestly. Trying to get to Lisbon and from there by boat to America would, in my case, be folly. It would mean crossing German-occupied territory—fatal, given Burhan's recent anti-Axis radio broadcasts. The safest route for me would be via Bulgaria. I listened and acted accordingly.

THE journey took me four months. On February 15, 1941, I left Budapest on the Orient Express with twenty-one pieces of luggage. Before I could say good-bye to Europe forever, the train flew through Hungary and into the center of Sofia, just hours before Hitler's SS marched into the city. All along the route, refugees desperate for shelter in Palestine flocked onto our train—only to be thrown off at the border because Palestine refused to admit them.

Ironically, my journey led me through Ankara and I waited with trepidation during our stop at the station, every second expecting Burhan to appear and drag me home. Not that he would have had an easy time of it because I was set on reaching America, Eva, and freedom. At the station, I noticed British flags flying everywhere, thought longingly for a moment of my mentor, Sir Percy Loraine, and his wife, and asked what was happening. The conductor made some inquiries and told me that the flags were being flown in honor of Sir Anthony Eden, who was in town.

I knew Eden from our London visit and liked and admired him. Fleetingly, I thought of abandoning this sad trainload of weary refugees who were probably doomed to a horrendous fate for the safety and security of my Ankara mansion—a haven where Burhan would welcome me and eradicate my fear of the future. But I knew that I, too, was now a refugee and that I belonged on this train.

The journey was endless. In Baghdad, the authorities didn't believe I was a diplomat's wife, detaining me for a month on suspicion of espionage. From there, I escaped to Basra, Karachi, and then Bombay where, as fate would have it, I met Princess Uma Chatterjee, one of my old friends from Madame Subilia's and another lifetime away.

Finally, Princess Uma and I boarded the S.S. *U.S. Grant.* The voyage took six weeks, during which I caused havoc amid a group of missionaries when, while dancing in the ship's ballroom, my sari unraveled—leaving me nude. The missionaries spent the greater part of their voyage praying for my soul. Had I known what lay ahead of me and the adventures I would encounter in my brave new American world, I might have asked them to pray harder.

AN American banker, Mr. King from New Jersey, a friend of Burhan's whom I'd last seen in Ankara and had wired from along my route, met me from the boat and took me straight to lunch at "21." There, listening to the latest society gossip, although I knew I had begun another life in a country far from home, I lost some of my bewilderment. I learned that today, in the early 1940s, New York was blazing with an excitement generated by an intensely cosmopolitan society.

There was Somerset Maugham, currently staying at the Ritz-Carlton, Emerald Cunard, hidden away at the Ritz in the suite next door to her lover, Sir Thomas Beecham. On the other side of Manhattan, Syrie Maugham was at the Dakota. Cole Porter was at the Waldorf Towers, and Baron Alexis de Rede was at the St. Regis, so was the famous society hostess Lady Elsie Mendl—a woman apparently so iconoclastic that, accompanied by her valet, she took a group of friends to the Automat for dinner and proceeded to deck the tabletop with her own linen and antique silver settings.

Deciding that the image of such grandeur was irresistible, in quest of my own, I invested a portion of my savings on two nights at the Plaza, never dreaming that in the very near future I would one day own it.

IN Los Angeles, Eva was waiting for me and together we spent many hours trying to find ways of convincing Mother (now the belle of Budapest with her boyfriend in tow) and Father to leave Europe. Eva's own marriage to Dr. Drimmer was in trouble and although I stayed with them, Eva and I did our best to spend most of our time away from home.

Remembering that I'd met Mr. and Mrs. Lawrence Copley Thaw in Ankara, I telephoned them and then followed up on their suggestion that I contact Basil and Ouida Rathbone—unaware that the Rathbones were the social stars of Hollywood. They invited me to dinner and, before I knew it, I found myself dining with David Niven, Cary Grant, Igor Stravinsky, Laurence Olivier, Vivien Leigh, and other stars I'd only seen on the silver screen in Budapest.

My English (which I'd learned in Lausanne) made conversation tolerable, but I was relieved when I could stop making conversation and instead dance with the tall distinguished man who had asked me to waltz with him. I thought I recognized him, but I wasn't sure. Then he told me his name was Douglas Fairbanks, Jr. Refusing to be flustered (after all, I had made love to a god) I relaxed a little in Douglas's strong arms and concentrated on my dancing. The entire room, all the stars and the would-be stars, stood still and watched as the great Douglas Fairbanks, Jr., danced with an unknown little Hungarian refugee named Zsa Zsa Gabor. And when the music stopped, Ouida Rathbone came to my side and whispered, "With your beauty, you can storm a fortress and conquer it." The subtext was clear: Hollywood, too, could be mine.

Two months later, Eva separated from Dr. Drimmer and together we rented a bungalow in the Hollywood Hills. At first, we had terrible difficulty making ends meet.

When I was about four, Father financed a good friend, Alexander Korda (who was also Hungarian) in his attempt to get into talkies. Daddy gave him something like one million dollars and Mother was furious at him. But he remained a good friend of Father's and I always called him "Uncle Korda."

Then, when I was a teenager, Father took me to London and we went to see Uncle Korda. Although I was still very young, Uncle said I was beautiful and that one day I should become a movie star.

When I left for America, Daddy said, "Darling, if we can't send you money, don't worry. Uncle Korda is in Hollywood, so go and see him and he will help you."

When I got to Hollywood, Eva had a $75-a-week contract with the studio but we were penniless. I called up Uncle Korda and asked if I could come and see him at the studio.

When I arrived, I said, "Uncle Korda, Daddy said to send his love." Then I asked for a contract like the one Eva had so we could make ends meet. Uncle Korda's reply was, "Take your clothes off." I was devastated and left.

AFTER I recovered from the shock of Uncle Korda, I started dating, something I'd never been allowed to do in Budapest and never had the opportunity for in my role as Madame Belge. I applied for an annulment from Burhan and suddenly I felt young and flirtatious and single again, once more the naive fifteen-year-old who had first boarded the Simplon Express with Burhan.

As Eva had a movie contract, we were invited to all the Hollywood parties. At one of them, just two weeks after I first arrived in Hollywood, I met Charlie Chaplin, who said I was charming and that I reminded him of his ex-wife Paulette Goddard. We went out together and he took me to an amusement park. At first I felt sorry for him because he told me how depressed he was about being fifty-three and going through a third divorce. Then he cheered up and we went on all the rides. It was obvious to me that Charlie longed to regain his childhood. I understood exactly how he felt.

WE went on about three dates, during which I grew to like Charlie more and more. Even though he was, in his world, as much of a god as Kemal Atatürk in his, Charlie was a simple man. I like simple people. That's why I have always loved actors. Actors are like children and children are simple. Many great actors I have known in my life—like Clint Eastwood and Robert Redford—are both simple and shy.

Charlie Chaplin and I spent most of our time together riding the roller coaster and eating hot dogs. I loved every minute. Charlie, however, telephoned one day to tell me, "You are too bright for me," and never asked me out again.

Years later, I met his daughter Geraldine (by his last wife, Oona O'Neill) at a party and she exclaimed, "My God! You could have been my mother!"

As a farewell present, knowing how much I loved dogs, Charlie sent me a cocker spaniel. But as Eva and I were virtually penniless, we couldn't afford to feed him. Our only alternative was to feed the dog orchids that our dates had presented us. From that moment on, I could never again look at an orchid without thinking of Charlie Chaplin.

MY first few months in Hollywood dazzled me. And although I never forgot my family in Europe, I couldn't help but revel in the kind of attention that I was now getting. However fulsomely I had been praised and admired in Ankara, I'd always felt as if the praise and admiration were for my role as Madame Burhan Belge, for my position in society and not for me, Zsa Zsa Gabor.

I was living in a moment of time when Hollywood was starting to blossom and burst forth with opulence. This was the era of formal dress and dramatic entrances. Jack Warner entertained lavishly at his Beverly Hills estate and Darryl F. Zanuck in Malibu. Samuel and Frances Goldwyn, Louis B. Mayer, and David O. Selznick threw immense parties for which gardens were adorned with tents, cut flowers were everywhere, and gigantic orchestras wailed the nights away as the elegant and the beautiful feasted on caviar washed down by French champagne, stealing passionate kisses from secret admirers for dessert.

IT seemed to me that although I was still so young, I had already lived many lifetimes. Now I was in America, becoming American; dying my blond hair a rich American red; learning to drive a compact American car; and discovering that American men with money seemed to think that every girl in the world belonged to them. Then I met an American man who appeared, at first at least, to belong to me.

I met him one night in December 1941, at the fabled Ciro's restaurant where celebrated attorney Greg Bautzer and his partner, Bentley Ryan, had taken Eva and me for dinner. He strode into the restaurant, a beautiful star on his arm, and I went white with a combination of shock and recognition. He was six foot two, exuded power, looked like Atatürk, my father, and an American cowboy from the Wild West—all rolled into one. For a moment I felt dizzy. The next thing I knew, I was dancing with him. He held me so close that I could hardly breathe. I looked up into his eyes and knew that I was going to marry this man, this Conrad Hilton.

HIS voice crackled with energy as he informed me, "I can't pronounce Hungarian, so from now on I'm going to call you Georgia." I was so enchanted by Conrad, by his personality, his blue eyes, his resemblance to Father, that the significance of what he had said utterly escaped me. Conrad Hilton, a man I'd only just met, had changed my name from Zsa Zsa—the Hungarian name I'd been given at birth—to Georgia, the name of an American state.

If I had paid more attention, I might have saved myself a great deal of heartache—because Conrad's decision to change my name from Zsa Zsa to Georgia symbolized everything my marriage to him would eventually become. My Hungarian roots were to be ripped out and my background ignored. It had been decreed that I was now an American state, with my past and my individuality erased forever. I was now annexed to Conrad Hilton, to his realm and to his power—like a small hotel with little importance other than that it was connected to the famous Hilton empire.

There were other false notes, too. During that first dance, Conrad Hilton offered me $20,000 to go to Miami with him. I was insulted and refused, but Conrad never really did get the message. Throughout our marriage he never realized who I was and where I came from and was everlastingly suspicious of the motives that led me—at seventeen—to marry him, at sixty-one. Quite simply, he thought I was after his money.

After we were married—before he took me home to his house in Bel Air—Conrad couldn't stop raving, "By golly! Georgia! You've never seen a house like it." I certainly hadn't. I'd never seen such bad taste. My mother and father's mansion was far superior. So was Burhan's palace on the Bosphorus. Conrad believed he was taking a poor Hungarian Cinderella and, by dint of his wealth, transforming her into a princess. He never took the trouble to find out about my background and how I was raised. He was far too busy making money.

THAT night at Ciro's, though, all I could see was Conrad. Ignoring his tacky necktie (with pictures of his three hotels embroidered on it), all I could see was his similarity to Father. Years later when we were long divorced, bemused visitors to my Bel Air home would see photographs of Father and ask why I still had pictures of Conrad Hilton everywhere. He was Father, Atatürk, and even more. I thought to myself, This man *is* America, rough, rugged, dominating, a blue-eyed Texan who wears a ten-gallon hat, spurs, and always gets his way. The words were out before I could stop myself: "I think I am going to marry you."

Years later, in his own book, Conrad remembered his reaction. "I, the confirmed bachelor, to whom marriage, from a religious standpoint was forbidden fruit, thought that was a fine joke. 'Why don't you do that?' I challenged with a roar of laughter. Four months later the joke was on me."

WE were married before a judge in Santa Fe, New Mexico, in a civil service which the Catholic Church would not recognize on account of our respective divorces. The reception at the Hilton was lavish beyond belief, with the rooms garlanded in white flowers. Although I was Catholic, I was not disturbed. Conrad, however, was devastated that he was now barred from taking the Sacrament. I didn't feel too guilty; I'd seen Conrad in action, his ruthlessness toward other people. And I believed his statement to me one day: "Anybody who double-crosses me, I kill." I could see him carrying out his threat and then assuming he would be forgiven at confession the day afterward.

I was afraid of Conrad and knew that the main reason he had married me was because I had refused to go to bed with him, that he was obsessed by me, by my body, and that he burned to have me. We spent our wedding night in Chicago, where Conrad was trying to buy the Blackstone Hotel. That night, we became husband and wife in every sense of the word. Conrad was a wonderful lover, virile, well-endowed, and masterful.

For a moment, my mind went back in time to a house in old Ankara and to the first man who'd ever loved me. Snuggling up to Conrad, I reminded myself that that was all over now. I had found a new god. Still dreamy and ecstatic, floating on cloud nine, I gazed ardently into Conrad's clear blue eyes and whispered, "Conrad, what are you thinking of?" expecting a torrent of amorous declarations. "By golly!" said Conrad, "I'm thinking of that Blackstone deal!"

I threw myself into my new role as Mrs. Conrad Hilton, redecorating the house and refurbishing my husband's image by telling him, firmly, "Conrad, take off your boots and your ties with the hotels on them. I'm taking you to the best tailor in New York, who will transform you into a 'big style man.' " Grumbling all the way, he agreed.

My wedding present from Conrad was unique, but one I recommend to every new bride. When I met Conrad I'd also made the acquaintance of his beautiful young secretary, a twenty-eight-year-old glamor girl with long blond hair and a big bust accentuated by her tight sweaters. On our marriage night, in the afterglow of passion and exhilaration (over what Conrad termed his "package deal"—marrying Georgia and buying the Blackstone in the same day), I made my move, announcing, "My first wish as Mrs. Hilton is that your secretary must go." Conrad—albeit unwillingly—acquiesced. The blonde was fired and replaced by a lady named Mrs. Olive Wakeman, a treasure who revolutionized Conrad's business—removing all his papers and files from the stove where he had been prone to store them and creating some semblance of order. Conrad was overjoyed.

He grew to respect my opinion, one day coming home and asking, "I can buy the National in Cuba or the Plaza in New York. Which one do you think?" Remembering my first night on American soil at the Plaza, I instructed Conrad to buy it. He never regretted it, although sometimes he still rebelled against the European grandeur that I so loved, complaining, "I hate all those people in the lobby, I am going to put on my big Texas hat and shoot them all!"

Instead of shooting the guests, using me as bait he set about charming backers for yet another New York hotel purchase. His first step was to buy me a navy blue lace Hattie Carnegie gown, which I was to wear with my sapphires and diamond wedding ring. The wedding ring, by the way, did not overpower the sapphires, as on our engagement Conrad had offered me a choice of two rings—one of which my father would have approved and another, far more minuscule diamond. Opting for judgment rather than desire, I picked the smaller ring. Conrad, as expected, was delighted.

The dinner at the Plaza that night was for E. F. Hutton and my appearance seemed to have the right effect. At the end of dinner, E. F. Hutton stood up and announced, "We have to finance Mr. Hilton. Anyone who has the taste to marry such a young and beautiful European girl is destined for great things!" Conrad got his financing—but I can't take all the credit.

He'd just come back from Texas, bringing with him a brace of wild duck that he'd shot himself and had ordered the cook at the Plaza to prepare the duck and serve it to his important guests. When the duck was brought in, arranged artistically on glittering silver platters, Conrad went scarlet and boomed, "Where is the duck's back? And where the hell are the legs?"

The maître d'hôtel looked terrified, but then rallied, drew himself up to his full height and, summoning every bit of *hauteur* he possessed, said, "Mr. Hilton, here in the Plaza we serve only the very best segments of a duck to our guests." In a fury, Conrad roared back, "I shot this duck and by golly I want my guests to eat all of it—legs and back included." E. F. Hutton was so impressed by Conrad's thrift that he decided to back him.

I soon discovered that my marriage to Conrad meant the end of my freedom. At a moment's notice, I would receive an order to meet him in New York and then be dispatched on a train and shipped across the country like a piece of Louis Vuitton luggage that its owner had suddenly decided was indispensable and had sent for. My own needs were completely ignored; I belonged to Conrad.

Conrad, however, did not always want me. Continually haunted by his rift from the Church, he also persisted in believing that I was with him for money. He couldn't have been more wrong. I have always known how to be thrifty and clever with money and have never needed an excessive amount to survive. Even on the night that Conrad and I first met, I had been wearing a symbol of my thrift. At the time, I hadn't been able to afford a cocktail dress, so my friend the Hungarian writer Bundy Solt took me to a dressmaker on Sunset. The dressmaker made me a simple black dress, to which I had attached a white gardenia on the night that I met Conrad. Since then, as I owned no other cocktail dress, I altered that one black dress each and every time Conrad and I went out. Once I wore a red rose on it. Another time I sewed a white collar on it. Another time I shortened the dress. Then I lengthened it. I was proud of my resourcefulness and, despite being a movie star, I still retain some of this quality today.

I always dress for myself. I change a lot during the day—sometimes as much as four times—but I do it for me, not because I want to impress a man. I don't treat my dresses as sacred either. I am not afraid to wear a designer dress twice and then just turn it back to front to make it look different so I can wear it again. I am just careful that it flatters me. If anything, I spend money on a dress because of the material. The design can always be adapted by adding jewelry or flowers, but one can never change the material. All in all, I have never been frivolous or unnecessarily extravagant about clothes or anything else. But Conrad never knew, nor would have believed the evidence if he had. His mind was already made up; I had married him for money.

There was the matter of my car. Conrad asked what kind of car I wanted and when I picked a Cadillac (just having seen one that I particularly admired) he sank into a depression. It was only afterward that I discovered some of his golf cronies had been laughing about me and joking, "I bet that your little Hungarian gold digger will ask for a Cadillac."

I can't remember which car I eventually ended up with. I only know that one day, while driving my car in Hollywood, I was sent a sign that there might well be other fish in the sea than Conrad. I'd never really learned how to parallel-park and was struggling to fit my car into a tight parking space when a tall, unshaven man in tennis shoes came up and said, "Pretty girl, can I park the car for you?"

I sized the shabbily dressed man up, came to the conclusion that he was a far from debonaire car thief, and haughtily refused. Leaving the car exactly where it was, I locked it and walked across the street to the friend I had come to see, photographer Paul Hesse who, with awe in his voice, said, "I'm very impressed. I had no idea that you knew Howard Hughes."

NOTHING happened between me and Howard Hughes. Nor did I fall prey to Errol Flynn's much vaunted charms. Errol came to one of my parties in Bel Air. Conrad was out of town and Errol and I danced together. Then Errol whispered to me, "Darling, come to my house and sleep with me tonight." Before I could reply, he went on, his voice pulsating with passion, "When you wake up in the morning you will look out of my window and see stallions outside—and then you will see what a stallion I am." I laughed off Errol's approach and changed the subject. I was in love with Conrad.

From the day that I first met him, on that fateful night at Ciro's, Conrad Hilton had dominated my heart, my thoughts, and my feelings. At the time, though, he hadn't been my only eligible suitor. I was also being courted by Bill Paley, who was handsome, intelligent, and rich. Bill used to come to Hollywood every two weeks and take me to dinner. He seemed to like me a great deal, but virtually hypnotized by Conrad, I didn't really have eyes for anyone else. Bill didn't seem deterred by my rejection, stayed on good terms with me, and asked me to cut the ribbon when he opened the CBS building on Fairfax in Los Angeles. Years after that, I met him again accidentally on Park Avenue and Bill—by now a legend—whispered to me, "What about making love today? I'll give you a wonderful TV show if you sleep with me." I refused. Ironically, I had, indeed, been tempted, but by Bill himself and not by the TV show. It was the mention of the TV show that stopped me from succumbing to Bill Paley. Without the mention of the TV show we might have become lovers.

MONEY was Conrad's god and white supremacy, not only Catholicism, appeared to be his religion. He always struck me as having Nazi tendencies—especially in later years when I discovered that one of his most trusted employees was a former *Gauleiter*—and once or twice I made the terrible faux pas of introducing him to someone as "My husband, Conrad Hitler." Conrad laughed uproariously, which I found chilling.

On the other hand, he couldn't have been kinder and more compassionate when my mother finally arrived from Hungary after escaping from Europe. Secretary of State Cordell Hull had facilitated her escape after I went to his office in Washington and dissolved into tears, imploring him to help me save my parents. Pronouncing, "Little girl, you don't have to worry, I will help," Mr. Hull was true to his word and Mother at last arrived in America—with only a sable coat, some antique Portuguese silver, and a hundred dollars in her pocket. As Eva and I rushed into her arms when the boat docked in New York Harbor, Mother removed the hundred dollars from her purse and, with a flourish, presented it to the porter who had just unloaded her bags.

Conrad gave her a suite in the Plaza, courteously examined the silver and elected to buy it from her. Conrad needed that silver like he needed to grow another three feet, but he was aware that Mother was too proud to accept money and wanted to help her. Using Conrad's money, she found a small store on Madison Avenue—between 62nd and 63rd streets—and opened "Jolie Gabor"—selling exquisite costume jewelry modeled after the Maria Theresia pieces so popular in Europe. Through the years, Mother made millions of dollars, also employing in her stores—she opened another in Palm Springs—Maria Callas's mother, and many impoverished members of European aristocracy.

FATHER came with Magda, my sister, two days later on a different boat. And although Magda took to America immediately like Mother did, Father couldn't adjust and went home to Hungary where he married his secretary and lived happily.

When the Communists took everything away from him, we all bought him an apartment on the Danube.

Every year (until my father died in his sleep in his eighties) all of us would travel to Vienna to meet him and were amazed and happy to discover that Father was just as content without his former grandeur as when he had been living with all the trappings of wealth and success. As Mother put it, "When I was married to him he was rich and was always worried about taxes, horses, and everything. But now he lives a simple life, he is happy." On one trip, Father took me to the airport alone (as I was going to London) and gave me a beautiful diamond crown, asking me to promise, "Don't tell your sisters. I always wanted you to have this and I don't have anything for them." That was the last time I ever saw my father. And the crown he gave me was and remains my most treasured possession. He truly was a "big style man."

MY marriage to Conrad wasn't making me happy. And perhaps part of it was my fault. Although I had chosen him over Bill Paley and had resisted the charms of Howard Hughes and Errol Flynn, another man—a boy really—who was the image of Conrad, was beginning to replace him in my heart. If Conrad ever discovered the truth, he never, in his entire life, breathed a word to me. He was far too proud. Perhaps, in a strange way, Conrad understood. After all, Nicky, his son, was the image of the young man Conrad had once been.

I was seventeen when Conrad first brought me home to his house in Bel Air. And his two sons, Nicky and Barron, were far closer in age to me than their father was. Although I was their stepmother (years later Nicky would sit in the front row during my Vegas act and say, "That's my ma! Isn't she beautiful!"), we were more like sister and brothers. We went swimming, played tennis together, and rode horses together. Sometimes it seemed that Conrad was our grandfather.

Throughout our marriage, Conrad treated me like a child, bringing me baubles and bonbons when he came home from doing business outside in the real world. On one occasion, Conrad presented me with a box of chocolates, I kissed him and Nicky—not able to control his jealousy—said, "What does a man have to do, Dad, to get a kiss like that from Zsa Zsa?" Conrad whacked him so hard that I was afraid

Nicky might suffer concussion. It was the one and only time that Conrad ever revealed his true emotions about my relationship with Nicky.

I was in love with Nicky, but he wasn't as exciting as Conrad. I still loved Conrad and wasn't unfaithful to him with Nicky until our marriage really began to flounder dramatically after a dreadful sequence of events. The first related to my jewelry. Early one morning in Bel Air I was awakened by a thief brandishing a gun. "This is a stickup, get up," he ordered.

"Come back later," I said—still not quite awake, "I'm sleeping."

"No," he barked. "This is serious."

"But I'm naked," I pleaded. "Please let me put on something."

"Stay nude. I'm not a sex maniac."

As he ransacked my drawers, I tried talking some sense into him.

"Look," I said, "this is America. You're still a young man. If you stop now, you can still become President of the United States."

My words, of course, made no impact. He continued looting my bedroom, taking all the jewelry I owned. Just before he was about to leave, he noticed a small green velvet pouch hidden in one of my lingerie drawers. Snatching it up, he left without a glance, taking with him the Hand of Fatima—and with him, it would soon transpire, my good luck.

I survived the loss of my jewelry but I still felt violated. There was worse to come. When I was out of town in Washington, I heard on the radio that our house in Bel Air had caught fire. I was overcome with nausea when I discovered that my beloved dog—Ranger—had perished in the fire, burned to death by the flames. Later, I heard that Conrad had learned about the blaze while he was playing golf. "Mr. Hilton, your house in Bel Air is burning!" he was told by a terrified messenger.

"I'm insured," said Conrad, not missing a stroke.

We came from two different worlds, and our souls, too, were worlds apart. Nicky and I, it seemed, had far more in common.

In the future, Conrad was to write about our marriage, "Being married to Zsa Zsa brought me, in many ways, more laughter and gaiety than I had ever known in my personal life. But it brought headaches and heartaches as well. It was a little like holding on to a Roman candle, beautiful, exciting, but you were never quite sure when it would go off. And it is surprisingly hard to live the Fourth of July every day." Conrad went on to bemoan the fact that his marriage to me—a divorcee—had separated him from the Catholic Church and made him ineligible to receive Holy Communion. The marriage continued to deteriorate and I discovered that Conrad's guilt in abandoning the Catholic Church had led him to be unfaithful to me. One day a messenger arrived at the Plaza with an elegant-looking invitation to a party on Long Island. Conrad decreed that, although we didn't know the name of the host, the party might be fun. And so we went.

The first thing I saw when we entered the mansion was a vast indoor swimming pool, filled with lotus blossoms floating on the water. In the midst of all the blossoms I discerned the nude form of our hostess, a beautiful blonde with long, flowing hair. I was startled but attributed the unconventionality of the situation to America, to my unfamiliarity with strange American customs and even stranger American parties.

Still, I felt dazed, lulled into a semi-stupor by the lotus blossoms, by the handsome young men, by the beautiful girls clustered around the pool. Sex and steaminess were in the air and I was overtaken by a kind of languor and after dinner became light-headed. Perhaps noticing and taking advantage of my momentary disorientation, Conrad disappeared. Out of the corner of my eye, I saw him slip behind a red velvet–curtained door. Perhaps, I told myself, Conrad had gone to the men's room. Yet the door had no sign on it, no marking to indicate what was beyond its portals. I was overtaken by an unfamiliar sensation of shyness—almost afraid to follow him.

Eventually, my innate curiosity won over timidity and I made my way to the red velvet door. I opened it and came face-to-face with Conrad—in the process of zipping up his pants. A beautiful girl lay curled up on a bed in the corner, her face flushed. Clearly, I had not blundered into the men's room. Nor was I at a conventional American party thrown by an average Mrs. America. Far from it. By the end of the evening I had discovered that our hostess was a madam, and that Conrad Hilton—my husband, the love of my life—had taken me to a whorehouse.

IN the past I'd always had the ability to turn a negative into a plus, but this time I couldn't cope any longer. With hindsight, I believe I was suffering a severe depression as a result of confronting the truth about my marriage. In today's world, therapy would have been the solution. Instead, Conrad had me committed to a sanitarium.

I was there for seven weeks and during my stay, my attorney, Barnet L. Arlan, and my friend Hamlin Turner visited me. Later, Turner made a sworn affidavit saying he'd seldom seen a woman in worse condition. These are the exact words of his affidavit:

"She was in shocking physical condition. She'd been brutally assaulted about the face, nose and body; she had been given insulin shock treatments tri-weekly and, as a result of the hypodermic injections, she displayed to me two large, infected areas on both thighs which resisted healing and which were open and festering."

Budapest and my childhood, Ankara and Atatürk's pink marble palace, all seemed to have existed light-years ago.

I recovered the only way I knew how—by taking refuge in the love of my animals. I rented a house in Bay Shore, Long Island, and spent happy hours riding horses on the beach, breathing the clear air, and doing my best not to think of what might have been.

Then Nicky found out where I was and, aware that my marriage to his father was virtually over, flew to my side. I had always loved Nicky Hilton, my stepson; now I began to love Nicky, the man. He was sexy and exciting, but not quite as dazzling as Conrad was. And when Nicky died I felt that he had always known the truth—that he could never eclipse his father and that he was doomed to be second best and to live in his shadow.

My love affair with Nicky began in Bay Shore and ended one day during his marriage to Elizabeth Taylor. Nicky came to see me in my house at 938 Bel Air Road. At the time, I was married to George, Nicky was married to Liz, and both of us were unhappy with our respective spouses. We spent the first few hours complaining bitterly about them. Then we both started crying and ended up by consoling each other in bed. Nicky Hilton was the first of a series of men I would have in common with Elizabeth Taylor.

Elizabeth and I have always had a great deal in common—not only men. Neither of us can ever truly be dominated by a man—which makes the men in our lives insecure. We are both famous for our diamonds and for our many husbands and our paths have often crossed—not always happily.

I knew all about Liz from the moment that Nicky met her. Although I was already divorced from Conrad—we still remained friends (I stayed friends with all my ex-husbands, with the exception of Michael O'Hara)—he told me about the girl his son was about to marry.

"By golly," he exclaimed, sounding greatly impressed, "my son is marrying a young actress called Elizabeth Taylor who earns $5,000 for a radio show."

"But Conrad," I said in surprise, "Elizabeth Taylor is famous. She is one of the most beautiful actresses in America today."

Conrad's sole response was "She makes $5,000 a radio show!"

THEIR marriage was doomed from day one. Nicky had been spoiled by Conrad, but Elizabeth had been even more spoiled by both MGM and by the trappings of stardom. When he got back from his honeymoon, Nicky immediately came to see me and confided all his problems.

"We were in Monte Carlo," he reported bitterly. "And all she wanted me to do was serve her night and day. She acted as if I were her butler. She was drinking and I was miserable." I felt a certain amount of sympathy for Elizabeth, knowing that Nicky, too, liked his drink. In later years, when I also became an MGM star, I understood Elizabeth even better. She may have been cold—but MGM made her that way.

Nick may have complained that "Liz still thinks she is at MGM," but I sympathized; by the time the studio had finished with me, I didn't even know how to dial a telephone, because someone at MGM had always dialed for me. I was told what to wear, how to dress, how to walk, how to talk, and in the end I felt like a puppet and almost forgot to think for myself. I was only at MGM for two years, but Elizabeth Taylor grew up there, so, in a way, I empathized with her.

Then again, I also felt for Nicky—who badly wanted a child—when Elizabeth refused to have a baby.

Conrad told me that the MGM bosses had dictated that Elizabeth avoid pregnancy, and Conrad—from the vantage point of his Catholicism—was appalled.

IN the future, Liz was to shock another one of my husbands, George Sanders. George told me that when he was in London filming *Ivanhoe* with Liz, he was staying at the elegant Savoy Hotel and one evening played cards with a group of English actors, including Michael Wilding.

As George described it to me, "All of a sudden, the door of the suite burst open and there stood Liz, dressed only in a see-through nightgown. She looked at each of us, one by one, with those phenomenal violet eyes, as if to say, 'Which one of you am I going to sleep with tonight?' " According to George, Liz picked Michael Wilding, who would become her next husband. Meanwhile, though, George, normally so urbane and unshockable, was totally dumbstruck. Later he said to me, "I couldn't believe it. Here was this beautiful young American actress acting almost like a French *cocotte*. I couldn't have slept with her, she was much too obvious."

WHEN Nicky and I made love in Bay Shore, I was convinced that my marriage to Conrad was totally finished and that we'd never sleep together again. But I was wrong. One day he sent a limousine for me, with instructions that I visit him in the Plaza. I obeyed, simply because by now obeying Conrad Hilton had become a habit for me.

When I arrived at his suite, I discovered that Conrad was in bed, his leg in a cast after an accident. First we had coffee. Then (incredible as it sounds, but quite believable if you had known Conrad, his forceful nature, and his intense virility) he raped me. His Hungarian valet came in, saw his master in bed with the soon-to-be ex-Mrs. Hilton, and was speechless with surprise.

NINE months later, our daughter, Francesca Hilton, was born and when I held her in my arms it was one of the happiest days I've ever known. I'd never dreamed about motherhood or babies, but when I looked into Francesca's little face I felt complete.

Since then, I've loved Francesca every day of her life, even if our relationship has sometimes been stormy. She is strong-willed and talented, intelligent, a gifted comedienne, and a good horsewoman. Currently Francesca is writing her autobiography and will tell her own story in her own words and in her own way.

I was unmarried now, which was a new experience for me. Francesca and I were living in New York in a brownstone on the East Side. Despite Francesca's company, I did get a bit lonely, but now and again, I was able to console myself. The King of Saudi Arabia (whom I'd met in Turkey) invited me out for the evening in New York. I suggested we try the Stork Club, forgetting that Sherman Billingsley admitted only the whitest of white members. And when we got there, Billingsley *did* refuse to let us in, declaring, "Mrs. Hilton, we would love to have you, but we can't let a Negro into our club."

We ended up going to Schrafft's and proceeded to sup on the best ice-cream sundaes in the world, served in clear bowls and smothered in homemade hot fudge and butterscotch sauce. The service was sublime—with three motherly Irish ladies looking after us, immaculate in tailored black uniforms with white lacy aprons, gracious and friendly. When we finally left, they actually curtsied to us. Of course, they had every reason: the King had tipped each one of them $1,000.

I was divorced from Conrad Hilton but, in a strange way, stayed connected to him for the rest of his life. When Nicky and Elizabeth divorced after only seven months of marriage, Conrad telephoned me in a fury, scandalized that he, a devout Catholic, had fathered a son who was now a divorcé. I tried not to laugh or to remind Conrad that he himself had been divorced twice. Conrad—a man who believed himself to be an absolute monarch—would not have appreciated the reminder. Nicky went on to marry for the second time. Trish Hilton, Nicky's second wife, became a very good friend of mine and I love her. And I was shattered when Nicky died.

Many years after my divorce from Conrad, I was appearing in the Flamingo, Las Vegas, and Conrad brought Francesca to see my act. This was his first visit to Las Vegas and by the time he left he had made up his mind to buy not only the Flamingo but also the International from Kirk Kerkorian. The Las Vegas Hilton and Flamingo hotels turned out to be the biggest money spinners in the entire chain—but I was never asked by Conrad to appear there again. Not only that but my agent always said that I was indirectly responsible for the Hilton Hotel's success in Las Vegas and that we should have been paid a finder's fee!

But I still couldn't be bitter at Conrad and was always able to laugh at the fiasco of our marriage. That night, on his first visit to Las Vegas, in my act I had the line, "When Conrad Hilton and I divorced, he gave me five million Gideon Bibles." Standing up in full view of the entire showroom, Conrad roared, "Then why don't you read one!" My divorce settlement from Conrad, by the way, was not gargantuan: a cash settlement of $35,000 and a monthly income of $2,500 until if and when I remarried.

I hadn't married Conrad for money and I didn't divorce him for it either. I think, at the very end, Conrad finally realized the truth. I went to see him when he was dying in Santa Monica, at St. John's Hospital. The very last time I ever saw him I brought along a little tree as it was Christmas. His toupee was on but he didn't have his false teeth in, and seeing him that way—Conrad who had been so big, so strong, and so powerful—was one of the saddest moments of my life. He couldn't talk anymore, but the priest who was by his side said, "The only time Mr. Hilton ever perks up is when he sees you."

I thought to myself, It is Christmas. Why should he die in the hospital? Why should he die alone? Two days later, Conrad died, aged ninety-one, leaving $365 million to the Catholic Church. I hope all that money bought him the place he so craved in heaven. I did love Conrad. And even today, I still cry about Conrad, about his death, and I miss him. He was a part of my life, my youth, and my first years in America. In a way, Conrad was my father.

IF Conrad Hilton was my father, George Sanders was my brother, my son, my lover, even my grandfather. He was infuriating and charming, intelligent and educated, a cad and a gentleman, a man who knew how to treat women and how to torture them, a disdainful prince, cool, remote, and elegantly contemptuous. I loved George from the moment that I first saw him up on the screen in *The Moon and Sixpence*—and made up my mind to marry him.

I didn't quite know how I'd accomplish my goal. After all, George was a well-respected British actor and I, the soon-to-be ex-wife of Conrad Hilton who was, at the time, pregnant with his child. Then, just six weeks after Francesca's birth, fate led me to George.

I was at a cocktail party thrown by banker Serge Semenenko at the St. Regis Hotel and there, literally across an extremely crowded room, stood George Sanders, my dream man, the man I wanted to marry. That night, I was wearing a clingy black jersey silk dress, designed by Alexis, and, of course, my diamonds.

Aware that I was dressed to kill, I opted for a spontaneous approach and walked over to George. Coolly, he looked me up and down. My voice shaking with nerves and excitement, I said, "Mr. Sanders, I'm madly in love with you." And George, without skipping a beat, answered, "How very well I understand you."

IT seemed that the whole world admired George. Even a few years ago, Clint Eastwood—whom I met with his then wife Maggie—told me, "George Sanders has always been my ideal. I've always admired his looks, his acting, and have always wanted to be like him." Men wanted to be like George and women, quite simply, wanted to have him. And many did.

At the time that we met, George was ricocheting between the ample charms of Dolores Del Rio and the even more alluring Gene Tierney. I didn't know any of that. All I knew was that George and I were meant to be. And despite the years of heartache and tragedy that followed, I was not wrong. For if I could live my entire life over again, I would spend every minute of it with George. If I live until the end of time, I'll never find another George Sanders.

HE came home with me that night, with writer Erich Maria Remarque, of *All Quiet on the Western Front* fame. We had caviar and vodka and Erich finally left at two A.M., leaving George behind. Hypnotized and overwhelmed, I didn't question anything but just succumbed to George and surrendered to the fascination he held for me.

There are those who have labeled the Gabor sisters as gold diggers, as blond sirens who target only the wealthiest of men and then envelop them in their charms. My choice of George Sanders—a man not wealthy and so stingy that he refused even to buy cigarettes or flowers when I was in the hospital—as the love of my life, as my third husband (so ending all alimony payments from Conrad Hilton, which in those days were worth over a quarter of a million dollars), must surely negate that entire image.

George and I were married on April Fools' Day, 1949, in a little Las Vegas chapel. We spent our wedding night playing chess after George flatly informed me, "I don't know if I can ever make love to you again. Yesterday you were the glamorous Mrs. Conrad Hilton. Now you are just plain Mrs. George Sanders."

FAR from being the archetypical Englishman he came to epitomize in films like *Rebecca* and *The Picture of Dorian Gray*, George Sanders was, in fact, a wild Russian, with a temperament as fiery as that of Vilmos himself. Born in St. Petersburg, although his ancestry dated back to Scotland, George grew up in St. Petersburg and was educated in England.

His family background was extremely colorful: as George wrote in his memoirs, his mother was an heiress and his father played the balalaika. Part of his family fled the Revolution and ended up penniless in Vienna. There, one of his uncles wandered the streets one day in the dead of winter, wearing the one and only possession he had managed to salvage—a sable-lined winter coat.

A drunken Russian *mujik* accosted him, put a gun to his head, and demanded the coat. And although he owned nothing else in the world, George's uncle handed the coat over. The cossack grabbed it, throwing his own flea-bitten rag of a coat onto the pavement, where it lay, covered in mud and ice. Shivering with cold, George's uncle, a once proud man, reluctantly retrieved the coat, wrapped himself in it, and trudged home. After breaking the news to his wife that this flea-bitten coat was now their sole possession, he instructed her to clean it. Always the obedient wife, she complied—only to find that the lining of the coat was full of diamond and gold jewelry worth hundreds of thousands of dollars. They promptly sold the diamonds and, on the proceeds, moved to America and started a new life.

George himself began life working in a Manchester, England, textile company before moving to Buenos Aires and a cigarette-manufacturing company. Already a lady-killer, George dallied with one female too many, got thrown out of South America as a result, and, instead, ended up in London. There—partly because of his stunning singing voice—he was discovered and, soon after, became a star.

His romantic exploits kept pace with his career success; George loved to tell the story about how he once made love to an aristocratic English lady on her drawing room couch, only to be interrupted by her butler bringing in the tea. "Put it over there, John," the lady was said to have instructed, before continuing her lovemaking. According to George, he was henceforth completely unable to make love to her ever again.

GEORGE had a sister, Margaret, and a brother, who acted under the name of Tom Conway. There was a certain amount of rivalry between Tom and George—although

George was definitely the bigger star. Just before our marriage, George was finishing Cecil De Mille's *Samson and Delilah,* co-starring Hedy Lamarr. At first, I was dazzled at the prospect of meeting Hedy—whose beauty had assumed almost mythical proportions in my mind after I'd first caught a glimpse of her in Vienna, all those years ago.

However, I soon came plummeting down to earth and was forced to deal with the fact that, far from being a goddess, Hedy Lamarr was an intensely real woman—one whom I suspected of having designs on George. But George being George, he did a masterful job of disguising it by complaining, "Oh dear, how am I ever going to say lines to Hedy like 'What a dimpled dragon you can be, flashing fire and smoke'? The writers are alliterative assholes!"

I tried to reassure him, cooing, "Never mind, darling, your gold armor and blond beard set off your blue eyes marvelously. And in your tunic you can show off your wonderful legs. No one will pay any attention to the dialogue." George's legs, indeed, were one of his best features, displayed to their advantage by Edith Head's costumes. Edith did not, however, succeed so well with Hedy's clothes. De Mille—who wore riding britches to work—insisted that Edith follow his own ideas regarding women's clothing and the result was that poor Hedy ended up looking like a stripper.

I felt less sorry for her, though, when I came on the set and she called out, "Who is this beautiful blond bitch? Get her off the set." George said, "This is the woman I am going to marry, Mrs. Conrad Hilton." Hedy looked momentarily taken aback, then rallied, shook hands with me, and said, "Can I meet Mr. Conrad Hilton?" Nice as Hedy became to me, my initial instincts about her had been right; George later confessed that he had made love to Hedy, but that she had screamed so loudly that the neighbors subsequently complained, which put him off.

A few years later, Hedy came to visit us in Bel Air. She arrived early in the evening, just as Francesca—who was three at the time—was going up to bed. Francesca's nanny (my wonderful friend Elizabeth Keleman) was off that night. Hedy volunteered to say good night to Francesca, started going upstairs, then, as an afterthought asked, "Does Francesca know the facts of life yet?" Perturbed, I shook my head.

The next morning Francesca came downstairs with a balloon stuck inside the front of her dress and informed me that she was now pregnant. Hedy Lamarr had told my three-year-old daughter the facts of life. I was livid. George had once said of Hedy, "She is lovely but stupid"—and he seems to have been right. My final memory of Hedy Lamarr, the great beauty who had once so dazzled me, was hearing her comment, "If a man sends me flowers, I always look to see if a diamond bracelet is hidden among the blossoms. If there isn't one, I don't see the point of flowers."

JEALOUSY was a facet of our relationship from the moment we went on our delayed honeymoon. In the years to come, George would do his utmost to airily dismiss the seriousness of any man who wanted me and pretend not to be threatened, but now, in Formentor, Majorca, he began our marriage with a virtuoso display of jealousy.

Each night, we used to love listening to the orchestra, and afterward often chatted with the guitarist, a young man named Jose. Soon after we arrived, I developed terrible toothache and George—who was in Majorca to make a film called *Blackjack* and was busy that day—asked Jose to take me to the dentist. It transpired that I had an impacted wisdom tooth—which the dentist extracted swiftly. Once I'd recovered, Jose drove me home. On the way, our Mercedes overheated and broke down. While we were standing by the roadside, George drove by in a station wagon with Herbert Marshall by his side. Instead of stopping to help us, George drove by, waving.

The moment I walked into our hotel room, George flew into a rage, shouting accusingly, "You tart. You slept with him." Protesting my innocence through lips swollen with Novocain and the aftereffects of a wisdom tooth extraction, I begged George to believe me. He didn't. The fight went on for hours.

Finally, George grabbed me by the collar of my dress and hung me out of the window. Luckily, I was still able to talk, pleading, "George, think about it. If you drop me, you will end up in Sing Sing. And I might survive." George pulled me back into the room. I thanked my lucky stars, first for my own eloquence in the face of what, literally, might have been my last moment on earth and also for the expensive Balenciaga model I was wearing. A cheaper dress might have ripped apart, sending me hurtling into eternity.

I wiped my eyes, applied my makeup, but was still aware that their puffiness and redness from crying almost equaled my swollen mouth, and walked into the dining room for dinner. To be confronted by none other than José, playing his guitar as usual. George smiled at him, said "Good evening," and acted as if nothing had happened. That was my George, infuriating, stormy—a roller coaster of a man—my great love and my tormentor.

WHILE George was filming in Palma I flew to Paris for a few days to buy clothes and see friends. One night, I went to dinner at Maxim's with Joan Bennett, Walter Wanger, and Elie de Rothschild. Elie was very seductive toward me and I decided to tease him by pretending I didn't know who he was or that he owned the most famous vineyards in the world. I said, in a wide-eyed way, "What kind of shop do you own?" Joan Bennett, who seemed very full of herself, looked shocked.

After dinner, we went on to Freddie's, the most fashionable nightclub in Paris, run by a woman so chic that all of Paris was in love with her. Both men and women.

Freddie was quintessentially French, but with her short brown hair, blue eyes, and penchant for dressing in tuxedo suit with navy skirt, looked like a German teacher. Not just any German teacher, though, but a German teacher who was so chic that she might have been designed by Coco Chanel herself. Freddie was so strong and so fabulous that everyone who met her fell in love with her.

When Elie and Joan took me to the club, I was prepared to be shocked, but I wasn't prepared for the animal attraction that Freddie herself exuded. I'd never been attracted to a woman before, but when Freddie asked me to dance with her, my immediate reaction was, Why not? Freddie and I started dancing and I couldn't take my eyes off her. I saw that although she was so chic, she was wearing absolutely no makeup—she didn't need any because her presence was so all-embracing.

I understood that Freddie was a good friend of Marlene Dietrich's. Joan Bennett told me that although she was such a great star, Marlene used to help out at the club whenever Freddie asked her.

Marlene Dietrich and I didn't meet that night, but we were destined to tangle in the future. First, though, we had a fairly cordial meeting when I wasn't yet an actress and George invited her to dinner. Marlene took one look at me, kissed me, then demanded the telephone and called her husband, Rudi. Without further preamble, she announced, "Rudi, I've just met a woman you'll love and who could replace me in your life—Mrs. George Sanders." I talked to Rudi for a few minutes because Marlene asked me to—but we were both extremely embarrassed.

When I became a movie actress, I had a part in Orson Welles's *Touch of Evil* in which Marlene was the star. During shooting, she got sick and Orson asked me if I could play an older woman. "Of course, Orson, I'd love to," I said, without hesitation. Marlene was running a 104 fever, but the minute she discovered that I was playing her part, came right back to work because she so hated the idea of being replaced by me.

WHEN George heard about my evening at Freddie's—he wanted to hear about every detail of the club and all about Freddie, especially when he was making love to me. Later, Freddie and I became friends—platonic friends, that is.

My only other flirtation with an attractive woman didn't end in bed either—although I did find Greta Garbo very attractive. I first met Garbo at Brian Aherne's house in Santa Monica when George and I went to a party there. The other guests, Sylvia Ashley Gable, David and Hjordis Niven, and Clifton Webb, had already arrived when Garbo breezed into the room. She was alone and I almost fainted. George, being George, made things worse by informing Greta, "My wife has a wild crush on you." I blushed scarlet. Dispassionately, Garbo responded, "She's a very beautiful girl, your wife." At the end of the evening, George escorted Garbo to her car. When he came back into the house, he (rather maliciously) whispered to me, "Zsa Zsa—you don't have to be so in love with her anymore. I kissed her and she smelled of cheap soap."

The next time I met Garbo I was alone at a party at Brian's house on 62nd Street in New York. At the time, Rex Harrison was appearing on Broadway in *My Fair Lady* and he was guest of honor. Garbo spent most of the evening standing behind the bar flirting with me. Rex was all over Garbo and

Garbo was all over me. I nearly melted. Then Rex had to leave and Garbo said, "Let's bring Rex's coat." The coat was beige and the pockets were so full of vitamins that we could hardly carry it. We took it to him, Rex left, and Greta asked me if she could drive me home. I said yes, but I was afraid of her. We got to my hotel (I was living in the Savoy Plaza) and for a moment I felt like inviting Greta in. Then she said, "Darling, would you like to come to my apartment?" I was paralyzed. Then she kissed me straight on the mouth. And I couldn't help kissing her back because she was so overwhelmingly strong and so beautiful. I've never had lesbian tendencies—but if I had ever had them, the woman of my life would definitely have been Greta Garbo.

AFTER that first night at Freddie's, Elie de Rothschild drove me home and on the way to the Plaza Athénée, stopped his car, and proceeded to try to get me to make love to him. In desperation, I whispered, "My room number is 305. I'll go upstairs first and then you follow discreetly. After all, you're married and I'm married." The next morning, I came downstairs into the lobby and found an irate Elie waiting for me. "Oh you bitch. I knocked on the door and waited and a woman finally answered. She had curlers in her hair and her husband nearly beat me up." Elie eventually forgave me for my deception and we became good friends after he understood that, as a new bride, I'd never had any intention of being unfaithful to George.

Back in Hollywood, George was waiting for me and we began our life together. From the start, we were totally compatible; both of us had the same tastes, laughed at the same jokes, and liked the same friends. I was open and honest to George about my feelings for him. He, on the other hand, was unwilling to reveal his emotions to me, always keeping me off balance and insecure. Then again, he really did seem to understand and sometimes, even admire me. In later years, he was to write in his own book, *Memoirs of a Professional Cad*,

> Zsa Zsa is perhaps the most misunderstood woman of our times. She is misunderstood because she is guileless. She allows her vitality and instincts to spring from her without distortion. She doesn't disguise her love of amorous entanglements or jewels or whatever else catches her fancy, because her character is pure. . . . Not for her the conventional mask of studied behaviour. Her behaviour is spontaneous and genuine. . . . No one is a better date than Zsa Zsa. No one is a better companion on a trip even if it involves roughing it. . . . Every age has its Madame Pompadour, its Lady Hamilton, its Queen of Sheba, its Cleopatra, and I wouldn't be surprised if history singles out Zsa Zsa as the twentieth century prototype of this exclusive coterie.

Despite George's laudatory description of me and our social life—with friends who were among some of the most radiant stars in Hollywood—my marriage to George was, ultimately, fairly mundane. George wanted me to be the classic housewife, to rub his back, bring him milk, and fetch his slippers and I was eager to comply. George and I would start many an evening intending to go to one of the many glamorous parties to which we'd been invited. We'd dress in the most elegant of clothes, then when we arrived at our host's house, drive around three times, not go in and, instead, drive right home again and spend the rest of the evening in bed. Not that we would make love. Sometimes, but not always. Just talking to George excited me and we didn't necessarily need to have sex to be happy. We spent lots of evenings in bed having caviar and iced vodka as George read the plays of Noël Coward (whom he'd once understudied) to me. Or I'd watch as George thumbed through *Webster's* dictionary.

At first, I used to joke that my only rival for George's affections was *Webster's*. But early on in our relationship, I discovered that I was wrong.

MANY of Hollywood's glamor queens were mad about George. Gene Tierney, his leading lady in *The Ghost and Mrs. Muir,* was one of them. The first time George took me to a party at Gene's—when we still weren't married—she saw us arrive together and the blood drained from her face. In embarrassment, I realized that George hadn't told Gene—who had wanted to marry him—that he was now otherwise engaged.

One glamor queen who *had* been told about me—but didn't care—was Marilyn Monroe. At the time, George and I weren't married and he took delight in torturing me with tales of Marilyn. "Poor girl," he would say, his voice resonating with supposed pity for Miss Monroe. "She always has lunch in the commissary but nobody wants to sit next to her. The poor girl is writing poetry and she wants to share it with someone." I couldn't bring myself to find much sympathy for her, aware as I was that George, like most men, was hopelessly hooked on women with oversized bosoms and undersized brains. Eventually he explained that Darryl Zanuck and Joe Schenk—two of the most powerful moguls in Hollywood—had both made love to Marilyn (arranging plastic surgery for her in the bargain) and that every other actor was afraid to go near her.

Not my George, of course. Joking that "Marilyn is so insecure that if a man takes her out to dinner and doesn't go to bed with her afterward, she thinks there is something wrong with her," he was not in the least bit immune to Marilyn's charms. I was in New York on a visit to my mother when George first sampled them.

We weren't yet living together and he had a little apartment house on Shoreham Drive. When I came back from New York, George regaled me with the following saga. "You can't imagine what happened the other day! The doorbell rings and there stands Marilyn in a beautiful sable coat. I asked her what she wanted and she opened her coat. Marilyn was stark naked underneath."

Suffering with every fiber of my being, I waited for the rest of the story, wanting to know, yet hoping against hope that there was nothing *to* know. Smiling sardonically, George said, "Who am I, darling, not to make love to a woman like that?" I didn't answer and George hurriedly went on, "It was wonderful, but really Marilyn was far too professional. I like you a lot better because you are naive. But Marilyn knows exactly how to make love to a man. And I didn't have to pay her afterward either."

The only comment I was capable of mustering through my tears was "Did she give you the hot oil treatment as well?" He had always told me that at 20th Century-Fox there was an extra who was a part-time hooker and specialized in giving all the actors hot olive oil treatments at $20 a time. According to George, Marilyn had not included that particular variation in her sexual repertoire because she hadn't had time. I fervently hoped that she would continue not to have time for George and that I had heard the last of her. But I was wrong.

JUST after our marriage, George signed for *All About Eve,* to play the part of Addison DeWitt—a role that would win him an Academy Award. Co-starring with him was Bette Davis and, in a bit part, none other than the ubiquitous Miss Marilyn Monroe. I was not elated.

I met Marilyn for the first time in the commissary and noted that she was extremely adept at wiggling her ass and batting her eyelashes. When we came home that day, George made violent love to me. Normally, violent love wasn't

George's style and, almost without thinking, I said, "George, I bet you were fantasizing about Marilyn all the time we were making love." Livid, George picked me up, carried me out into the garden, and dumped me into the swimming pool.

I recovered with sufficient alacrity to fly to San Francisco with George—who was scheduled to film a sequence for *All About Eve* in the Curran Theater there. On the plane, I had the window seat, Marilyn the aisle—with George, appropriately, sandwiched in the middle. Marilyn spent most of the trip batting her eyelashes at George, who turned to me when we were alone and said, with a mixture of sympathy and pride, "Poor girl, she has it bad." "George," I said, in fury, "don't flatter yourself, she's having sex with everybody."

Later that evening—with Marilyn's unwitting cooperation—George's voyeurism got the better of him and I was able to prove my point. Our hotel suite was right next door to Marilyn's and I took George aside and said, "Why don't we keep our door ajar tonight and watch how many men go into Marilyn's room?" Ever the voyeur, George agreed and watched with me as four different men from the movie's crew each, in turn, visited Marilyn's room and made love to her.

The next day, George spoke Addison DeWitt's vitriolic lines with added venom—especially when they were directed at Marilyn, and I breathed a sigh of relief. I had seen the last of Marilyn as far as George was concerned, but through the years, our paths still crossed. I made *We're Not Married* with Marilyn.

Then, when she was one of the biggest stars in the world (seeing her on screen, I could finally appreciate her and understand why) and was having an affair with French actor Yves Montand (then married to Simone Signoret), Yves spent one entire evening at my house, talking on the phone to Marilyn. I felt deeply sorry for Simone, who was a friend of mine and who worshiped Yves. But I couldn't help smiling at Yves romancing Marilyn with the words "Mon amour, ma chérie," when poor Marilyn had no idea what any of that meant and probably thought it was all some dirty French words.

When Marilyn died, our mutual friend, the great hair designer Sydney Guilaroff, said, "I'm glad she died young. She could never have stood getting a wrinkle on her face. All she had was her beauty."

I liked Bette Davis, though, and admired her acting. At the time, she was madly in love with Gary Merrill, who was co-starring with her in the film. There was a bed on the set and every time we came back after lunch, it was obvious that Gary and Bette had been using it during the break. Bette was a star—with a capital *S*.

So was Merle Oberon, another of our Hollywood friends. George told me that Merle was also having an affair with Joe Schenck, then president of 20th Century-Fox and married to Norma Talmadge. To counteract negative publicity, Joe concocted a love affair between Merle and a dashing English officer around town, rented them a love nest in Malibu, and broke the story to all the Hollywood press. The officer's name was David Niven.

David was part of the English crowd that congregated around George for obvious reasons. I liked him tremendously and I also admired Merle. She was so elegant and ladylike—although I once had a unique glimpse behind her dignified facade. I was making a film in Madrid, *Sang et Lumière,* and a photographer came to town to shoot a layout of me. I knew Merle was staying at the samc hotel, that she was alone and eager for company, so I said to the photographer, "Why don't you shoot some pictures of me with Merle?" The photographer (a gorgeous Italian) obediently went off in search of Merle and didn't return for two days. When I asked him what had happened he blushed, then confessed, "I rang the door, Merle opened it and then kept me there for two days!"

OUT of all the English circle, George and I were closest to James Mason and his wife Pamela, who became a great friend of mine. I loved James in *The Seventh Veil*—playing just my kind of man—but when I met him I was disappointed that he wasn't more exciting. As I got to know him better, I discovered that James was henpecked, bored, and spent most of his evenings listening to television through headphones because he didn't want to hear what we were all saying.

When James and Pamela first arrived in Hollywood, George telephoned James, told him how much he admired his acting. Later James invited us to dinner at their house. We duly arrived there, rang the doorbell but when the servant finally opened it, nearly fainted. The stench of cat civet was overpowering. It seemed that the Masons had never heard of air freshener. I was dressed in a gray velvet Dior gown, with emeralds as a contrast to my then red hair and George was, as always, debonair in his tuxedo. We felt as if we'd arrived at Tobacco Road and not 1018 Beverly Drive—a classic Hollywood mansion that had once belonged to Buster Keaton.

"My God," whispered George in distaste. "Why on earth did we come here? Our clothes will smell of cat into the next century." Then James emerged from his cat-infested study wearing a pink jacket and Pamela, dressed in a flowery negligee, joined us. Noticing that all the furniture was covered in plastic to protect it from the Masons' twenty-eight cats, George muttered, "My dear, these are not our kind of people."

Dinner was abominable. Pamela was a terrible cook and George said afterward that he was afraid that we were eating cat food. Nevertheless, we became great friends with the Masons and I took Pamela to all the best dressmakers. James appeared to be amused by me and one day said to George, "Why don't you have her go on one of those new TV talk shows? She'd soon become a star."

Quick as a flash, George countered dismissively, "She's too stupid. She'd never make it." His words hurt me deeply. I knew that he was wrong but that he just didn't want an actress for a wife. Intent on making him happy, I didn't bother to argue and forgot James's suggestion instantly.

*

*

*

JAMES and Pamela eventually divorced, with the lion's share of James's money going to Pamela. Vivien Leigh and Laurence Olivier were another English couple George and I liked—whose marriage was also doomed to disaster. The first time I met Vivien, I was in London. I wasn't an actress at the time and George took me to see Vivien and Larry in *The Prince and the Showgirl* on the London stage. We went backstage afterward. Vivien was absolutely gorgeous and very kind to me. She took my hand and said, "You are a beautiful young girl and you are married to George Sanders. . . . He's a difficult man."

The Oliviers invited us to have dinner with them. I sat in their Rolls-Royce (I, who had seen Vivien as Scarlett O'Hara in *Gone With the Wind* before I ever set foot on American soil) with Vivien, George, and Larry and felt as if I were in heaven. I have never been so impressed in my life. We had dinner at their London duplex. Normally, Vivien made Larry's life hell because she was so jealous of his career (two married people should never both be in show business), but that night was peaceful and perfect. We had a beautiful dinner and then Larry turned to Vivien and said (and I'll never forget this as long as I live), "Go upstairs, my darling, and make yourself ready for me." I thought I would faint—I was so impressed.

Things turned to ashes for them and, a few years later, Bundy Solt rented a house to Vivien and was very disappointed in her, telling me, "She was so superficial, you always had the feeling she looked over your head." At the time, although no one knew it then, Vivien was ill. And Bundy told me that the police were called one night after Vivien—who was now divorced from Larry—was found fencing in the street—completely naked.

My final meeting with Vivien was during the last years of her life when she was starring in *Tovarich* on Broadway. I went to see her backstage after the performance. There, I found Vivien, her hair short and dyed red, her back to the door, facing the mirror, unable to turn around and look at me. Instead, she stared into the mirror and, almost as if to herself, said, "Darling, look at that face. I can't believe I'm getting so old." Her words—and her life—were a tragic commentary on the devastation that can be wrought on the beautiful and the talented once stardom is over.

*

JUDY GARLAND, too, couldn't cope with old age and the end of superstardom. The first time I saw her, we were at Bogart and Bacall's house in Holmby Hills and Betty took me into one of the guest rooms and begged me, "For God's sakes, darling, watch Judy—because if she goes into the bathroom she'll eat up every single pill I have in there." I knew Judy well through the years—she was crazy about my fourth husband, Herbert Hutner, and he spent many an evening playing the piano for her while she sang. Judy used to call me "my sister." And when I was making my first film, *Lovely to Look At,* a segment of which was directed by Judy's husband Vincente Minnelli, I looked up at the boom one day and saw a tiny little person with enormous black eyes sitting up there, his daughter, Liza. She was adorable and always came to Francesca's birthday parties.

I also liked Bogie and Bacall very much. I first met Betty—her real name—when she was a young actress and I was still Mrs. Conrad Hilton. Joe Schenck and Louis B. Mayer used to take us both out and complain that we were the only two virgins left in Hollywood. The last time I saw Bogie, he was at Irving Berlin's house and he had cancer and was as thin as a skeleton. I couldn't believe how terrible he looked and I avoided him all evening because I was afraid he would notice how shocked I was. He died very soon afterward. I will always regret that I didn't kiss Bogie good-bye that night, because I never saw him again.

C**ARY GRANT** was another English star we liked. He was shy but friendly and once confided to me, "I love going to the dentist because he gives me laughing gas and then I feel very happy and secure." Years later, I hired his ex-secretary, who told me that Cary was the stingiest man in the world.

George, however, could probably have given Cary (or anyone else for that matter) a good run for their money. He was chronically stingy. At the start of our affair, I gave him a gold cigarette case (I think a woman in love should give the man she loves a present) engraved *I'm so glad I met you.* Once I asked George for something minor in front of Clark Gable and George refused. Clark picked up the gold cigarette case and said, "Say, why the hell are you so stingy with Zsa Zsa? Look how she treats you."

Clark was a simple, down-to-earth American male. He could disassemble a car and put it back together. He was at our house almost every other day because he adored Elizabeth Keleman's Hungarian cooking and loved George and me as well. He was a heavy drinker and a chain smoker, but loved to go riding.

We once went horseback riding together on his ranch in Thousand Oaks. George and Clark's British wife, Lady Sylvia Ashley, were sitting under a tree, having tea. As we rode over the crest of a hill, Clark looked down and said, "Just look at those two English people sitting there drinking tea. Wouldn't they have more fun riding horses like we are!"

We had a little gray poodle called Harvey Hilton and Clark used to give him brandy. Harvey became the only alcoholic dog in the whole of America, but I still adored him and Clark as well. Clark always loved Hungarian sausages and a week before he died, I brought him some.

GEORGE'S friends always treated me with great respect—once they knew who I was, that is. One morning, I put a red rinse in my hair, put on a revealing black velvet swimming costume, and sashayed down to the pool where George was chatting with Gary Cooper—whom I'd never met before. Gary took one look at me, turned to George, and asked, "Who is that sexy number?" "My wife," said George, dryly.

NO ONE—not Gary, Cary, nor Clark—could eclipse George in my heart. Nevertheless, life with him remained anything but stable. He was a prisoner of his own passions, his own disdain for Hollywood, and ultimately, his own shyness. George was a paradox. The story of George's reaction to my appendix operation—one that could have been life-threatening—sums up the enigma that was George Sanders.

As I was being wheeled into the operating theater, George, usually so cold and remote, stroked my face tenderly, then whispered, his voice breaking with anguish, "Darling, don't you dare die because then I'd die too."

Just a few hours later, George strolled jauntily into the ward where I was recovering from the operation, presented me with a mangy bunch of faded flowers, and said, "I stole these from someone's garden because I couldn't afford to buy any for you."

I owe my entire Hollywood career to George—indirectly, that is. He refused to take me to London where he was slated to start filming *Ivanhoe.* Announcing, "I won't take you, because you'll spoil my fun if I do," George made his exit, leaving me feeling rejected and bitter. Later, I found that my bitterness had been justified when, on his return, in my good-wife persona, I unpacked his suitcase and one of his handkerchiefs fell out. Picking it up, I saw that the imprint of full, crimson-stained lips had been left in the middle of the handkerchief. I confronted George, who began to chuckle heartily.

"Oh that, darling, that was Pamela Churchill. She told me she wanted you to see that I knew her." Seeing my chagrin, George relented and added, "She's a big success with men, but she's not really beautiful at all."

LEFT alone in Hollywood, grappling with my misgivings about George's fidelity, I was prey to the manipulations of George's younger brother, Tom Conway. Although George had helped Tom, having made the initial suggestion that he move to Hollywood and suggesting him for the series "The Falcon," Tom was jealous of him and enjoyed needling him. With George out of the way, he formulated the perfect scenario by which to undermine him.

I can't say that I was totally innocent. Still smarting from George's comments to James—that I was too stupid to appear on one of those new television talk shows—I jumped at Tom's invitation to go on *Bachelor's Haven,* a TV pilot he was hosting.

The day of my appearance dawned, and I duly arrived at the studio, dressed in a black off-the-shoulder Balenciaga model, plus the diamonds, which I'd always worn in my respective roles as Madame Burhan Belge, Mrs. Conrad Hilton, and Mrs. George Sanders. The format of the show demanded that I open viewers' letters on camera, and instantly answer them with as much spontaneity as I could muster.

I'd never been in front of a television camera before, wasn't sure what to do, but made up my mind just to be myself. The show was live and when the red light went on, I just plunged in, devil-may-care, with nothing planned, just to be Zsa Zsa.

*

I don't quite know what happened. All I know is that that night I became an instant star. And I couldn't even go out on the streets of Los Angeles without being mobbed by crowds of fans. It had all happened so quickly—as everything in my life seems to happen. Things happen to me faster than lightning. And, inevitably, I always hit the headlines. Like it or not, encourage it or not, I seem born to make headlines. A week after I first appeared on TV, my picture graced the cover of both *Life* magazine and *Cosmopolitan*. And within a month, I was offered an MGM contract. My success was what is known in show business as "overnight"—only in my case it was "over half an hour."

Looking back, I realize that all I did was do what I have always done: flout convention and say what I really think, no matter what the consequences—and poke fun at myself while I'm doing it. The first question was "I've just broken off my engagement to a wonderful man who gave me a beautiful home, lingerie, a mink coat, diamonds, a stove, and an expensive car. Now that we are no longer engaged, what shall I give back?" Suddenly, I was thirteen years old and back at Madame Subilia's again, surrounded by up-market English girls, hanging on my every word, eager to hear the wickedly worldly pearls of wisdom that dropped from my Hungarian lips. Instinctively, I answered, "Give back the stove." Tom

Father, Mother, and the three Gabor children in Budapest. I am the one sitting on Mother's knee. At the time, I hated having my picture taken.

My father, Vilmos Farkas Gabor, in Budapest.

George Sanders and I by the swimming pool in the first house we lived in together, at 1000 Bellagio Road.

The young Mrs. George Sanders, not yet an actress but about to host a dinner party at her Bel Air home.

With Francesca on her birthday in the Bel Air house, which burned down. At the time of this picture, my hair was red.

One of my first television appearances on *The Jack Paar Show* in New York. My Yorkie, Mr. Magoo, is on the desk.

My very first picture at MGM, *Lovely to Look At,* in which I co-starred with Red Skelton, Kathryn Grayson, Howard Keel, Ann Miller, and Marge and Gower Champion. I played a French model who doesn't speak a word of English. (*above*)

A scene from *Lovely to Look At.*

A break with Francesca and Eva during filming of *Lili* at MGM.

A scene from *Lili* with co-star Leslie Caron.

Lili, in which I co-starred with Leslie Caron, Mel Ferrer, and Jean-Pierre Aumont.

As Jane Avril singing the famous "Song of Moulin Rouge" at Shepperton Studios in London.

Rubi and I in Paris after flying in on his B-25 clipped-wing plane—the one that Barbara Hutton had given him.

Larry Harvey at a party at my house.

Francesca and I in London during the filming of *The Man Who Wouldn't Talk.*

Shooting *The Man Who Wouldn't Talk* in London with Sir Anthony Quayle.

Jolie Gabor and her three daughters at her home in New York.

George Sanders and I in a scene from *Death of a Scoundrel.*

Joanne Dru and I in the film *Three Ring Circus,* in which Dean Martin and Jerry Lewis co-starred. During filming in Arizona, Rubi continually called me—even though he had just married Barbara Hutton.

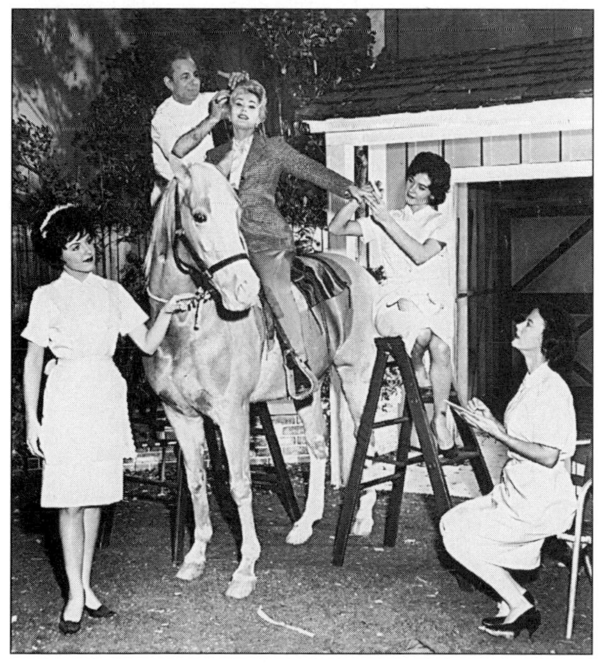

Rehearsing with the Beatles for "Night of a Thousand Stars" at the London Palladium.

Guesting on Mr. Ed's television show.

Herbert Huttner and I at a costume party at Les Ambassadeurs in London. Herbert is dressed as Der Rosenkavalier and I am dressed as Catherine the Great.

The *Queen of Outer Space* poster.

A scene from *Queen of Outer Space.*

My "wedding" to Tony Curtis filmed for *Arrivederci, Baby!* in Cannes. Six months later I wore the same Christian Dior dress when I married Joshua Cosden, Jr. (*above*)

On location in Capri shooting *For the First Time* with Mario Lanza, in his last film.

Conway roared with laughter. The other panelists looked momentarily bemused.

The questions followed in quick succession.

Question: "Do you think large families are a good idea?"

My answer: "Oh yes, I believe in large families. Every woman should have at least three husbands."

Question: "I've just broken off my engagement. Should I return the ring?

Answer: "Yes. A woman should always give back the ring. But keep the stone."

By now, Johnny Jacobs, the moderator, had joined in, commenting on my diamonds. Almost without thinking, I cracked, "Oh these! These are just my working diamonds."

I was just being Zsa Zsa. I always have been and I always will be.

NOËL COWARD used to say that he had a talent to amuse. It seemed that I had a talent—of sorts—to shock in a comical way and to ad-lib without the help of scriptwriters. Throughout the years, I've never lost that ability. In his book

I Owe Russia $1,200, Bob Hope wrote of our 1960 tour to Guantánamo Bay, succinctly describing what I did and how I did it—all in the most flattering terms.

> Finally, even Zsa Zsa deigned to grace our stage. She looked beautiful, but then I've never seen our Hungarian mantrap when she didn't look great.
>
> And she really flipped the guys. We'd do a set routine and then, for an encore, she'd just ad-lib answers to questions from the audience. I don't recall all of her zingers, but here are a few that I made a note of:
>
> Question: What's more important, love or money?
> Gabor: Love. Money doesn't help you in the evenings.
> Question: Who are you going to marry next?
> Gabor: You sound like my mother. I want a man who appreciates the finer things in life ... diamonds, furs, and me.
>
> I could go on like this for twelve pages, but you know how she hates publicity.

Bob's words—as always—were very kind to me. But, in one respect, the last sentence, sarcastic as it is, still perpetrates the legend that I am an obsessive publicity seeker. Which isn't true. I don't seek publicity. It has always, right from my very first appearance on *Bachelor's Haven,* sought me.

MY first film part was in the MGM musical *Lovely to Look At*. I was to play Mignon, a French model. My lines were all in French and when I spoke, there would be English subtitles. My salary was a staggering $10,000 a week—a sum that would eventually prove to be the first nail in my marriage—for George, then already a star, had been paid just $250 for his first Hollywood role in *Lloyds of London*. I knew he would resent the disparity in our debuts and I soon discovered that two actors should never be married. The clash of egos is far too deafening and destructive.

Soon I would upstage George (a man who had once declared, "I wouldn't want a wife who was more famous than I") and he would never forgive me. He came home from London one month later to find that the little wife he'd left behind had become a star. Ultimately, the birth of my career would mean the death of our marriage.

MY first day at MGM dawned and I was petrified. Before I left home, Elizabeth Keleman tried to infuse me with courage by saying, "If an American girl can act—if an American girl can do it—so can you!" But I was still terrified. First I was dispatched to makeup—only to find myself sitting at a long table, in front of an even longer mirror. Next to me sat Ava Gardner, Elizabeth Taylor, Lana Turner, and Grace Kelly. I soon found out that the modus operandi at the studio was for actresses to apply their own lipstick, on the premise that no one, not even the world's leading makeup artist, is capable of applying a woman's lipstick the way she can apply it herself. (MGM was full of such folklore, e.g., soak white underwear in tea so that it assumes a realistic flesh tone.)

On that first day, just as I was about to embark on the lipstick process, Ava Gardner (whom I liked immediately), leaned over conspiratorially and said, "Sydney will make his entrance any minute." Sydney was Sydney Guilaroff, the legendary hair designer, who swept into the makeup room a moment later, glanced at the collection of world-famous Hollywood stars, and contemptuously commanded, "Girls! Put your lipstick on! I don't fix up dogs!" I adored him instantly, and still do.

However, despite Sydney's hair artistry, I arrived on set practically speechless. I was given my cue, but I was so scared that (one of the only times in my life) I couldn't even open my mouth. The leading lady, Kathryn Grayson, who had been watching me, cried out, "I have a run in my stocking. Can we have a break so that I can go and change?" The director agreed and, on her way to the dressing room, Katie put her arm around me sympathetically and asked if I'd come to her dressing room with her.

I followed her, grateful for the reprieve, yet still feeling crestfallen and inept. Once in the dressing room, Katie invited me to sit down, made a certain amount of small talk to give me time to compose myself, then poured me a stiff shot of vodka, telling me, "Drink up." When we went back onto the set, my performance was virtually flawless. And Kathryn Grayson became my best friend.

THAT first day at MGM, I met another woman who would become deeply important to me and would become a friend. I have always needed and cherished friends. I am very perceptive about people and I start out liking everybody. I give all my friendship, my advice, and my loyalty to a friend. But most people end up coming out with some kind of angle and take energy from you and hurt you. Jorja Courtright was an exception. She was a young actress who worked with Elsa Stanoff helping actresses with their lines and we became close friends. Sometime later, when we were shooting *Lili,* I introduced her to one of Bundy Solt's friends—a man named

Sidney Sheldon. Six weeks later, they were married. Jorja and Sidney's marriage became one of the happiest in Hollywood and they loved each other until the day Jorja died. At the memorial service, Sidney Poitier gave the eulogy, ending with the words, "Let's all get up and give Jorja a big hand because that is what she liked best." Jorja deserved every iota of applause she ever got. I loved her dearly.

WHEN I came home from the set, after the first day's filming, despite Kathryn Grayson's divine intervention, I was still shaking with nerves. Clark Gable was waiting for me, sitting with George at the kitchen table sampling yet more of Elizabeth Keleman's wonderful cooking. I cried on his shoulder, telling him that the whole experience of Hollywood had terrified me, that I wanted to give up acting and never see a single studio light again. Smiling his irresistible Rhett Butler smile, but sounding more like an understanding uncle than a sexy heartthrob, Clark patted my hand and said, "Don't worry. Just play Zsa Zsa. I always play Clark Gable. And I didn't do badly, did I?"

Apart from a brief pep talk, Clark went on to offer further practical advice, telling me to invest in some private coaching. That was how I ended up with Elsa Stanoff, one of the greatest geniuses ever to arrive in Hollywood, an acting coach par excellence. Elsa lived in the Hollywood Hills. She was a former director who was married to another drama coach, Michael Stanoff. The Stanoffs provided further confirmation of my growing belief that both partners being in show business did not help a marriage. Elsa used to say of Michael, "He's good. But not as good as me."

I can't challenge her statement, because I studied only with Elsa, not Michael. And to me, she was unbeatable. Gregory Peck studied with her. So did Gary Cooper and Patricia Neal. I studied with Elsa till she died—and although, like some of the actors in Hollywood, I delighted in calling her by her nickname of "Applestrudel"—she taught me everything I have ever learned about acting.

*

THE conflict between George and me over my fledgling career began to escalate dramatically. In the meantime, in quick succession, I had gone on to make *Lili,* with Leslie Caron and Jean-Pierre Aumont. Jean-Pierre played a French magician in a traveling carnival. I played his assistant, Rosalie. In one of my scenes, Jean-Pierre, with a wave of his magic wand, swept away my red sequined gown, leaving me dressed only in revealing sexy black lingerie. Years later, when MGM held their auction, the panties and bra I had worn in *Lili* fetched an incredible $7,000.

I had also made *The Story of Three Loves,* and *We're Not Married* with Marilyn, now a big star. The film was an anthology of stories about five supposedly married couples who suddenly determine that they aren't married after all. I played the gold-digging bride of an aging millionaire, played by Louis Calhern. Luckily, although Marilyn and I were deemed to be cast in the same dumb-blonde mold, we didn't have any scenes together.

*

BY now, though, I had even bigger, more fetching fish to worry about than Marilyn. George was beginning to cast his sexual net onto richer, more opulent waters. He was thoroughly demoralized by playing second fiddle to me at parties—like the one where Ethel Barrymore sailed over to us, George's eyes expectantly lit up in anticipation, only to find himself shunted aside as Ethel praised me for my appearances on *Bachelor's Haven*—where I was now a regular and for which I had been nominated for an Emmy. Despite George's chagrin, Ethel's exact words were not completely gushing. "I love your TV show—you are very talented, beautiful, and young. If you remain healthy, have endurance, and are lucky, then maybe you will make it."

We were at a party at Ciro's (ironically, given that it was here, too, that I had first met Conrad Hilton) when I observed a brief encounter that was the first chain in a link of events that would transform my life. George and I were about to help ourselves from the sumptuous buffet when Doris Duke, the tobacco heiress and one of the wealthiest women in the world, glided up to George, kissed him familiarly on both cheeks, and said, in a voice intended to be heard, "Darling, didn't we have fun this afternoon?"

As soon as Doris proceeded on to someone else, I turned to George, my voice trembling with trepidation. "George, I didn't know you knew Doris Duke. When did you meet her? You told me you didn't know her!"

Slowly and patiently (now that he had got the upper hand), George explained that he and Doris had been taking voice lessons with the same teacher and that, sometimes, today as it happened being one of those times, they had a drink afterward.

The subsequent arguments between us about George—who loved money—and Ms. Duke—who possessed it in magnitude—were marathon and culminated in me hiring a detective and tracking George and Doris to a motel in New Jersey. The shock almost tore me apart. But I confronted George, swearing revenge. Striking out at random, I accidentally stumbled on the instrument of that revenge—Porfirio Rubirosa—Doris Duke's ex-husband, a man she still loved and desired and wanted to remarry. Spitefully, at that point blaming Doris far more than George and wanting to hurt her, even if she never knew it, I lashed out with "I'm going to have an affair with Rubirosa." Not knowing that, if I carried out my threat, I wouldn't merely hurt Doris, but that I'd destroy George, the husband whom, despite his cruelty to me, I still loved so much.

THE turning point came when producer Jimmy Woolf, a thirty-five-year-old Englishman, offered me the part of Jane Avril in *Moulin Rouge*. My first instinct was to refuse. Accepting meant spending six months in England—six months during which George and I would be apart. George, for whatever reason, insisted that I accept.

Jimmy, too, was extremely persuasive. He came to Hollywood in an attempt to convince me to take the part and I decided he was one of the brightest men whom I'd ever met. Jimmy and I soon became great friends (although he fast developed a marked antipathy to George, whom he labeled as "that bastard").

One of Jimmy's friends, actor Laurence Harvey, was in town and we all had dinner at Romanoff's. In the future, he went on to marry Joan Cohn—the widow of Columbia studio chief Harry Cohn—because he said he felt like getting some stock in the studio. Joan adored Larry and spoiled him immensely.

She threw a spectacular Christmas party to which we were invited. When we arrived at Joan's mansion, Larry was standing outside looking extremely petulant. Pointing at a brand-new station wagon parked in the driveway, he announced, "That bitch. She bought me a station wagon! And I wanted a Rolls-Royce!"

Larry had been so spoiled by his overnight success in the British film *Room at the Top* that he had evolved into an insufferable snob. At a dinner party I gave in Bel Air, also attended by Rex Harrison, Larry pronounced that the wine was not up to par. "I don't like the wine at all, my dear. Can I send my butler back to my home for some real wine?"

Later, Rex, who had known Larry for years, wryly commented, "I remember when he didn't have enough money to buy a Coke with."

On another occasion Rex enlisted George's help in deflating Larry's outsize ego, when all three of them were co-starring in *King Richard and the Crusaders*. First, though, conscious that Larry considered himself to be one of the world's best actors, Rex approached him and asked, "Tell me, dear boy, am I playing this scene properly?" "Well, Rex," said Larry, taking him seriously, "I can't teach you how to play it—but I *can* give you some good advice."

Piqued but not surprised at Larry's reaction, Rex got his revenge. In one scene, the script called for Larry to lift George's "dead" body high into the air and carry him off. But when it came to film the scene, Larry, to his consternation, discovered that he couldn't move George at all. The director declared, "Mr. Harvey, I'm surprised and disappointed. After all, you're a strong young man." The entire cast and crew burst into laughter at Larry's discomfort. Rex and George laughed loudest, knowing full well that they had put weights into George's pocket.

With his classic wit and intelligence, George summed up the enigma that was Larry in the following poem:

How to take young know-it-all Larry?
A cross between Shakespeare and Madame Du Barry.

Despite George's opinion of Larry, I thought he was a genius. When he died, Larry left a will that was written entirely in Hebrew.

I finally capitulated and accepted Jimmy Woolf's offer to appear in *Moulin Rouge*. Before I left for Paris, I found out that John Huston, who was directing the picture, had been against casting me in it, but that he had been overruled by Jimmy and his brother, Sir John Woolf. John Huston was not a man who liked to lose and I knew that this did not bode well for me.

On my first night in Paris (where the exteriors were to be shot) John took me to Maxim's and after dinner, with no preamble, said, "Now I am going to sleep with you." He was leaning toward me, almost into me, and his hoarse voice rasped, "I must have you." He had a very macho nose that he'd broken in a boxing match, he appeared to be about ten feet tall—and it seemed as if every inch of him was wrapped around me. Looking straight into his eyes, I said, with as much resolution as I could muster, "No, John. I'm not going to sleep with you. I'm madly in love with my husband, George Sanders."

John didn't like being rejected any more than he relished having been overruled in his casting. On the first day's shooting, he took me into the upstairs room of Maxim's, opened all the windows, stood at one end of the room and ordered me to project. Elsa Stanoff had instructed me never to project in a movie, only onstage. But John continued to order me to project, forcing me to scream until my voice had almost disappeared.

Soon the room filled up with extras—European aristocrats, many of whom were friends of my parents' from Hungary—whom John had hired for the film. John did his best to humiliate me in front of all of them. Dropping the end of a sentence is a Hungarian habit I hadn't yet lost. And John made the most of it, yelling, "Stop dropping the end of your sentences," then telling the cinematographer, Ossie Morris, "Move in close. I mean close. If they can see how beautiful she is, they won't notice that she can't act."

Once we arrived in London, where we were shooting the interiors at Shepperton Studios, John meted out yet more of the same treatment. When I was about to shoot the scene in which I walk down the staircase, singing the title song, I made the mistake of asking John how to play it. His only advice was, "Darling, as you know nothing about filming or acting or singing or dancing, I'm going to put a heart on the camera and then you come down the staircase, wiggle your Hungarian ass, and just look into the heart."

I was so miserable, lost so much weight (which pleased John, who liked "his" women to be thin), that I called Elsa in Hollywood. John found out, which infuriated him. "That bitch in Hollywood ruined you," he grumbled, before sending me for coaching to the great actress Constance Collier. Her coaching gave me more confidence and, as a result, John spent most of my scenes playing poker, looking up occasionally and pronouncing, "That's right, Zsa Zsa." Soon he mellowed sufficiently to take a friendly interest in me.

After spending the weekend in Stratford-upon-Avon with Jimmy Woolf and Larry Harvey, John asked benevolently, "Now tell me, little girl, what did you do over the weekend?

"We went to Stratford-upon-Avon."

"Did you go to Anne Hathaway's cottage?"

"Yes," I replied eagerly, "I believe we had tea with her."

He started laughing heartily and I was offended. Then I read up on Shakespeare and felt really embarrassed. Then again, what the hell would a Hungarian know about The Bard? I'd been brought up on Goethe and Schiller. In any event, John had a souvenir made up for me with the inscription *Zsa Zsa, she had tea with Anne Hathaway.*

ON my last day of work, John came onto the set looking like a dried-out monkey with a hangover. He confessed that he didn't know how to handle Jane Avril's last scene in the film, so when they started shooting, I leaned over Toulouse-Lautrec's deathbed and improvised, saying airily, "Toulouse, darling, I hear you are dying. I just came to say good-bye. I will see you soon. Now I have to run—I have the most beautiful man in the world waiting for me at Maxim's." When the cameras stopped rolling, I looked at John and saw that he was smiling through his hangover. "You wrote and acted it in one take," he said.

"I can do it better. It just needs a little bit of warmth to make it perfect."

John refused to let me reshoot the scene, and later was highly amused that I caused great controversy when the director of the Tate Gallery, Sir John Rothenstein, invited me to view the Toulouse-Lautrec paintings on display there. I accepted and was photographed in front of Toulouse's paintings in the gallery and created a major controversy. In Parliament, Viscountess Davidson attacked me, objecting to my using the Tate and its national treasures to publicize a film. After that, *Moulin Rouge* was world news.

WHEN *Moulin Rouge* opened in New York in the spring of 1953, I was alone, staying at a suite in the Plaza, where my life in America had first begun. George had abandoned me, leaving me in Manhattan on New Year's Eve, after refusing to attend the film premiere. His rejection of me, my career, and his unwillingness to be associated with what would turn out to be a triumph for me, left me feeling drained and hopeless. True, he had gone to Italy to make a film with Ingrid Bergman and Roberto Rossellini. But I had asked to go with him and he hadn't wanted me. Moreover, he could have delayed his journey and taken me to the premiere. George's message was clear—he didn't want me to be an actress and would have no part in supporting my new career.

Perhaps I should have given in, should have given up acting and tried to be the wife that George wanted. But I was too insecure, too unsure of his love or his loyalty. After all, the specters of Doris Duke, Hedy Lamarr, Marilyn Monroe, and yet more assorted lovelies, still haunted me. If I gave up acting and then George gave up me—what would I have left? So I had concentrated on my career and had guest-starred on the Bob Hope, Bing Crosby, Frank Sinatra, and Red Skelton shows.

I'd even signed for the first of many Las Vegas nightclub appearances—this one at the Flamingo Hotel—for which I would receive a princely $35,000 a week. I'd done all that—and now I was paying the price. I would attend the *Moulin Rouge* premiere without George. I would be alone. But, as it turned out, not for too long. I hadn't bargained on fate—for what Atatürk, my first love, would have called karma. For on that night—the night of the *Moulin Rouge* premiere—I came face-to-face with my own particular karma—a man named Porfirio Rubirosa.

PORFIRIO RUBIROSA was machismo incarnate. The facts are these: Born in the Dominican Republic, the son of a general, Rubi (as he came to be known) was educated in Paris, then expelled from school for drinking, nightclubbing, and seducing beautiful women. At twenty, his adventures had already become legendary in Santo Domingo. Soon he was appointed aide-de-camp to President Trujillo, married his daughter, Flor, but divorced her for the beautiful French actress Danielle Darrieux, who became his second wife. And I was, of course, extremely aware that his most recent wife was Doris Duke, whom he had divorced, even though she was still in love with him. I knew that now he was a leading diplomat, traveling the world representing his country. I also knew that he raced cars, flew planes, and played polo. He was a playboy and a Casanova, a Don Juan and a charmer—a man whom other men longed to emulate and every woman longed to love.

I knew all this, but none of it impressed me. After all, I was the ex-Mrs. Conrad Hilton, the ex-Mrs. Burhan Belge, Atatürk's lover and, above all, George Sanders's wife. I'd been involved with some of the most charismatic men in the world. The myth of Porfirio Rubirosa, I told myself, had nothing to do with me except that when I had threatened George that I might go to bed with Rubi—he had momentarily dropped his guard and had gone pale. No, Porfirio Rubirosa interested me only on account of George and not on account of himself.

We met in the Plaza elevator on the night of the *Moulin Rouge* premiere, he sent me flowers, then—after the premiere—invited me to the Persian Room for drinks with Prince Bernadotte of Sweden. I was still not impressed—not by Rubi, or by the idea of meeting him. But I accepted, feeling miserable and alone without George by my side. Mother and I went to the Persian Room and it was then that I met him. It was then that Rubi finally impressed me. He was dark, magnetic, as mysterious in his own way as Atatürk had been in his, as cool and composed as Conrad Hilton, and as sophisticated and urbane as George Sanders. Before we ever even touched, Rubi mesmerized me.

RUBI and I spent one night together at the Plaza and in the morning I knew that I never wanted to leave him again. I was madly in love with George, but after one night with Rubi, I lost all sense of reality. He was exciting, sensual, passionate, primitive yet incredibly sophisticated. In time, I was to discover that he was also a daredevil, risking his life riding horses, flying planes, racing cars, and challenging other men by seducing their women. In his own way, Rubi was as much of a rebel as I had always been. Sometimes, when I looked into his eyes, I saw myself.

THE day after the opening, John Huston sent me a telegram saying, "You and Technicolor saved our picture! Congratulations, John Huston." Delighted as I was, I was nevertheless disturbed by a second telegram I also received. Usually pointedly indifferent to me, this time George suddenly became psychic. He telegraphed me to join him in Italy, where he was making the film *Journey to Italy* for Roberto Rossellini with Roberto's wife, Ingrid Bergman.

Bogie once gave an interview to *Ladies' Home Journal* in which he said that the two women he most admired in America were me and Ingrid Bergman. Unfortunately I was unable to share his admiration of Ingrid. Before Ingrid and I first met, my friend Bundy—who had written her movie *Joan of Arc*—told me everything he knew about her. According to him, she had been unhappy with her first husband, Petter Lindstrom, but hadn't been slow in consoling herself. Bundy told me, "There was hardly an electrician on the set that she didn't sleep with. When she was finished with them, she had them fired."

At that point, Ingrid and Roberto had already had three beautiful children, but their artistic collaboration had proved to be a disappointment in films like *Stromboli* and *Europa '51*. By this time, the only way in which Roberto could finance his films was to cast a world-class name like George to co-star with Ingrid.

George met me in Rome and we took a train to Naples. Although my mind was full of Rubi, I didn't mention him or give in to the urge to confess my affair to George. On the journey, George spent the whole time complaining to me about Rossellini. "He is the least professional director in the world," muttered George. "We just wasted five days with Ingrid wandering through a museum, looking at pictures, aimlessly. She loathes all the other films they've done over here, but she gave up everything and now she's stuck with him. I hate working with her; she's a conceited bitch."

George's litany of complaints continued. "I want a director who knows what he's doing. I want a shooting schedule. I want some order and discipline! Rossellini looks on moviemaking as a picnic. The other day he went off spear fishing, right in the middle of shooting. Roberto Rossellini is an asshole. He never gives me a script. He makes up the story on the set. There's no prepared dialogue. I'm an English actor and I can't work like that. Neither can Ingrid. I don't know how she puts up with it, film after film."

The day we arrived, Ingrid, noticing me, sailed over and said, "Oh, I want to meet George's wife." Given my burgeoning career, it felt like a slap, so I replied, "And I'd like to meet Roberto's wife." Our first meeting was not auspicious, but I felt sorry for Ingrid when Roberto began to hurl abuse at her. I admired her dignity and restraint. George was less composed, yelling, "I can't go on. I can't do this *commedia dell'arte* and invent and get the lines at the last minute."

George sank into a terrible depression. "I might as well go ahead and have a nervous breakdown," he threatened. "I've nothing to look forward to but this dismal movie." I looked at George appraisingly, and, always the perfect wife, eager to please and to placate my husband, hit on a unique way to make him happy.

Flashback:

On the Train from Rome to Naples

GEORGE was in the midst of his anti-Rossellini tirade when the compartment door opened and a priest entered. For a moment, I thought it might be a divine sign, that the priest might be able to help George out of his depression and prevent a nervous breakdown. Both George and I nodded to him, and he smiled courteously. I hoped George would pour his heart out to him, but he did not believe in God and was much too proud to ask for help.

Instead, he started whispering in my ear, a suggestion so profane that I was shocked: "Darling, my secret fantasy has always been to see you making love with a Catholic priest."

"But George," I pointed out helplessly, "they're celibate."

"Allegedly," said George, raising an eyebrow. Suddenly he

was smiling at me—no longer so intensely melancholy. I was relieved to see this mood change.

"Anyway," he went on, "with you, my dear, anything is possible. Every man can be laid, count on it."

"But a priest . . . ?"

"Priest or not, notice how he's looking at you. He's looking at you like a woman. You're a religious girl—surely holiness is the ultimate aphrodisiac."

"Isn't that blasphemy?"

"Afraid of turning into a pillar of salt?" countered George gleefully, then adding, "Besides, it's my heresy, not yours. Now, look into those piercing eyes. The father is positively burning for you!"

I took another look at the priest, who was, indeed, sizing me up. George continued whispering in my ear, his breath getting warmer, exciting me.

"See the veins on those muscular hands." George sighed, his moist lips lasciviously nuzzling my earlobe. It was my husband I wanted, and I wanted him now, but George continued, "Imagine those hands stroking your breasts, darling. He's yours for the taking."

This priest had the boldest bedroom eyes I'd ever seen. He was a striking young man, with an athletic build, radiant green eyes, and a glossy mane of black hair.

Moving even closer to me in the train, George begged me, "Darling, try to make love to him. Nobody ever turned you down."

*I smiled at the priest, and he smiled back at me. "*Bella signora,*" he said. "Will you be getting off the train in Naples?" "Yes," I said. "And you?"*

"Also Naples."

"My name is Guido," he said, extending his big, warm hand.

"And mine," I said, smiling at George, "is Cokiline"—a pet name George sometimes used to give me, meaning "spicy cookie."

Meanwhile, George was staring out of the train window, pretending to study some cows chewing the cud in a distant field, but I could feel his body tensing with excitement beside me. I stood, smiled again at Guido, and left the compartment.

In the passageway outside the door, I lit a cigarette and gazed out at the fields. The next minute, Guido was standing beside me.

"Cigarette?" I asked.

He laughed and said, "If you say so."

After I lit it for him, he stood there holding it awkwardly. I took it from him, crushed it under my heel, and moved close to him. Behind us, George watched from behind the compartment curtain.

He spoke of his family, his collegiate sporting triumphs, and his time in the army before he became a priest.

Guido was handsome and charming, but what really excited me was the pleasure our encounter was giving to George, so near us, just behind the curtain.

Guido didn't seem in the least bit concerned about George except to ask, "Your husband, isn't he jealous?"

"Yes," I said, smiling provocatively, then adding, "But not today. Today he'll forgive me anything."

"Signora Cokiline," Guido said. "When I took my vows I did not imagine I would see an angel, golden and fair. With you, nothing would be profane. Ask anything of me, I will do it."

Guido understood. He suggested we get off at the next station, book into a hotel, and make love. I refused but instead gave him the number of Rossellini's production company where he could leave a message for me.

GEORGE'S depression deepened and he began talking of suicide—which terrified me. I wondered whether, with his uncanny intuition, he had divined the truth about my affair with Rubi. I couldn't bear the thought of losing George and I was willing to pay any price to keep him. I thought once more of Rubi and my infidelity and made up my mind to do the ultimate penance and, in the bargain, to make George happy. So that when Guido's message arrived, begging me to meet him in Ravello, and knowing how thrilled George was at the prospect of our profane liaison, I accepted.

Before the meeting, George tried to persuade me to make love to Guido that day, but I refused, hoping that the lunch-time rendezvous would satisfy him and reverse his depression. But knowing George, I was afraid it wouldn't and that he would want more. We met at a terrace restaurant, while

George, complete with sunglasses but otherwise unconvincing disguise, sat at the next table, listening.

Guido, it turned out, was even more impatient. He arrived dressed in jeans and sweater, set on taking me to his friend's house. Over lunch, I discovered he was as bright as he was attractive, able to speak good English, and that he loved horseback riding. Glancing over at George, I saw that he was waiting, expectantly. I arranged to meet Guido—ostensibly to go riding with him—the very next day, when George was not filming and could be around to savor the denouement.

Early the next morning, George got a call from the set asking him to report for work after all. There was no way out, but I promised, "Darling, everything I do with Guido, I'll do with you tonight." George bounded out of the room, happier than I'd seen him since I first arrived in Italy. I toyed with canceling the meeting, but knew George would never forgive me.

Guido and I spent hours riding and talking and laughing. Toward midday, we came to a stream and got off our horses. Without a moment's hesitation, Guido took me in his arms and devoured me with kisses. For a moment, I forgot that George wasn't watching us and congratulated myself on playing the scene so well for his benefit. But George was miles away, dancing to Rossellini's tune and missing the experience of his life.

Guido's kisses grew more passionate, we were totally isolated, with no one around for miles, and, slowly, he began to pull me onto the ground. I tore myself away from him. "Guido," I asked gently. "How long is it since you've had a woman?"

"Never—I've never had a woman."

Then I told him that I was sorry but I could not be his first—his only woman. I was in love with George, George had incited me, inveigled me into this situation, I found Guido intensely attractive, but knew I had to stop myself, that I couldn't lead him to break his vows, that my conscience wouldn't let me.

Guido's first reaction, "I'm grateful to have aroused your desire," made me feel sad. After all, would it have been so terrible for me to give in to my desires? Then he went on and I knew I'd been right. "But I love you unconditionally. Nothing is different now than when we met on the train. My love has no strings attached. As for my lust, I now surrender it to God. He knows better than I what to do with it." We parted.

That night, I greeted George with the words "Don't ask me what I did with Guido. Let me show you." When we finished, George's only comment was "I assume Guido is leaving the church." His depression was over. Guido and I remained friends—platonic friends—and even to this day, whenever I go to Italy (where he is adored by his parishioners) I still see him.

MY ostensible "sacrifice" infused George with a newly awakened passion, defused his depression, and seemed to herald a renaissance for our marriage. That is, until Rubi sent me a romantic telegram. George found it, I got an offer to fly to Paris and make a film with the great French comedian Fernandel and I accepted it. Soon I was back in Paris and back with Rubi.

I was in Paris because of my career, because I had signed to make *The Most Wanted Man* with Fernandel. In theory, I was in Paris for my career—but in actuality, my stay in Paris undermined it. At a time when I was riding the crest of my *Moulin Rouge* success and should have been in Hollywood meeting with all the many producers who wanted to sign me up for parts that may well have made me into an international star, I was in Paris, scandalizing society with my adulterous affair with Porfirio Rubirosa.

Professionally, I missed my moment. If I hadn't followed my heart and hadn't capitulated to my passion for Rubirosa, and had, at that moment, concentrated on my career, my life might have been completely different. As it is, I did follow my heart, I did let passion overrule judgment but I didn't care and, to this day, I still don't care. Out of all the many lives I've lived up till now—my life with Rubirosa was the most exciting.

WE were like two children: pleasure-seeking, hedonistic, perhaps spoiled and selfish, but full of an unquenchable lust for life and an insatiably strong appetite for excitement. For Rubi and I both suffered from the same curse: Life held too many possibilities for us. It was as if there was too much potential surrounding us, too much love, too much excitement. We were too greedy for life and too greedy for each other.

Rubi was renowned for his charm, his machismo, and, above all, his sexual prowess (which owed more to the strength of his desire, his warmth, and sensitivity than to his anatomy). I was famous for my diamonds, my looks, and my husbands. Both of us far transcended our public images and, underneath, were far more simple, far more childlike than anyone knew. Rubi understood that. He also understood me. Which made him irresistible.

I was obsessed by him, addicted to him, he was in my blood and he possessed my soul. But life had to go on. In the early days of our romance, when we were together in Paris, I tried hard to concentrate on filming, tried desperately to snap out of the potent sexual trance I was in and to break the powerful spell Rubi seemed to have put on me. But although I was supposed to be staying at the Plaza Athénée, I found myself spending more and more time with Rubi at his house on the Rue Bellechasse, close to the Seine, which Doris Duke had given to him.

Rubi's house, like Atatürk's secret hideaway in old Ankara, was a romantic dream, an oasis of beauty and sensuality, where we would spend hours making love, where Rubi played soft music, serenaded me, even bathed and dressed me.

We were in Paris for three months, then we were together in Rome, Deauville, Cannes, with Rubi, all the while, begging me to divorce George, marry him. He was wildly, passionately in love with me. But I couldn't decide because somehow, I didn't know which of the two men in my life, the two men whom I loved, was best for me. I felt George wasn't enough for me because he wasn't Rubi. And that Rubi wasn't enough for me because he wasn't George. I was caught in an agonizingly exquisite dilemma. As yet, George wasn't prepared to fight for me. But I knew that despite my infidelity, he wanted me back.

THOSE years in Paris with Rubi took on a dreamlike quality. The days were enchanted, sparkling, with life, with love, and with diamonds. Unlike other men—men who didn't adore women as Rubi did but who thought of them as ornaments lacking in any life or passion of their own—Rubi didn't shower me with gifts chosen at random, but spent hours of thought and care on mementos designed to forever commemorate our love and our passion. From Van Cleef & Arpels, he selected a turquoise and diamond necklace, from Bulgari he purchased a diamond brooch, with the reddest of rubies fashioned into roses, which he himself designed specially for me. And from Cartier he chose a bracelet fashioned out of the most sparkling of blue diamonds, crowned with a cluster of red rubies—a rare art deco gem that he deemed perfect for me.

Rubi had the rare ability to recognize quality and appreciate it, be it in a stone, in a horse, or in a woman. He didn't care how much time or energy or money he spent on pursuing quality and pleasure, prepared to spend hours at Christian Dior not only ordering the entire collection for me, but also inspecting every design to ensure that it flattered me as he felt I should be flattered.

When I wasn't filming, we would sleep till eleven, then drive in Rubi's Mercedes to the Champs-Elysées and eat oysters for breakfast. Next we went to the Bagatelle to play polo. Rubi was a four-goal player (the world's best are ten-goal players) and he made up his mind to teach me to play. He had a little polo pony flown in for me from the King Ranch in Texas and gave her to me. We called her Little Sister and Rubi taught me to play on her. Polo players invariably wear white helmets—only Rubi wore red. Even today, all those years later, whenever President Trujillo's grandsons play polo they still wear red helmets in memory of Rubi.

After polo, we rushed home, spent hours making love, then dressed for the evening, before going out again with friends for cocktails before dinner at Maxim's—ending the evening at a club—usually Jimmy's, or the Eléphant Bleu. Rubi never wanted to leave. There was always more champagne, more caviar, another dance, another romantic refrain for him to strum on a guitar handed to him by some admiring orchestra leader, eager to see the legendary Rubirosa serenade his Zsa Zsa Gabor.

Our friends were the cream of society: Queen Elizabeth of Yugoslavia, Ingrid and Pierre Smadja, Mr. and Mrs. Jean Roi, Geneviève Fath and a Portuguese prince, one of the richest men in Europe. They were all attractive, celebrated, wealthy, and not one of them mentioned George or my desertion from him. Instead, they watched as Rubi held me close to his side, romanced me and hypnotized me as he whirled me through the Parisian dusk and into the early dawn, from party to party and nightclub to nightclub. We never went to Freddie's though. For some reason, Rubi, who guarded me more closely than any sultan ever guarded the queen of his harem, was jealous of my friendship with Freddie.

That friendship remained innocent, but Rubi was undeterred. Part of his power, part of his charm, and part of his hold over me was due to the sense of danger he wore around him like a sinister cloak. For when Rubi became jealous, he was transformed from aristocratic charmer to something akin to Jack the Ripper. He blazed with anger, erupted in fury, a hot, sexual volcano exploding with jealousy and an unquenchable lust for control—to tie me to him forever.

I first tasted the sting of Rubi's jealousy and felt the lash of his rage one night after we drove Prince Jimmy and Geneviève home to their house. I was finally leaving for Hollywood the next day and kissed the Prince good night. We watched Geneviève and the Prince walked into the house, Rubi turned the key in the ignition, then suddenly, without warning, his eyes blazing like hot coals, slapped me hard around the face. I screamed in shock, Geneviève ran out of the house and, without a word, helped me out of the car and into the house. Without looking back, Rubi started the car and roared off into the heart of Paris.

My nose was bleeding, I was hurt and humiliated and let Geneviève lead me into one of the guest bedrooms, where I lay down on the white satin sheets. Geneviève was shaking. "How can he do that to a beautiful girl like you?" she said, wringing her hands in despair. "How can he! I am going to call the police." The Prince came in and, seeing my nose, insisted that he was leaving that minute, was going to search for Rubi and was going to kill him. I convinced them not to do anything, but said that I needed some sleep.

All of a sudden, the doorbell rang. It was three in the morning and we all exchanged glances, knowing it could only be Rubi. Geneviève looked at me imploringly and begged me not to let him in. But I had no choice. Rubi owned me, I had lost my will, I was a part of him and I no longer belonged to myself. Geneviève let him in. He knelt in front of my bed and asked for my forgiveness. Then the next minute we were in bed again, making love, while I told myself, This can't be me. This can't be happening to me. I'm married to George, I love George, I can't be this lost, this much in love with another man, I can't be. And I shouldn't be. But I was.

I had a bruised nose and I didn't know what George would do when he saw it. The press had daily reported my affair with Rubi, I had made a fool of George, and now, to top that, was finally coming home to him complete with bruised nose as a testament to the storminess of my illicit passion. Luckily, though, my plane stopped at Shannon Airport in Ireland and I stayed there for a few days until my bruises disappeared.

I arrived in L.A., outwardly free from bruises, but inwardly quaking. George had told me, "Darling, sexual passion lasts only two years. You'll be back with Daddy." Now I was back, but I knew Rubi was bound to follow. For the moment, at least, George appeared to have forgiven me, telling me, "You've made me look rather ridiculous with your

Rubirosa and your love affair. But I forgive you because you always make me laugh."

We went back to Bel Air. I observed that George was putting on weight. "Not at all," he retorted. "It is just that your lover in Paris is much slimmer than I." Even if I had wanted to forget Rubi, George was determined not to let me. And in 1953, he filed for divorce. Despite Rubi, despite Doris Duke, despite everything, I had somehow imagined that George and I would stay married until the day we died, and I was devastated.

I didn't believe that George would ever divorce me and I kept telling myself that he was bluffing. Late in 1953, the Last Frontier Hotel in Las Vegas made an offer for Eva, Magda, and me all to appear there in a nightclub act. We began rehearsals in Los Angeles and, in the midst of them, Rubi appeared. We all spent Christmas Eve together, at my house in Bel Air, celebrating Christmas early because we were due to fly to Vegas on Christmas Day.

Again, Rubi begged me to marry him but, even as he asked, he knew the answer, that I wasn't ready, so he changed the subject. There was also, he confessed, a new element in his life—a new player whom destiny had set on the stage of our melodrama—Barbara Hutton. Startled, I thought back to Deauville, the elegant resort where I had recently gone with Rubi and watched him play polo and remembered Barbara, her field glasses trained constantly on Rubi. Then, after the match, Barbara had come over to our table, started blatantly flirting with Rubi and had all but flung herself at him then and there, announcing, "Rubi, I am going to marry you."

Trying to look unconcerned, I accepted an invitation from an admirer, Sweeney (who was once married to Margaret of Argyll), to play roulette with him and, late that night, we left the casino together. Sweeney took me home to our hotel and I waited all night for Rubi in the suite. And when he finally came back in the morning, he was blind drunk. In despair, I went to Deauville beach with my friend Lulu Hakim, who said, "I'll bet you any amount of money that Rubi is going to marry Barbara Hutton. He wants to prove to the world that he can marry the daughter of the president of his country, Doris Duke, Barbara Hutton, and get you . . . !"

At the time, I had laughed, convinced that Rubi would always want me and that I would always want him. Even when the calls came from Barbara, calls from all over the world, pursuing Rubi, I still laughed. But now, today, on Christmas Eve, things were suddenly different. George had filed for divorce, whether he meant it or not. And now Rubi was telling me, "My darling, I have to leave you. I need money and Barbara Hutton has offered me five million dollars if I marry her. Then I'll come back to you in a few weeks."

Until then, I hadn't understood why the world had labeled Rubi as a kept man, but I had never really accepted the truth. But now I was experiencing it for myself, now it was inescapable. Rubi came from a different world, from a world in which his other mistresses, the women with whom he had dallied before me, French aristocrats and *cocottes* alike, would have merely shrugged their elegant shoulders and said, "Naturally, *chéri.* But when you come back to me, remember to buy me much jewelry." Rubi's world and Rubi's women had not prepared him for me and for the fact that I would look down on him for marrying Barbara Hutton.

WE talked until four in the morning. And we would have talked longer, had there not been an almighty shattering of glass, which came from the direction of the French windows. Suddenly, my bedroom door burst open and George appeared, accompanied by two detectives. In shock, I jumped out of bed, forgetting that all I was wearing was my diamond earrings, and stood there, stark naked. George, who hadn't seen me for months, couldn't take his eyes off me.

Rubi, also naked (a sight that George was to dine out on for years, explicitly describing Rubi in all his fabled glory), locked himself in the bathroom. Meanwhile, George and I stood there, staring at each other. George had grown a beard, he was bronzed and his blue eyes seemed suddenly to be sparkling, lit up by the drama of the moment. The break-in, he explained, was to get evidence so that he could cite Rubi in our divorce in the eventuality of my applying for alimony.

I had no intention of asking for alimony. Or, for that matter, of divorcing George. And as he left, with a farewell,

"This visit, Cokiline, is my Christmas present to you," I knew that I still loved George. Then Rubi came out of the bathroom, we made love, and I knew that, despite George, my passion for Rubi remained undimmed.

RUBI followed me to Las Vegas. There he issued me with an ultimatum: either I marry him or he would marry Barbara. Screaming that I still loved George, I lashed out at Rubi. And he hit me back. The next I knew, I was sitting on the floor, my right eye swelling up to what seemed enormous proportions, and Rubi had left—for New York and for Barbara.

That night, I went onstage wearing a black patch to hide my eye. The press were not deceived. They knew Rubi had been in Vegas, that he had been with me, and that he was, even now, on his way to New York to marry Barbara Hutton. The resultant uproar was overwhelming. And when, just a few hours later, Rubi—holding a cigar in one hand and a glass of champagne in the other—married Barbara, the avalanche of publicity surrounding me was unparalleled. Nothing—not even my encounter with the Beverly Hills police—has ever surpassed it.

I was besieged by newspapermen, shops all over America began stocking up with eye patches, and Marlene's show girls all appeared on stage the next night wearing black eye patches in recognition of the entire controversy. Not only that, but throughout it all, George kept telephoning, his passion for me re-ignited, offering to drop the divorce, desperate to win me back again. And, just a few days after his marriage, I began to receive calls again from Porfirio Rubirosa.

WHEN Barbara married Rubi, her father, E. F. Hutton, called her and said, "Have you gone out of your mind, Barbara? Do you know what this man is? And do you realize what that makes you?" Generalissimo Trujillo, Rubi's former father-in-law, however, was delighted, immediately reappointing Rubi to his old post as Dominican ambassador to France. Not that he had much need of power, position, or wealth anymore. According to *Fortune* magazine, Barbara was then worth $25 million. Moreover, she was determined to spend a large part of it on Rubi. During their marriage, she was to gift him with a twin-engine North American B-25 plane, a four-hundred-acre citrus plantation in the Dominican Republic worth $450,000, fifteen polo ponies, a Lancia car, ruby cuff links and a diamond stickpin.

There are those who say that money buys everything. But that isn't true. The world thought that Barbara and her money now owned Rubi and that I, Zsa Zsa, had merely been a fling—eclipsed in Rubi's heart by Barbara and her millions. Rubi was later to tell me that he never slept with Barbara, declaring, "Darling, how could I—it was impossible—she was on drugs—but more than that—I only loved you." For although the saying goes, "A woman can never be too rich or too thin," I think that I have proved it wrong—I have never been very thin or very rich, but I always have gotten every man I ever wanted—and Rubi was no exception. For Barbara Hutton's marriage to Porfirio Rubirosa lasted just seventy-two days. And on many of those days, Rubi spent his time on the telephone to me, begging me to come back to him, begging me to marry him.

Meanwhile, George went ahead with his plans to divorce me. Our divorce hearing took place in April 1954. And I cried most of the way through it. After the hearing, George telephoned me and said, "Cokiline, you looked like Francesca, like a little girl." He came home, we kissed, then went straight to bed. We may have been divorced, but George and I were lovers again. And we were lovers forever—until the day he died.

RUBI and I announced our engagement just after I'd finished filming *Three Ring Circus* with Jerry Lewis and Dean Martin. But we were slow to marry and instead, lived out our mutual wildness all over the world. We were always flying somewhere, speeding in a car, or making love. It was like being caught in a whirlwind, but I loved it.

It seemed as if the whole world was our home. We never settled anywhere for long. There was always a polo game to attend, or a tennis match or a car race or a rugby game. My favorite moments were when Rubi would play his guitar and sing the songs of Charles Aznavour and Gilbert Bécaud. In those moments, he was all feeling and heart and it was a dream to be with him.

Our affair—with its volatile quality—seemed to set the world on fire. Even literary legend Dame Edith Sitwell took an interest, asking a reporter, "When do you think Rubirosa and Zsa Zsa will marry?" then confiding that she considered Rubi to be "a charming man" but bemoaned that it was "a pity he doesn't read more." Incensed, Rubi retorted that he was a voracious reader and an authority on Napoleon, his favorite historical figure.

The controversy raged on to such a degree that, for a time in Paris, Rubi and I couldn't go out into the street without photographers and journalists pestering us. Rubi even was forced on one occasion to disguise himself by dressing in my mother's fur coat and going out in drag. Which didn't disturb him at all—Rubi was so masculine that very little could undermine his masculinity.

Except, perhaps, my career. After the Fernandel film, Rubi had accompanied me to work one day on the set of a French and Spanish co-production I was making called *Sang et Lumière*. In the film, I played the lover of a Spanish bullfighter, portrayed by the French star Daniel Gélin. Ironically the love scenes had to be shot twice, first in Spanish—with me dressed in high-necked clothes, acting with restraint and decorum. And then in French, with me wearing low-cut dresses and acting in a far more risqué way that would appeal to the French.

That day, with Rubi watching, we shot a love scene in which I wore a black lace nightgown, and Daniel threw himself on top of me and—according to the script—began to tear my nightgown off. The cameras started rolling and Daniel began tearing—ripping my nightgown so enthusiastically that my breasts were completely exposed. Rubi grew scarlet, insisted I stopped filming immediately, and made such a scene that he was ordered off the set. I was his love, and his passion and his urge to possess me drove him wild. As Elizabeth Keleman later observed, "Miss Gabor, Mr. Rubirosa is the one who loved us the most."

There were other suitors in my life during that time who were not intimidated by Rubi and his legend. Cornelius Vanderbilt Whitney was one of them. Sonny (as his friends call him) and I met at a party when Rubi was in Paris. Merle Oberon had pointed him out, saying, "Look at that man. He has the most beautiful eyes." Dutifully, I looked in the direction in which Merle was pointing, at a man whose eyes were not striking. I asked Merle his name. And she replied, "Cornelius Vanderbilt Whitney." Sonny and I started talking then we danced together and he grumbled, "Please can we go and have a drink?" Afterward, Eva and her husband, Anne Baxter and her husband, and I all went to my home. We ate a baked ham, which Rubi and I had brought from Spain where I had just finished making *Sang et Lumière.* We became friends and he was soon baby-sitting for both Francesca and Portland Mason. When I appeared in Las Vegas, Sonny was always in the front row. Joey Adams (who was opening for me) used to joke, "Let's invite Sonny for dinner—he never invites us anywhere." Sonny knew about the gag and soon took to calling me and saying, "This is Sonny. Can I invite you for a peanut butter sandwich?"

As time went on, Sonny continued to pursue me fairly relentlessly. I was surprised when he decreed, "I want you to know, when I marry a woman I wash my own underwear." At one point, I went to Arizona to star in *Blithe Spirit* and spent time there with my good friend Mary Lou Hosford—who is wonderful and to whom I am eternally grateful as she once hid Rubi during the days when the press was stalking us. As usual, Sonny was in the front row of the theater, watching me for the umpteenth time in *Blithe Spirit*. One night, Mary Lou took me aside and said, "Zsa Zsa, Sonny has seen the show a million times. Do you mind if I take him to dinner?" I said, "Of course not. He must be bored stiff." I didn't see either of them for at least two weeks. Sonny fell madly in love with Mary Lou that evening. I didn't blame him because Mary Lou is the world's best cook, the world's best mother, and turned out to be the world's best wife to Sonny.

DURING my time with Rubi, I also made a picture called *For the First Time,* with Mario Lanza. We'd never met, but I had already had an unfortunate experience that didn't endear Mario much to me. In the middle of the night, he had once called me and, in explicit terms that left nothing to the imagination, informed me that he wanted to make love to me. But, as I traveled to Rome to start filming, I made up my mind to forget the incident and start afresh. Soon after my arrival, several reporters interviewed me at the Rome Opera House. Out of the blue, one of them asked, "It is rumored that Mr. Lanza uses dirty language. Is that true?"

"I've never heard him," I lied.

Suddenly, Mario burst into the auditorium, yelling at his agent, "I won't do it, you son of a bitch!"

"What timing, Miss Gabor," the reporter observed, "Now we can say that you confirmed the rumor."

Mario had rented Mussolini's house in Rome and I went there for dinner. He and his wife had four children and they and Francesca spent most of the evening bicycling around the house, skillfully avoiding Il Duce's marble furniture.

Before I left for America, Mario told me he was going to a fat farm to lose some weight. I didn't think that he needed to lose any weight—I've never liked skinny men—but I didn't say anything. When I got back to L.A., Kathryn Grayson told me that Mario was dead. The rumor was that a gang of Philadelphia gangsters had ordered him to sing at one of their gala evenings, that Mario had refused and that, in revenge, they had hired a nurse at the fat farm to inject air into Mario's veins one night while he was sleeping and killed him.

*

*

I was shattered by Mario's death—but in later years came across two other situations in which people I liked died under mysterious circumstances. When I was married to Joshua Cosden, Teamsters' boss Jimmy Hoffa approached my agent at William Morris and offered me $10,000 and all expenses if I went to his wife's birthday party in Miami. I went without Rubi and I found Hoffa and his lovely Polish wife whom he adored, to be charming and intelligent. Later, when he disappeared, I was horrified.

Another acquaintance of mine who met with a mysterious end was Johnny Stompanato. When George and I were married, we wanted to go to London for a while and decided to rent out our house in Bel Air. One day, three gentlemen appeared to look over the house. It transpired that they were part of Mickey Cohen's gang—and that one of them was Johnny Stompanato. George was extremely excited by the idea of gangsters renting the house. For my part, I found Johnny to be very attractive.

Although we ended up not renting the house at all, a short while later, I ran into Johnny at a bakery on Wilshire. He invited me for coffee and, as I didn't want to be rude, I accepted. Afterward, he started to phone me—just to chat—and one day told me all about his relationship with Lana Turner and that Lana wanted him to go to London with her.

"She's making a picture and she begged me to come with her because she's very lonely. What should I do?" he asked.

"Go," I urged him. "You're a little Italian-American kid. You will learn some manners in England."

"Well, I don't know," he said, "I can take her or leave her." I tried to talk him into going because I felt he could use some polish. "I strongly advise you to stay with Lana," I said. Though he'd been working for Mickey Cohen, he was not a gangster. Eventually, he followed my advice.

Then he was killed by Lana's daughter, Cheryl Crane, after allegedly threatening to carve Lana up. I liked Johnny a great deal and, later on, developed an uneasiness about his whole relationship and about having encouraged him to get involved with Lana.

As always, my mother saw right into the heart of my dilemma with Rubi. One night, when Rubi was drinking, he had complained to Mother, "Zsa Zsa is so cold to me." Causing Mother to approach me and say, "Rubi is not for you. He drinks a lot. At the most you have a white wine spritzer. He loves nightclubs. You don't smoke. You hate nightclubs. For a husband he is not good."

I listened to Mother intently as she went on. "You are ruining your career. He's chasing you all over the world, you are staying up late, getting no sleep. You're exhausted! Your eyes are red-rimmed. Don't throw your wonderful career away."

I did my best to follow her advice. During the next two years that I spent with Rubi—after my divorce from George—I made fifty TV shows, appeared on the covers of thirty-two magazines, and starred in six motion pictures. One of those motion pictures, *Death of a Scoundrel,* also led to the end of my romance with Rubi.

D***EATH OF A SCOUNDREL*** was a delicious *film noir* in which I was to play a woman who—along with three other women, played by Yvonne de Carlo, Nancy Gates, and Coleen Gray—was used by a man named Sabourin—an impoverished immigrant turned financier. Charles Martin directed, the gowns were by Waldo, Max Steiner wrote the score, and George Sanders played Sabourin. I couldn't wait to work with him.

Rubi was adamant, telling me, "*Chérie,* if you work with George on this film, I will never see you again." I was sad, but I knew what I had to do. I wanted to get away from Rubi. He meant society and nightclubs, polo fields and jetting around the world. Whereas all I really wanted to do was to act. Especially with George, whom I still adored. I accepted, knowing that it would mean the end of my relationship with Rubi. I flew to Los Angeles where George and I carried on with our roller-coaster relationship and, yet again, became lovers.

AFTER *Death of a Scoundrel* I flew to Rome to shoot *The Blue Contessa,* with an old suitor in hot pursuit. Before I married George, I had dated "young" Bill Hearst. Bill was in Rome with his sons, I was there with Francesca and soon the two of us were spending a great deal of time with Bill. His father had been the great press lord William Randolph Hearst. When I first came to Hollywood, in the forties, Marion Davies (Hearst's mistress) and I became friends and Marion took to referring to me as "my daughter—by Calvin Coolidge."

I had given a party for Marion when Hearst died and she married Captain Horace Brown. Bill had always liked Marion and had gone to Europe with her in 1934. He told me about that trip and how, as Marion was an alcoholic, his father, Bill, kept drink away from her, but that he—Young Bill—used to slip Marion a Coke bottle full of booze. He also told me that at San Simeon, the fairy-tale castle Hearst had built for her, Marion hid her gin bottle in the toilet tank. Bill was down-to-earth and always had a friendly grin. He was sweet and charming, but I refused his offer to marry me and we remained good friends.

Although I may have started to console myself and recover from my four-year romance with Rubi, filming didn't always go exactly as planned. In one scene shot in Naples, I was dressed as a vamp, in Theda Bara style, and the script called for me to walk onto the set with two pumas. My secretary had brought my Yorkie to the set that day, and she was holding him in her arms.

When I came in with the two pumas on a leash, they smelled the Yorkie and went crazy. The dog leapt from my secretary's arms and the pumas took off after it down the street. I ran after them, screaming, "Stop those pumas! They're going to eat my dog." The young Italian men watching couldn't believe the sight—a blonde running through the streets half nude, chasing two wild animals. *"Bella signora!"* was their sole response.

*

IN 1956, Rubi married Odile Rodin, a nineteen-year-old French girl, and I didn't expect ever to see him again. But not long afterward, a letter arrived from Rubi in Paris, asking me to introduce Ramfis Trujillo, the son of his president, to Hollywood and to help him fulfill his dreams of mingling with the stars.

Ramfis was twenty-four years old and currently attending military staff college in Kansas. He was Rubi's best friend—but not on an equal level, because for him, Rubi was god. We met at the Mardi Gras, in New Orleans. Ramfis arrived on his yacht, formerly *The Sea Cloud,* now called *The Angelita* after Ramfis's sister. In New Orleans, we both attended a big party during which the mayor of the city, Chet Morrison, gave me the keys to the city and crowned me queen of Mardi Gras. Dressed in a red chiffon evening gown I'd bought at Martha's in Palm Beach, holding the orchids Chet had given me, I was tempted momentarily by both the mayor and by Ramfis himself.

But he was Rubi's friend so I didn't want to get involved with him. Instead, I suggested introducing him to Kim Novak. After asking if she was like me, Ramfis agreed. He met Kim and took her out on a date. Afterward, Kim called to bemoan the fact that Ramfis hadn't slept with her. Impatiently, I said, "For God's sakes, be a little patient. He's a Spanish gentleman who respects you. And you are a big star."

Kim obviously didn't follow my advice, because Ramfis didn't marry her. But he did give her a Mercedes 190SL and even once rented a private plane for her that cost him $40,000. She fell madly in love with him and why not? Ramfis was young, tall, dark, handsome, and the son of the president of his country.

After that Ramfis wanted to meet Joan Collins. Rubi arranged it. From the first, Joan set her sights on the most glittering prizes available. Joan and I met in Hollywood when she was dating Arthur Loew and we were both the European girls around town. Joan was always very beautiful, but no one wanted to marry her. And every time I would see Joan, she would wistfully ask me, "Zsa Zsa, how can I catch Arthur?"

She and I were friendly and I knew that she was a strange mix of very tough and very insecure. She was always complaining to me, "I can never hold on to a man." I understood exactly why. It seemed to me that Joan was like a man herself. You can't chase a man. He has to chase you. Let him chase you until you catch him. I always tell a man I want to marry him. But I only tell him when I'm sure he wants to marry me. Joan never understood my philosophy of love or marriage, but she definitely knew who and what she wanted.

Years later, Joan and I clashed when she accused Francesca of flirting with her then husband, Ron Kass. Which was ridiculous because Francesca was much too young and even now doesn't really know how to flirt. Then, about five years ago I gave a dinner party for the exiled King of Tunisia and invited Joan and her new husband, Peter Holm. Peter was much younger than Joan and was what they call a "toyboy." I hate toyboys. I need to respect a man and to admire him. I don't think it is that easy to admire a man who is your toy.

Throughout the whole evening, Joan was draped all over Peter and insisted on sitting next to him during dinner—which is completely contrary to the European custom of seating husband and wife separately. She spent the entire evening holding Peter's hand so tightly that he could hardly eat.

When the marriage ended in divorce, Joan cried and cried and I advised her, "Joan, you're a big star. Don't say he left you. Say you left him! What's the difference? You're telling the whole world he left you for another woman. Are you crazy? Say you left him because you are sick and tired of him." I can't remember the outcome of the whole thing but I do know that what Joan Collins wants, Joan gets.

When Rubi broached the subject of meeting Ramfis, Joan's reply was "I only want to meet him if he gives me a beautiful present." Tactfully, I relayed the message to Ramfis, who shrugged and said, "Okay, if she wants something, call up Van Cleef and Arpels and order a diamond necklace for her." I obliged, ordering an item that today would cost in the region of $100,000. The date was duly arranged.

Afterward, I asked Ramfis if he had had fun with Joan.

"I picked her up in my yacht in Miami," he said tersely. "She was so boring that I put her ashore in Palm Beach."

I said nothing, having quickly come to the conclusion that the clever Miss Collins had probably taken the diamond necklace and then proceeded to make herself appear to be so boring that she didn't have to do anything with Ramfis afterward.

RUBI asked me to throw a party for Ramfis and I willingly agreed, refusing his offer to pay for it. The purpose of the party was to introduce Ramfis to Los Angeles. And I certainly did my best. The guest list included Kim Novak (Ramfis's date), Jimmy Stewart, Maureen O'Hara, Hedda Hopper, Conrad Hilton, Ann Miller, David Selznick, Charles Vidor, James and Pamela Mason, Robert Mitchum, Kirk Douglas, Van Johnson, Louella Parsons, Beatrice Lillie, Shirley MacLaine, Jeanne Crain, and Kathryn Grayson. The waiters were all dressed in red livery, the whole evening cost $10,000 and was catered by Fred Heyman, who later, with his wife Gail, founded Giorgio's, then later sold the name for millions.

George and I were still very much in love and he stood with me on the receiving line and helped me welcome our guests. I looked away for a moment, only to turn back and see Rubi, with his new wife, Odile, by his side. In embarrassment, I introduced Rubi to George, forgetting that they had already met. Which, given the circumstances, was probably just as well. The two men, George and Rubi, whom I had both loved and—to some extent—lost, shook hands so heartily that for a moment it seemed that they might be joined together forever. George broke the spell by nervously pouring his Scotch down my dress.

Rubi and Odile walked away (although Rubi spent the entire evening gazing at me as if I were still his fiancée and he was still in love with me and not Odile). I was left talking to Conrad and George. Whereupon David Selznick came over and whispered, "You are the only woman alive who could have two ex-husbands and a famous ex-lover to the same party."

MY party for Ramfis Trujillo was a great success. But it also had far-reaching consequences. Ramfis thanked me by sending me a floor-length chinchilla coat worth $80,000, as well as a red convertible Mercedes 220S. The press found out and an uproar ensued. The Dominican Republic had just been given $10 million worth of American aid and now it appeared that Trujillo's son was squandering a part of that aid on gifts for movie stars.

The controversy reverberated in the U.S. Senate itself, when during a debate on foreign aid, Ohio Democrat Wayne Hays said of Ramfis, "If he keeps on fooling around with Zsa Zsa Gabor, who apparently is the most expensive courtesan since Madame de Pompadour, the old man is going to have to raise the ante." Later, he went on to suggest that all the millions borrowed by the Dominican Republic might just as well be directly sent to me and Kim.

I asked Bill Hearst for his advice on how to reply to these charges and Bill said, "Ask him to come out from behind his congressional immunity." I did and heard no more from Wayne Hays—or anything else about him—until sometime in the seventies when he fell from grace after his indiscretion with his secretary, Elizabeth Ray.

AFTER my notorious Trujillo party, I only once saw Rubi again, in Maxim's. He was with Odile, but the moment he saw me, he left her side and gravitated toward me like a moth to the heat and light of an alluring flame. We talked for a moment, then Odile pulled him away. Our eyes met for the last time.

Flash Forward

*

IN 1965, Rubi died in a car accident in the Bois de Boulogne. He was driving his Ferrari and crashed into a chestnut tree. Afterward, the papers said that had Rubi been wearing a seat belt, he would never have been killed.

But I knew that Rubi in a seat belt would not any longer have been Rubi. He didn't wear one and he was pinned to the ground by the car and died a few hours later.

My sister Magda called and told me about Rubi's death and I felt numb. Later, I went to Paris and a friend told me that Rubi's very last words were "Zsa Zsa." For the first time since I'd heard about Rubi's death, I cried for him, cried for his charm, for his passion, his verve, for our love, our romance, and for the absurd idea that during his last moments of life, Rubi would cry out my name. An absurdity, I realized, that had been fabricated by a friend who was still enthralled by the romantic saga of

Porfirio Rubirosa and Zsa Zsa Gabor. I had been enthralled by it all myself, had luxuriated in every minute we were together. For in my heart I knew that no one ever loved me as much as Rubi did.

A few years later, when I was married to my fifth husband, Joshua Cosden, I went to Paris—to see Rubi's grave at the Père Lachaise cemetery. At first I couldn't find it. I got lost among the tombstones, the last resting places of Colette and Oscar Wilde. Eventually, I did and saw that no flowers marked the last resting place of the most famous playboy the world has ever known. Instead, there was just a small headstone, marked with Rubi's name and birth date. An old Christmas tree had been placed on the grave. It was July.

I immediately paid for perpetual care for Rubi's grave, buying red flowers (red for Rubirosa) and placing them in two black marble urns. Later, I received word that Rubi's widow, Odile, had banned me from beautifying Rubi's grave.

After the Divorce from George

*

I didn't seem to have much luck in dealing with the women who replaced me in my lovers' and ex-husbands' affections. For although it was not her fault, my first meeting with George's next wife, Benita, was not very successful.

In 1959, out of the blue, Louella Parsons called me and told me that George had become engaged to Benita Colman—Ronald's widow. At first, I couldn't believe it and cabled, "Georgie, it can't be true, is it true?" George cabled back, "Unbelievable as it sounds, Cokiline, it is true," and then followed up with a letter that read,

"Dearest Cokiline,

"Don't be unhappy. I am really much too old for you. You need someone closer to your own age, someone who can respond to your admirable effervescence, someone who can identify himself with your goals, someone who has a little more vitality.

"I shall always love you, and yield to no one in my admiration for your many qualities.

"A big kiss for Francesca, a hug for you.

"George."

I was forced to accept the truth—I had lost George forever. But perhaps, somewhere deep inside, I still didn't grasp that George was now married to Benita. Not until I met her myself in London, during a dinner with Jimmy Woolf and Alec Guinness, whom I adored. Ever thoughtful, and knowing that it would break my heart to see Benita, Jimmy decided at the last minute not to go to Les Ambassadeurs for dinner, saying, "I know that Benita and Lady Sylvia Ashley are going to dine there tonight." Instead, we chose to go to Annabel's. So, it transpired, had Sylvia and Benita.

Tactfully, Benita approached the table and, bending down conspiratorially, said, "Zsa Zsa, don't worry. I'm going to take good care of the old boy." I think she went on to compliment me on looking lovely and that I said, "Benita, I love your hat." When she left, Alec wryly informed me, "My dear, Benita is not wearing a hat." My nerves and shock at finally meeting Benita had betrayed me.

Flash Forward

George and Me: 1959–1972

In time, I grew fond of Benita and was glad that she always welcomed me to the home she had made for George. She did, indeed, take good care of him. She was also extremely kind to me, telling me, "We want to adopt you," graciously referring to George as "our husband" whenever the three of us were together. Benita was the perfect wife for George, the perfect wife for any man.

Sadly, in later years, Benita grew sick. At one point, she broke her hip and never again walked without crutches. Eventually, she was diagnosed with bone cancer. She and George went to live on her farm in England. George didn't know how to cope with Benita's final illness—but remembering my own reaction to Bogie just before he died—I fully understood when George told me he couldn't any longer be in the same room as Benita. He said in horror, "She looks like a skeleton." He said, "I couldn't go in, couldn't look at her. The shock would show on my face, and she doesn't know how sick she is so she'd know and lose hope the minute she saw me."

***GEORGE'S** brother, Tom Conway, too, remained a part of my life. When I was married to Herbert Hutner, my fourth husband, he and Herbert became friends. George contacted us to give us the tragic news that Tom had cirrhosis of the liver and that he was dying. I was very fond of Tom and we had a family reunion. At the end of it, George said, "Here, old boy, take this $40,000. Go to Capri and die there happy."*

Tom did exactly as George said, except that he didn't die. On Capri, Tom met a German scientist who had discovered a new serum that he wanted to test. He told Tom, "Let me try it out on you since you're dying anyhow. It may kill you or it could, conceivably, cure you." He persuaded Tom to try it and miraculously, he was cured.

George, however, was now in a difficult situation—particularly when Tom asked him for money. His voice ringing with determination, "I'm sorry, old boy," said George. "You're my brother but you are supposed to be dead. I never want to see you again."

After that, Herbert and I supported Tom every time he was broke. One day, his ex-wife called and said that this time

Tom was, in earnest, on his deathbed. Francesca and I visited him at the hospital in downtown L.A. and when we left, I gave him $200, telling him, "Tip the nurses a little bit so they'll be good to you."

The next day the hospital called me and informed me that Tom had disappeared. I found out later that he had taken my $200, had gone to see his girlfriend, had gotten drunk, and then went to bed with her. Then he died, right there in her bed. I contacted George, but he was still so livid about his $40,000 and Capri that he wouldn't help me or even show up at the morgue to identify Tom's body.

AFTER *Benita's death in 1967, George started drifting and we grew even closer. Then in 1969, when I was starring in* Forty Carats *on Broadway, George, who by now had had a light stroke, would sit quietly in the audience and watch the show. During the run of* Forty Carats, *George was with me every night. The show was a tremendous hit and so was I. Humbly, he told me, "My God, I'm getting such a complex. You're now the big star and I just sit backstage and wait for you."*

One night, he took actor Michael Nouri—who was playing my husband—aside and said, "You're not kissing my wife hard enough." That night, Nouri, heeding the advice of the great George Sanders, proceeded to make love to me so vio-

lently that he tore my clothes. Afterward, George was elated, the fire rekindled, declaring with almost paternal pride, "Now that's a proper kiss." For a moment, he was once more the George of my youth, the same George who had once traveled with me from Rome to Naples and begged me to make love to another man for his pleasure, the George who had broken my heart.

We were invited to go on the David Frost TV show together. Like most actors, George was so accustomed to relying on a script that he was terrified. When the camera started rolling, he clutched my hand and I could feel how much he was perspiring. Every time David looked at him, George demurred, saying, "Let Zsa Zsa talk." After the show he congratulated me with the words, "Somebody who is talented is talented in everything." For a moment, I glowed, basking in the triumph that George—the same George who once said I was too stupid to succeed as an actress—had acknowledged my talent at last. For a second I felt like a conquering heroine, then the emotion died as I realized that George's compliment was the compliment of an old man. That he was an old man, an old man who could no longer hurt me, an old man who needed me.

Soon George was wanting me again, suggesting that we remarry. But I followed the advice of friends like Pamela Mason and refused. George was crestfallen, so I tried to soften the blow, saying, "But George, half the richest women in America want to marry you. I know a millionairess in Bel Air and a society lady in Palm Beach who would marry you tomorrow. And even my sister Magda has a crush on you,"

"All right," said George. "Then I'll marry Magda."

I didn't know if he was serious, but just in case, called Mother and with obvious incredulity said, "George wants to marry Magda."

"You're all insane," she snapped—ever the voice of common sense, then added, "This is ridiculous."

The following day, George drove to Palm Springs to talk to Mother.

Then he went to Magda, proposed, and she accepted. My sister, Magda Gabor, was going to be Mrs. George Sanders. I thought I was going to go insane and I realized that George was marrying Magda because he wanted to hurt me, because I had wounded his pride, and because he had finally accepted the fact that we had no future together.

*T**HEIR** 1970 wedding turned out to be a big one and it took every iota of Elsa Stanoff's training for me to stand there, smiling, as my sister married my ex-husband. But smile I did. And I went on smiling when all three of us ended up at the same party and I heard Magda and George announced as "Mr. and Mrs. George Sanders." I was jealous, confused, bewildered, and wished that I hadn't listened to anyone, had followed my instincts and had married George again myself.*

George, it seemed, clearly felt the same way, phoning me on a daily basis as soon as the wedding was over. First he tried the excuse, "Darling, come down to Palm Springs. Magda can't cook and I want you to cook something special for me." After I'd refused often enough, George uncharacteristically let his defenses slip and simply asked, "Cookie, please come to see us. I need you."

The situation wasn't easy for Magda either, especially when George started calling her Zsa Zsa. I felt sorry for both of them. Finally, when I was in Palm Springs on a visit to Mother (who lives there in winter), George asked me to go shopping with him and I agreed. Palm Springs, despite its aura of glamor, is still a small town and before I knew it, the news got back to Mother, who was outraged. "The whole town is talking about you going out with your sister's husband."

Before I could stop myself or think about what I was saying, I burst out, "My ex-husband, you mean?"

In my mind, George was still mine—no matter how many wives he had. George felt the same way about me and, soon after our Palm Springs outing, he annulled his marriage to Magda. They had been husband and wife for just six weeks.

A few months later, George came to stay with me in California and waited around while I talked to agents and producers. I tried to tell him that he didn't need me anymore. But I knew that wasn't true. George had been talking about suicide for years and I'd often worried about him taking his

own life. Through the years, I consulted doctors and psychiatrists and most of them told me that people who threaten suicide usually don't carry out their threat. Later, I found out that I had been misinformed.

In April 1972, I was in London playing Mata Hari in the film Up the Front *with the brilliant British comedian Frankie Howerd and George came to see me, en route for Barcelona, where he was scheduled to make a film. While we were together, he confided that he was terrified of having another stroke and becoming totally helpless. I took him to a psychiatrist, who said that George had suffered another nervous breakdown but that there was nothing to worry about. Relieved, I left George with his sister Margaret (who arranged for his stay at the Hotel Rey Don Jaime in Castelldéfels, ten miles outside Barcelona) and went to California, where I was scheduled to make a Bob Hope special.*

I was in Bel Air when I received the news that George had overdosed on sixty Nembutals. His suicide note read, "Dear World, I am leaving because I am bored. I feel I have lived long enough. I am leaving you with your worries in this sweet cesspool. Good luck." I had known and loved George Sanders for twenty-five years and I blamed myself for leaving him, for not marrying him again, for divorcing him in the first place. And I always will. I'll never get over George or his death, but as I said to Mother, "Now it won't be so bad to die. Wherever George is, heaven or hell, I will go there happily, because he will be waiting for me."

Career After the Divorce from George

*

I was free of Rubi now and free—as free as I'd ever be—from George. I began to enjoy life as a bachelor girl. The most important thing in my life, though, was still my career. I worked constantly. I made *Queen of Outer Space,* which was destined to become a classic. Written by Ben Hecht (of *Front Page* fame), *Queen* was one of the last films he wrote. The plot tells of a wicked queen—Iliana—who knocks out an American space station and takes the astronauts prisoner on the distant planet Venus. Iliana leads a band of fierce Amazon warrior women, who were all played by former Miss Americas. On Venus, so the story went, men had caused so much havoc that the women took over and banished all men to a prison colony planet.

I play Talia, a scientist who is against all of Queen Iliana's cruelties and wants to see her banished. The high point comes when I declare, "I *hate* that queen"—a line that even to this day, causes a great deal of mirth among many of my gay friends. I liked Ben Hecht and adored my costumes, designed by Edith Head and costing a staggering $15,000 apiece.

I also made another film in London called *The Man Who Wouldn't Talk,* in which I play a secret agent who pretends she is married to a scientist. The film was directed and produced by Herbert Wilcox and also starred his wife, Anna Neagle. The scientist was played by Shakespearean actor Anthony Quayle. Tony was a wonderful man. Stage actors are usually snobbish people, but not Tony. He had a sardonic sense of humor and we had a marvelous time making the film. At one point, impressed by the way he played one of our scenes together, I gushed, "You are such a big star!" In his unassuming way, Tony shrugged, "Nonsense, you are a star. I am just an actor." "But aren't I an actress?" I asked, a trifle petulantly. With a twinkle in his eye, Tony replied, "Maybe!"

Tony told me that he had made *A View from the Bridge,* which was written by Arthur Miller, and that Miller had talked to him about his marriage to Marilyn, revealing, "I don't approve of her or know how to talk to her but I find her overwhelmingly sexually attractive."

Tony and I always remained friends and when the British version of *This Is Your Life* did my life, the producer taped a segment featuring Tony reminiscing about working with me. At that time, he was in the hospital and when I saw it I was shocked to see how old and ill Tony looked. He was only sixty-eight. Three days later, he was dead of cancer. I sent roses to his funeral with a note saying that I would never forget him. And I won't because I can still see his big round, lovable boyish face smiling at me.

Interlude: The Men in My Life After George and Before Herbert

*

YES, I knew how to be single and I knew how to have fun. For a while, millionaire Hal Hayes wanted to marry me and become my fourth husband. He went as far as announcing our engagement and presenting me with a forty-carat diamond ring. Hal was a fascinating man: self-made, having started out as a timekeeper in North Carolina and ended as master builder in L.A., where he had constructed freeways and now lived in an incredible seven-level house on the side of a mountain. In his living room, Hal had a tree growing through the floor. Champagne flowed out of the faucets and, all in all, Hal understood the meaning of luxury. But I still didn't want to marry him and so returned the ring. Now Mrs. Gianni Agnelli has it.

My friend Aly Khan later cracked, "Why didn't you keep half of the ring!" Aly and I first met in Paris, during the days when I was apart from George and was making *Moulin Rouge*. John Huston and his girlfriend, French actress Suzanne Flon (who co-starred in the film), invited me to dinner and arranged for Aly to be my date. He didn't seem like a prince at all, but more like a nice American boy. For some strange reason, I felt as if I had known him all my life.

At the end of the evening, when John Huston demanded the bill, he discovered that Aly had already paid it. "We are not refugees," screamed John at Aly. I whispered to Aly to let John pay. He did and John's machismo was salvaged. When he took me home, Aly kissed me, but I didn't go to bed with him. The following day, he filled my suite with red roses. I did eventually have lunch with him at the Ritz and every few moments women called, wild for him.

Sometime later, Rubi and I met Aly again on the Riviera. At that point, he was having an affair with Gene Tierney, who was deeply in love with him. Rubi and I were often invited to Aly's beautiful Château de l'Horizon, overlooking the Mediterranean, where we also spent time with Aly's father, the Aga Khan. Mother and Francesca joined us all in Deauville and Francesca used to make me laugh by introducing our friend the Maharanee of Jaipur as "a real live princess."

One evening, Colette (who wrote *Gigi,* in which Eva scored one of her biggest successes) had dinner with us and Francesca announced to no one in particular, "This is the old lady who wrote *Gigi.* She lives in a wheelchair. Her husband is sixteen years younger but he adores her and pushes her around all the time!"

All of us had a lot of fun, except for Gene, that is, who was destroyed by Aly's refusal to marry her. Once I asked the Aga Khan why Aly didn't marry Gene, and he gave me the reasons extremely adamantly. "Aly has had enough trouble with actresses. After Rita Hayworth, why should he take on yet another one?" According to the Aga Khan, Aly had thought he was marrying Gilda—the character that made her so famous in the film of the same name. Instead she was a simple American girl who smeared cold cream on her face, wore rollers in her hair, and spent the whole day sleeping by the pool!

*

IN my opinion, marriages between Hollywood stars and members of the nobility have a strong chance of failing. I knew Princess Grace from the early days at MGM, when she was just plain Grace Kelly, a bricklayer's daughter from Philadelphia. Even then, I was aware that Grace had more boyfriends in one month than I had in a lifetime. Although she had risen to stardom as a chaste iceberg queen, Grace went to bed with anyone she fancied at the time. Conrad Hilton once told me that Grace had lived with one of his wine stewards in a little room at the Waldorf-Astoria and that she had had her nose fixed. And when I was married to George, he told me that

Grace had had a passionate affair with Ray Milland during the making of *Dial M for Murder* and that although Ray was married to a beautiful society girl, he left his wife for Grace. Then MGM stepped in and decreed that Ray leave Grace and go back to his wife.

Our paths crossed in Monte Carlo when I was there with Rubi and Grace was with French actor Jean-Pierre Aumont, with whom she was madly in love. One day, Prince Rainier sent a message to Grace and to me inviting us to Monte Carlo for a tour of his zoo. Rubi raged, "You are not going!" And so Grace went on her own. Afterward, according to Jean-Pierre, she said that Prince Rainier was quite charming.

When we all got back to Hollywood, Jack Warner gave a dinner party to celebrate Grace's engagement to Prince Rainier. That night, there were a dozen guests, including Roz Russell, her husband, Freddy Brisson, and de Gaulle's brother. Jack had a rare parquet floor imported from Versailles especially for the occasion. The party was small enough to be very chic—only Grace's closest friends were invited—and everyone was instructed to curtsy.

Jack was notorious for using dirty language and we all begged him not to use any that night. He agreed. We all arrived at Jack's Holmby Hills home looking elegant and everything went smoothly throughout dinner. Until the cognac was served, that is, when Jack (who had had a bit of wine by then) proclaimed, "Now, ladies, the *pissoir* is thataway."

Grace invited me to her wedding, but I couldn't go as I was filming. She sailed from New York on the U.S.S. *Constitution* with an entourage of 72 friends and family members, as well as 110 media representatives. During the Atlantic crossing, Grace entertained her guests one night by doing a great imitation of me. My wedding present to her was a gold ballerina brooch with precious stones set in the skirt.

I hoped that she and Rainier would be very happy—but they weren't. I saw Grace for the last time when she came to Los Angeles for a benefit at the Beverly Hills Hilton. She was overweight and, during the evening, drew me away from the crowds and told me how unhappy she was, confiding, "Darling, I never see my friends anymore. I miss Hollywood, I miss all of you. After all, I am an American."

DURING my single years, after I divorced George, I tangled with one of Grace's most famous co-stars, Frank Sinatra. But the experience was not pleasant. I know that Frank—particularly at that time—was the heartthrob of most of America—a dream man for women all over the world. But I saw another side of him. I'd met Frank at parties over the years—usually when I was with George—and he was very kind and complimentary about me, telling George that I was beautiful.

Now I was single again, and Mrs. Delmer Daves, the wife of a producer, invited me to a party at her home in Brentwood and arranged for Sinatra to be my escort for the evening. He came to pick me up from my house in Bel Air and Francesca—who was around eight at the time—nearly fainted at the sight of the great Frank Sinatra taking her mother out for the evening. I, on the other hand, was unimpressed; I admired

Frank, but he wasn't my type. Besides, I couldn't help noticing that he insisted on keeping his hat on all evening to hide his bald spot.

We were scheduled to have dinner alone first and then go on to the party. Frank took me to La Rue restaurant on Sunset and I can't remember what we talked about, except that he was entertaining, nice and—inexplicably—called the waiter "sir"—which puzzled me as I'd never encountered that before. We went on to the party, where everyone made a fuss over us. Then, at the end of the evening, Frank drove me home. When we got to the house, the maid Maria opened the door and I turned to Frank, expecting to say good night to him. Instead, he pushed himself inside.

In the hallway, I looked at him questioningly. Whereupon Frank calmly announced, "I am not going home until you make love to me." I was dumbstruck. He was transparent and made it blatantly obvious that, come hell or high water, he intended to score that night. At the time, I had the impression that Frank didn't particularly want me that night, but wanted to go to bed with a woman, any woman.

Despite my pleas, Frank refused to move from the hallway and we stood there, in what Americans call "a Mexican standoff." Finally, making a concession of sorts, Frank said stiffly, "In any case, I have a terrible headache, Zsa Zsa, and I have to lie down." Glimpsing a way out, I rang for Maria, tonelessly telling her, "Mr. Sinatra has a terrible headache. Put him in Mr. Sanders' room" (we always called one of the rooms in the house George's room) "and put some cold compresses on his head." Maria rushed off for the compresses and put them on Frank's head, which he hated.

Meanwhile, I locked myself in my room and prayed that Frank would recover from his headache and go home. I heard Maria go upstairs to her room and waited for the sound of

Frank leaving. But I was disappointed. There was a knock on my door. I ignored it. Frank knocked again. I still ignored it. Finally, Frank started banging on the door so loud, shouting that he was going to sleep with me, that in furious frustration I called out, "Frank, the answer is no! Go home and leave me alone." But Frank wouldn't take no for an answer and made so much noise that I was terrified that he would wake Francesca.

I wasn't in the least bit interested in him. The more he banged and screamed, the less I wanted him. I knew that many women would have loved the idea of hiding behind a locked bedroom door while Frank Sinatra was on the other side, begging to be allowed in. But I wasn't one of them. For a time, I lay down on the bed again and tried to sleep, hoping that Frank would go away. But I couldn't sleep and Frank didn't go away. Finally, at seven in the morning, I heard Elizabeth arrive, ready to make Francesca's breakfast and take her to school. Gingerly, I opened the door. For the moment, at least, Frank wasn't outside, but was in his room.

Creeping out, I met a surprised Elizabeth at the door. Before I could explain, she asked, reprovingly, "Miss Gabor, what shall we do. Mr. Sinatra's car" (a gold Cadillac) "is in the driveway. I can't send Francesca to school because she knows the car was in the driveway last night and if she sees it here this morning, she will have a very bad opinion of her mother." I knew Elizabeth was right. Casting around for a solution, in the end I said, "Put Francesca in the bathtub and read to her." Then I went to see Frank and begged him to leave. My begging took nearly an hour, and didn't have any effect. Finally, Elizabeth knocked on the door and said, "Francesca is mildewing in the bathtub!" But Frank Sinatra wouldn't leave unless I made love to him. So I did. I made love to Sinatra so that he would leave and from then on, I hated him. And Frank knew it.

FRANK knew that I hated him and he did his best, from then on, to get his revenge. When he had his television series, I was hired to guest-star on one of the episodes. I arrived at the studio punctually, as arranged, at eight o'clock. Two hours went by but Sinatra didn't show up. I walked out. Frank Sinatra had made me wait two hours—which was completely unprofessional.

Sometime after that, I was in Las Vegas, appearing at the Riviera. Frank was appearing at the Sands. One night, I was having dinner with some friends at an Italian restaurant and Frank walked in with Dinah Shore. Frank has a habit of coming up behind someone and blowing on their neck, which I despise. That night, Frank did that to me and I told him to stop, with "Frank, that's awful." Slightly taken aback, he paused, then rallied and said, "Zsa Zsa, why don't you come over to the Sands one night and act the end of my act, I'll introduce you and we'll do a little bit of comedy. Then, I promise you, I'll come over to the Riviera the next night and do the same for you."

Frank was a much bigger star than I was, so I went to my bosses at the Riviera and asked if they would let me end my show ten minutes early so that I could go to the Sands and do what Frank had asked, telling them that if I did, Frank would come over and do the same for me the next night. After a lot of persuasion, the bosses agreed. So I went over to the Sands and walked into the auditorium. I was wearing a beautiful white lace dress that Rubi had bought me at Balmain in Paris and Frank greeted me with the taunting words "Here comes Zsa Zsa Grabber. Oh boy, would I like to grab her!"

The next night, I waited at the Riviera for Frank to arrive and return the favor. He never showed up and my bosses—who were paying me $35,000 a week—were furious that I had entertained at the Sands for Sinatra's audience for free. I was embarrassed and humiliated and knew that this was Frank's revenge.

But he hadn't finished with me yet. Years later, when I thought his anger might have subsided, I accepted an invitation from Frank to go to a screening at his house on Mulholland. By then, he was married to Mia Farrow, whom I knew and liked. When we arrived, we all had drinks, then they began screening the film. In the middle, I went to the powder room. And Frank followed me, and pushed his way in, persisting, "My darling, you are so gorgeous and beautiful, I want to make love to you again." With that, Frank began to undo the buttons on my black silk blouse while I tried to reason with him. "Why are you doing this, Frank?" I asked imploringly, "Let's face it, I don't like you and you don't need me." "But I want you," he insisted, "I want to prove to you that you will love the way I make love to you. You will love it."

Suddenly, I remembered that I had somewhere heard how much Sinatra had admired Rubi. It was then that it struck me that it wasn't me Frank Sinatra cared about—but the reputation of Porfirio Rubirosa. And I knew, without a shadow of a doubt, that Frank's persistent attempts to make love to me (including our abortive moments together when he refused to leave the house before I made love to him) had been prompted by his burning desire to prove that he was as great a lover as Rubi had been. He wanted to use me to help him prove it, to reassure him that he, not Rubi, was the best in the world. And I couldn't do that.

Summoning all my strength, I pushed past him and out of the powder room, turning only to threaten, "Frank—I am leaving. Don't you ever, ever, try to touch me again." He didn't. Instead, Frank began dating my sister Eva. They were involved for six months and every time we met, Frank would sheepishly say, "I am taking good care of your sister."

Frank would probably have taken good care of me, too, but I just wasn't impressed by him. I think he is an intelligent man, but at the same time, his initial approach to me was so unintelligent. If he had taken me to the door, that very first evening, had kissed my hand and said, "Darling, it was wonderful. Let's do it again tomorrow," I might have eventually been charmed (because he did have charm) sufficiently to go to bed with him. We might even have been happy together.

PERHAPS Frank just wasn't lucky with me because (with the notable exception of Rubi) I have never been overly interested in Latin men. I am much more enamored of Anglo-Saxon men; when it comes to women, they can take it or leave it. Then it is a wonderful fight to get them to take it and not leave it. It is a challenge and I love a challenge. Frank Sinatra was not a challenge. Richard Burton, on the other hand, definitely was.

We met one New Year's Eve after Jimmy Woolf invited me to a party. Jimmy arrived at my Bel Air house to pick me up, Richard was with him and they both came in for cocktails. After a few moments, Jimmy left the room to make a phone call, leaving me alone with Richard. And before I could open my mouth to offer him a drink, comment on the weather, or produce any other suitable platitudes, Richard looked me up and down with so much intensity that I felt as if his blue eyes could see right into my heart and soul. Then, without any hesitation or self-doubt seeping through his deep voice, he said, "Instead of going to that party, why don't we go to bed, my darling?" And took my breath away.

I was extremely attracted to him; his facc was pockmarked, but he had an unquestionably masculine aura about him. Although he wasn't nearly as tall as George or Conrad, with his broad rugby player's shoulders, Richard exuded power and sex appeal. And although his conversation was erudite, peppered with references to his time in Oxford, he hadn't quite disguised his Welsh peasant origins. They simmered dangerously close to the surface and they excited me. Still, his approach had, to say the least, been startlingly abrupt, so I suggested a compromise, that we get rid of Jimmy, give the party a miss and, instead, go dancing.

Richard and I went dancing somewhere or other in Hollywood. I can't remember where, exactly, because the time and the place have been eclipsed by my memory of Richard in bed with me afterward, of his voice, his hands, and his powerful body. It was as if our time together was made in heaven and that circumstances had conspired so that, for a time, Richard and I could be together. Francesca was away and the servants were off on a New Year's vacation. They were scheduled to be away for three days. And Richard and I took advantage of every one of those days.

We arrived home just after midnight on New Year's Day and Richard pulled me down onto the white fur rug in front of my fireplace and made violent, passionate love to me, talking incessantly, erotically, all the time he made love. He had a violent, animal attitude to lovemaking that I adored, using his voice to excite me—sometimes romantically, sometimes crudely, telling me, "You bitch! I have to have you" as we made love by the flickering flames of the fire.

Richard was a wonderful lover. After my time with Rubirosa, it had been virtually impossible to describe any other man as a good lover. But Richard was wonderful. And we had such a wonderful time together. Rubi and I didn't have such a wonderful time. Rubi was morose with his horses and oysters and parties and drinking and could really only make love. Richard was amusing, adorable, and we laughed a lot.

On New Year's morning, we celebrated the New Year with champagne, caviar, smoked salmon, and Hungarian sausage as spicy and hot as our new romance. Then we made love. In the swimming pool, in the kitchen, and, finally, in bed. There, Richard told me about his life, his background and how poor he had been. How he had always wanted to be an actor, how he had trained his voice by shouting into the Welsh hills until he was hoarse with effort and how he wanted to storm Hollywood so badly that he had even had plastic surgery on his nose.

Richard was a total man, an inveterate womanizer, who relished telling me intimate details of his previous liaisons with actresses Claire Bloom and Jean Simmons. At the time, I was aware that I was yet another notch on the increasingly overcrowded Burton gun, but I didn't care. Richard and I liked each other so much, enjoyed each other so much, that neither the future nor the past mattered. We spent three wonderful days together before he had to leave Hollywood for some distant film location. We never made love again, but we always remained friends.

RICHARD **BURTON** and I met again in Bel Air, when he was married to Elizabeth and they both gave a party to which I was invited. Sydney Guilaroff escorted me and when I arrived, Richard came out and kissed me. Liz, on the other hand, ignored me and didn't even say hello. In retrospect, I imagine that she must have known about my fling with Richard. But at the time, I was livid and took Richard aside, telling him, "I want to leave. I don't stay at a party where the hostess won't say hello to me. Especially when it is Liz and we once used to be part of the same family—the Hiltons." Richard, trying to persuade me to stay, said, "Don't you see, darling, she is jealous of you. Liz is jealous of everyone." Even Sydney (who adores Liz) was compelled to agree that Richard was right.

Of course, Liz had every reason for jealousy when it came to Richard. When she and Richard went to Budapest (where he was due to film *Bluebeard*) for her fortieth-birthday party, my cousin who lives there wrote and told me all about what happened. According to him, Liz hardly ever left her room at the Inter-Continental Hotel—and when she did, insulted every Hungarian because she refused to look at the royal palace.

My cousin wrote that everyone in Budapest laughed because, according to him, Liz stayed in her room, drank only champagne, ate fattening Hungarian food (such as goulash, which is like chili, her favorite food) and cried all day. Meanwhile, Richard was out making love to all the beautiful Hungarian girls. And when she challenged him about his infidelity, Richard said, "Screw you." Everyone couldn't wait until they left Budapest and my cousin told me that when the Burtons left the hotel, the management had to spend hours cleaning the suite because Liz ate so much, drank so much, and broke lots of things in the suite—she was so jealous of Burton that she kept throwing things at him.

I don't really know whether Liz ever discovered that Richard and I had been lovers. But, starting with Nicky, many of the same men have fallen in love with both of us. Liz's third husband, Mike Todd, used to flirt with me like crazy whenever we met. He was charming, wonderful, and intelligent. I just wasn't too enamored of his cigars. He smoked them so incessantly that he once burned a hole in one of my red velvet Dior gowns and I wanted to kill him. We once traveled back to Las Vegas on the same plane together and Mike asked me to get married to him there. I didn't take him seriously and later, when he married Liz, went to parties at their house. At one of them, Mike announced, "I have to get the Academy Award for Liz next year."

Liz stormed out and went into the powder room. I followed her and she—and I don't blame her—said, "I am going to shoot that son of a bitch. I don't need him to get me an Academy Award. I am going to get my own Academy Award. How dare that son of a bitch say that!"

Of course Liz did exactly that. After Mike died, my drama teacher Elsa Stanoff confided to me that Liz had married Eddie because he was the best lover in Hollywood. I never thought that Liz stole Eddie Fisher from Debbie Reynolds but that Eddie had left her because, at the time, Debbie used to be so boring. He once said to me, "How can I live with a woman who is a big star, yet still insists that her mother sew all her clothes for her?"

After Eddie, Debbie married Harry Karl. Before that, Harry and I used to date. He was one of the most generous men I have ever known and seemed to be very much in love with me. He rented an apartment in Mother's building in New York and said, "Here, Jolie, take this $100,000 and furnish the place for me because I need a place in New York." When Mother got engaged to her last husband, Edmund, Harry said to him, "If you marry her, I'll give you the apartment as a wedding present." He did and Harry kept his promise.

He was kind and generous, and bought me diamonds and sables and once even sent me twenty embroidered handbags. Once, when I was in New York working on a television show, Harry found out that I missed Francesca, so he had her and Elizabeth flown out to New York at his expense. And when I appeared at the Riviera Las Vegas, Harry sent me $30,000 worth of purple orchids.

At that time, he was dropping $200,000 a night at the gambling tables. As a child, he had been orphaned and then adopted by rich parents, later inheriting Karl Shoes. But he never forgot his humble origins, and now lived like a king, right next door to the Bel Air Hotel. Harry was the most wonderful, nicest, sweetest darling, a "big style man," the most generous man who ever lived. On our first date, he bought me an emerald brooch. On our second, a diamond bracelet. But I didn't want to marry him—so he married Debbie.

At the time, he was very rich with a beautiful house in the Holmby Hills and he also sent her children to school in Switzerland. Harry used to complain to me that Debbie was never around, was never with him and was always working. He also accused Debbie's children, Carrie and Todd Fisher, of bugging his bed to check whether or not he was unfaithful while Debbie was away.

Eventually, Harry lost all his money. I don't know how Debbie took it, but when a woman marries a rich man, she has to be prepared for the possibility. And even if things do go well, a rich man may still need help; I once lent Conrad my last $17,000 so that he could buy a hotel. I never regretted it and Conrad repaid my loan with interest. I don't quite know why Harry and Debbie finally broke up, only that Harry ended up penniless, living in the Hillcrest Hotel. Soon after, he developed an embolism and died. When the press informed Debbie of his death, her sole comment was "No comment." Debbie did not attend Harry Karl's funeral. I know, because I did. Harry Karl was one of the nicest people I have ever known.

LIZ and I are so alike. When we are in love—we can't see anyone else, we are so in love. I remember that my mother saw Liz with her husband Senator John Warner at Regine's in New York. As always, extremely perceptive, Mother said, "I have never seen anyone as smitten with a man as Liz is with John Warner." Yet when she stayed with my wonderful friend—and godmother—Liz Whitney, in Upperville, Virginia, Liz Whitney told me that Elizabeth spent most of her time in the kitchen and never came out. Apparently she spent the whole day cooking and eating and not doing anything else.

My mother has always liked Elizabeth—ever since the days when she was married to Nicky. Nicky took Liz to Mother's shop on Madison Avenue and bought her an imitation Maria Theresia emerald necklace. And as Nicky was paying for it, Liz leaned over to Mother and said, "Don't worry, Jolie, I'll have a real one soon." Which, of course, she did. Liz is a lady who always gets what she wants.

In the late eighties I flew to Miami to work with Liz on an AIDS benefit. Frederick and I were invited to take part by the organizers and to attend the final party but then Liz's publicist called up and (using some triple-speak) indicated that Elizabeth didn't want me to be at the party because she wanted to be the only star there. I went on to help raise $6 million for the charity. On the final evening at the

Fontainebleau, although many people had contributed to raising the money, only Liz came onstage, as if she had done everything herself. The rest of us were left, like poor relatives, hidden away in another area, singing "The Best of Times" from *La Cage aux Folles,* while Liz basked in the glory.

Mother and Liz's mother, Sara, are great friends and Sara told her about how Liz thinks nothing of buying herself jewelry worth thousands of dollars.

Of course, Richard used to buy Liz incredible jewelry, including the famous Krupp diamond. Vera Krupp used to live close to me in Bel Air and they say that she got $25 million from her husband, the armaments king, Krupp. With it, she bought the most unbelievable diamonds. Vera wasn't in the least bit overwhelmed by any of her diamonds and used to wear them while gardening or doing the dishes. I always used to tell her, "Vera, I am going to put an arrow on my property saying 'Vera Krupp Lives Thataway,' so any burglars stay away from me and go where the jewelry is." But Vera lost all her money when she went to Las Vegas, fell in love with a croupier there, married him and gave him her entire fortune. When she died, she had her four black Great Danes cremated and buried in the coffin with her.

I saw Richard twice again twice before he died. First, in Chasen's when he was with his third wife, Suzy, and pitifully complained to me about his backache, "Zsa Zsa, you don't know how much I suffer. My back is killing me." I went away feeling sad and depressed that my wonderful effervescent Richard was so miserable.

The very last time I saw him was at a party for Lucille Ball. Richard was with his final wife, the former Sally Hay, and her parents, who were over from England. Richard came over to me and said proudly, "My wife is dying to meet you." Sally was very friendly and afterward, Richard whispered to me tenderly, "I really love her. Maybe she isn't as beautiful as Liz, but I like her a hundred times more because I can talk to her."

*

*

I'**LL** always think of Richard with affection and I'll always be attracted to his kind of man. In London, once, I met Peter O'Toole, one of Richard's friends, who openly informed me, "I used to hate you because I thought you were frivolous.

But now I've met you, I really love you." I felt the same way about Peter, but didn't get too enthusiastic about another one of his fellow British Isles countrymen, Irishman Richard Harris.

I rented my house in Bel Air to him for a time and before he moved in, I threw a party for him to introduce him to the neighborhood. Richard arrived late, wore an Indian headband, brought his butler with him, and his housekeeper had to spoon-feed him because he was so drunk.

At the end of the evening, everyone was in the process of saying good night, when Richard (in front of Rona Barrett, one of my guests) said, "I'm not going to go. I'm going to sleep with you." In the end, I turfed him out, whereupon Richard lay on my front lawn singing "If Ever I Would Leave You," from *Camelot*, until I was compelled to call the Bel Air Patrol to take him away.

R**ICHARD HARRIS** may not have been the man for me, but another Brit—Sean Connery—undoubtedly was. Sean and I met in a London studio and after the meeting, Sean began calling me five times a day but we never arranged anything. A few months later, back in Hollywood, I got another call from Sean, telling me that he was in town and desperately wanted to see me. I was due at the designer Rubin Parnis any minute, so I told Sean to be there as well.

I'll never forget the moment when Sean Connery, dressed in jogging clothes, his soft brown eyes alight with anticipation, strode into Parnis's shop on Melrose Avenue and all the salesgirls nearly fainted. I couldn't wait to leave with him. I found him sizzlingly handsome, intelligent, and wonderful, rippling with masculinity and virility. He also—I soon discovered—had an amazingly beautiful body, one of the most beautiful bodies I had ever seen. Sean's skin feels as soft as velvet, as sensuous as silk.

Sean was a very different lover than Richard. More romantic than sexual. He was extremely adroit at giving me the impression that I was the only woman in the world he ever wanted to make love to. I knew he probably worked the same magic on hundreds of other women before and after me, but at the time, the effect was potent.

Sean and I didn't just make love—we began to see each other socially as well. At one party, while Sean and I danced together, all the women in the room were after him, but Sean was patently uncomfortable, confiding in me later that he hates parties. At another dinner, Pamela Mason, her acid tongue much in evidence, commented, "Remember how much Rubi loved you, Zsa Zsa." Without a word, Sean got up and left. Later, he told me that Pamela's words had really upset him.

I sensed that under his gruff macho exterior, Sean was a romantic, capable of jealousy as well as of passion. Sean went back to London and our affair ended. He is now married to a wonderful and brilliant woman named Micheline and is very happy with her.

My romance with Sean was long ago, but in many ways, I wish I had met Sean Connery when I was seventeen. If I had, I believe we would still be married, with ten children—because Sean is the perfect man for me.

Life After George Continued

*

DESPITE my romantic entanglements, my career had always had first priority in my life—but even that had to take a backseat when tragedy struck. I was in London when my agent called me and gave me the shocking news that my house (at 1001 Bellagio Road) was on fire. Even as he spoke, fire was sweeping through Bel Air, hopscotching between the palatial mansions so that Vera Krupp's house escaped but mine burned to the ground—Burt Lancaster's blazed, but Kim Novak's didn't. My first call was to Francesca, who was shattered by news of the fire and began crying, "Mommy, mommy, stop the fire." I only wished I could. But the fire blazed on, consuming Francesca's dolls, her miniature Mercedes, all my clothes, my jewelry, my family photographs and the cherished letters from my parents in Hungary.

Anything that escaped the fire was looted a few days later (a month after the fire I was approached to buy back goods that had been stolen from the burned-out shell of my house).

When I came back to Bel Air and saw the ash-covered remains of the elegant Japanese trees that had surrounded the house, I cried. But I thanked God that my beloved dogs had not perished. According to eyewitnesses, my German shepherd, King, had tried to bite the fire, my Yorkie, Mr. Magoo, had chased the rats streaming out of the burning house, and my French poodle, Harvey Hilton, had jumped into the Rolls-Royce almost as if he were demanding to be driven away. The story of my pets may sound funny—but it does happen to be true. They did act that way and I was overjoyed that they were alive because I cared more about them than any possession that I lost in the house.

THE effects of the Bel Air fire were surmountable—but the next tragedy in my life was not—the tragedy of my sister Magda suffering a near-fatal accident. Magda and I had always been extremely close—a closeness that perhaps partly stemmed from the fact that she was so like Father and I had loved him so much. She had his red hair, his fierce temper, was superintellectual and far more interested in literature than Eva and I had ever been. At a very early age, Magda had married a Polish count, Count Jan Behovsky, who joined the RAF immediately and was shot down.

She then fell in love with the Portuguese ambassador to Budapest and became engaged to him. Fearless and courageous, Magda's relationship with the Portuguese ambassador helped her save the lives of two hundred and forty Jewish families during the Second World War.

Once in America, Magda, tall, slim, with green eyes, speaking eleven languages, a horsewoman and a brilliant tennis player, also started acting, winning parts in a variety of plays. Then she married again, after our godmother, Liz Whitney, invited her to her ranch in Virginia and paired her off with an Irish writer. Unfortunately, though, the writer was continually drunk, Magda complained to Father (then alive and on a trip to America), who promptly tore down to Virginia, horsewhipped the writer, then arranged for Magda to divorce him.

Next Magda met the man who became the love of her life, Tony Gallici. They lived in New York, where they had a house on East 71st Street as well as a wonderful house in Southampton. The centerpiece of the Southampton house was a spiral staircase specially imported from Italy. Whenever any of the family came to stay with Magda and Tony, before they went to bed she would remind them that Maxim, the dog, always slept on the staircase and to be careful not to trip over him. Ironically, late one night, Magda herself got up to get a glass of water, slipped and fell, hitting her head.

I was in New York when I got the call from Mother, telling me of Magda's accident. By some cruel trick of fate,

Magda hadn't just broken a blood vessel, but had traumatized the part of the brain governing strokes.

Now she was in a coma. All of us—Eva and her then husband, Dick Brown, Francesca, Mother, and I—rushed to Mount Sinai, where Magda spent six weeks locked in the coma. Mother's husband, Edmund, had a cousin, Professor Rosenthal (who was a top surgeon), and we consulted him. After a battery of tests, his somber verdict was "If we operate, Magda has a fifty percent chance of surviving. If we don't, she will survive, but her faculties will be impaired." We had a family conference, at the end of which our unanimous decision was not to operate.

Once she left the hospital, Magda began speech and physical therapy. Then (in the most terrible time of my entire life), her beloved husband, Tony, contracted cancer and died after a harrowing six months. We held a big funeral at St. Patrick's and Magda stood there, her face shrouded by a heavy black veil, and was unable to say a word. From that moment on, she gave up her therapy and Mother took her under her wing.

Today, Magda lives in Palm Springs, close to Mother. She can talk and I am able to understand her. On most weekends, I drive to Palm Springs to see Magda and to have lunch with her and Mother at Le Vallauris restaurant. Nevertheless, the shock of Magda's accident, and the death of her great love, was one of the saddest things that has ever happened to me in my whole life.

*

*

*

WHILE Magda was in a coma, lying helpless in Mount Sinai, I turned for comfort to a man who would become my fourth husband. Businessman Herbert Hutner was—and is—an angel. With his gray hair and kindly manner, he was the father figure par excellence, a gentle man, a solace for me amid my unhappiness at Magda's illness. We first met at the Plaza at a dinner for St. Jude's Hospital. I had sat at Danny Thomas's table and Herbert was seated next to me. His date had been a stunning Indian princess, which had intrigued me and caused me to conclude, "Any man who dates a girl like that must be fantastic." I wasn't wrong because, in his way, Herbert Hutner was a fantastic man. He just wasn't the man for me. He was a brilliant, worldly man, a graduate of Columbia, a former attorney turned spectacularly successful industrialist and Wall Street financier. Francesca adored him, Mother championed his cause and—ironically—my masseuse clinched the marriage.

After about three dates, a messenger appeared, bearing a gift from Herbert. But not just any gift. A twenty-three-carat blue-white diamond ring! (eventually valued at $3 million). At the time, I was having a massage, my masseuse tried the ring on, declared, "This ring we can't give back," and I listened and accepted the ring—along with Herbert's proposal. I wasn't sure that I could make Herbert happy, but I married him because he was kind, sweet, and everything that the doctor ordered.

Nevertheless, Herbert is the only man whom I did not marry for love or passion—I loved him as a human being, but I was not *in* love with him. After my marriage, I took the risk of appearing on *F. Lee Bailey's Lie Detector* show, still a little apprehensive, knowing that my propensity for honesty often got me into trouble. Bailey asked me which one of my husbands I had married for love. I replied "All of them, except Herbert Hutner." And the polygraph machine registered that I was, indeed, telling the truth.

HERBERT and I got married two weeks after we first met. I married him because he was kind and good and not because of his generosity in giving me jewelry. After all, I had already bought myself (with my own money) a necklace fabricated out of thirty-seven unbelievably perfect stones, graduated, matched rose-cut diamonds amounting to one hundred carats. At the time, Harry Winston wistfully informed me, "It took seven years to collect these stones. I could never do it again."

Herbert may not have been my grand passion, but I gave him a certain amount of pleasure. He loved meeting all my friends. When we gave a costume ball in London, at Les

A scene from *The Girl in the Kremlin* with Lex Barker. I played twin sisters.

George and I leave from the stage door during the Broadway run of *Forty Carats*. Even though we were long divorced, George escorted me home from the theater every night.

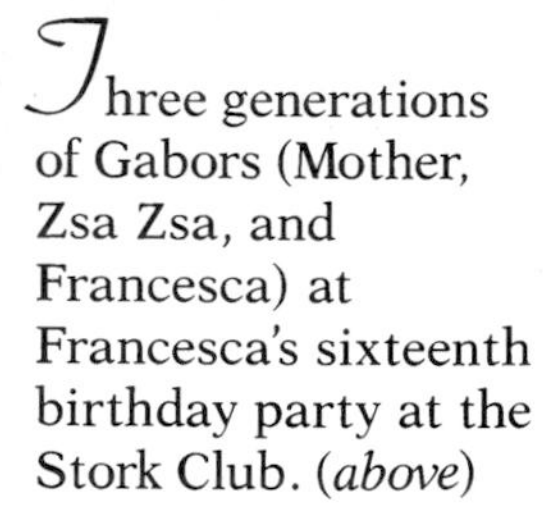

Three generations of Gabors (Mother, Zsa Zsa, and Francesca) at Francesca's sixteenth birthday party at the Stork Club. (*above*)

Francesca and her father, Conrad Hilton, at a party thrown at my house after her graduation from Marymount.

A portrait of Francesca that I love.

Making an entrance during my show at the Riviera, Las Vegas.

Appearing at El Rancho Vegas in Las Vegas.

Guest appearance at the Folies-Bergère, Paris, at a benefit performance in aid of the charity Le Petit Lit Blanc.

With Jimmy Stewart, Rich Little, George Jessel, and Bob Hope in Baltimore to take part in a benefit for flood victims.

With President Nixon at a birthday party he threw for me in San Clemente. The President even brought out the cake for me himself!

With Bebe Rebozo, Richard Nixon's friend, at a party thrown in San Clemente.

With Dr. and Mrs. Armand Hammer.

With President Ford.

In Anchorage, Alaska, representing Montgomery Ward.

The producers asked me to wear a dark red wig for my part in *Picture Mommy Dead,* as I was replacing Hedy Lamarr and the leading lady, Martha Hyer, was blond.

Meeting the Queen of England and Prince Philip at Nancy Reagan's party for them at 20th Century-Fox.

King Rechad, the son of the deposed King of Tunisia, at the party I gave for him at my Bel Air home.

My engagement party to Frederick in my house in Bel Air, with Magda, Merv Griffin, Eva, and former Tarzan, John Frederick.

Behind bars at the famous El Segundo City Jail.

Mr. and Mrs. Reagan's party at the Beverly Wilshire Hotel, three months after my clash with the police. Mr. Reagan was so sweet and kept holding my hand to reassure me.

With the children of the Macbride School for retarded children, rehearsing a French song I taught them.

Jolie Gabor at her ninetieth birthday party given for her on September 29, 1990, by Magda.

With my beloved Silver Fox, the World Undefeated Tennessee Walker Champion.

A corner of my dressing room at 1001 Bel Air Road.

Another corner of my dressing room in Bel Air.

Prince and Princess Frederick von Anhalt, Duke and Duchess of Saxony.

Ambassadeurs, even Princess Margaret attended. I wore a green sequined dress, a $2 million diamond necklace, a $3 million diamond ring, and $150,000 pear-shaped diamond drop earrings. Noël Coward observed afterward, "You're worth at least five million dollars walking." We also went to Ascot together and sat in the Royal Enclosure with the Queen of England.

Herbert was deliriously happy. I, on the other hand, felt trapped.

HERBERT took away my will to work. With his kindness and generosity, he almost annihilated my drive. I have always been the kind of woman who could never be satisfied by money—only by excitement and achievement. My decision to marry Herbert had basically been influenced and prompted by my mother, who had told me that I needed finally to settle down with a more conventional man, a man who wasn't a challenge, who would love me unconditionally.

Herbert didn't just love me. He idolized me. And I was bored. Forever a tomboy and a rebel, I still needed a rogue to love, a man who was a challenge and a marriage that was as stormy as my wild Hungarian soul required. I knew that my marriage to Herbert was destined to end in the divorce courts. My only problem was that my grounds for divorce were completely unacceptable to any judicial system in the world: divorce on the grounds of mental kindness!

MANY times, throughout our three-year marriage, Herbert had begged me not to accept film offers and had even once offered me $200,000 if I turn down a $100,000 salary for a film. I did manage to work sometimes, though. When Hedy Lamarr was arrested for shoplifting and I was asked to take over for her in the film *Picture Mommy Dead*—co-starring Martha Hyer—I took over the part at short notice, donning a red wig for the role. And when it came to *Arrivederci, Baby,* Herbert was amenable to the idea of my agreeing to take the part (opposite Tony Curtis) and to traveling with me to Cannes, where the film was scheduled to be shot.

Tony Curtis is also a Hungarian and we got on very well—especially when the unit moved to London and Tony and I shot our love scene at Shepperton Studios there. The script called for me to be in bed with Tony and I was semi-nude through most of it. After one take, the director said, "Let's do another take"—whereupon Tony ruefully admitted, "But I can't retake it. That would be impossible." Herbert was ecstatic and I couldn't help thinking back to Rubi and how he would have reacted.

*

THE problem was that Herbert was so easygoing, so delighted with me, so thrilled to be married to me. He was so kind and nice and considerate of me that I became deeply depressed. Soon, I almost stopped talking to Herbert altogether. And I felt fully alive only when I was working. I wanted out of the marriage, but couldn't quite work out how to manage a divorce without hurting Herbert too badly. I knew that Herbert didn't deserve to be hurt. But I also knew I couldn't survive in our marriage for much longer either.

Back in New York, I tried find a substitute romance for Herbert and gave a big dinner to which I invited Gina Lollobrigida and Princess Soraya. I wore all my diamonds and toward the middle of the evening, went into the powder room with Gina and Soraya and pointedly informed them, "You know, Herbert bought me all these diamonds. I want to divorce him and one of you two should go after him." Gina grew visibly excited, but as the evening went on, I could sense that Herbert wasn't interested in her. We went on to a disco and Soraya danced with Herbert. I so much wanted him to fall in love with her because she is so beautiful. But during the dance, she and Herbert didn't say a word to each other, so my plan to find a substitute ultimately failed dismally.

*

HEDDA HOPPER once acerbically commented, "If Herbert lets Zsa Zsa go for one day of his life he will never see her again." Herbert must have listened to Hedda, because he did his best always to stay close to me. But after three years of marriage, fate stepped in and led poor Herbert to break his leg in the same week when we were due to travel to Fort Worth, where I was scheduled as guest of honor at a museum opening benefiting charity. Arranging for Elizabeth Keleman to travel with me instead, Herbert insisted that I fulfill my obligations without him.

Once in Texas, my hostess, on discovering that I was alone, telephoned me in my hotel room. "Darling, I am going to send you a blind date," she said in a determined voice that wouldn't brook no for an answer. "He is very charming and divorced." With that, she rang off. With a sigh of resignation, I put on the outfit I had already planned to wear when I thought Herbert would be escorting me, a mint-green Guy Laroche gown decorated with bugle beads, long white gloves, and a long white mink coat. In those days, I was still wearing fur, but I haven't worn any for the longest time, as I don't believe in wearing fur anymore.

While I was fastening my diamond necklace (the one made entirely of stones from Harry Winston), the doorbell rang. Elizabeth answered it and, after a moment, came back into my dressing room looking extremely elated and exclaimed, "Miss Gabor, I'm afraid we've found our next husband!" Flustered, I didn't have time to ask her what exactly she meant by that, but made my entrance into the drawing room, where Joshua Cosden, Jr., was waiting for me.

HE looked exactly like a young Jimmy Stewart: tall, slim, with gray hair and blue eyes, closer to Conrad in appearance than to any of my other husbands. He looked like a Texan prince. In fact, he was a Texan prince. Later, I learned that in the twenties Joshua's father had been worth $300 million but that nowadays the family fortune was all but gone. Nevertheless, it seemed that Joshua had grown up in the most privileged of worlds. He hadn't merely been born with a silver spoon in his mouth, but with jewelry at his feet—as a child even permitted to walk on the $500,000 precious-stone-encrusted Persian carpet that decorated the family's Palm Beach mansion.

That first night, Joshua didn't reveal much about his current financial circumstances. Not that that mattered. Far from it—for I was riveted by Joshua himself, by his nonchalance, his style, his intellect (he had been educated at the Sorbonne), and his obvious interest in me. As flashbulbs sparkled at the museum opening, I couldn't help glancing at Joshua out of the corner of my eye and thinking that he really did seem to be the man for me.

The climax of the evening was dinner—a dinner so grand that it rivaled any function held at Buckingham Palace itself—at the home of Texans so wealthy that they had three Renoirs hanging in the powder room. By the time Joshua took me home to my hotel, the atmosphere was heavy with romance and in the limousine, Joshua gazed at me with those haunting blue eyes of his and in a husky voice said, "Zsa Zsa, you are the kind of woman I like." Spellbound, I replied, "And you are the kind of man I like." Then, the spell broken, we both burst into giggles.

Elizabeth was still up, waiting for me in our suite, as if I were a naughty teenager who had been out dancing and was slinking home at dawn. In front of her, Joshua kissed me good night. Then he left. I couldn't sleep all night, thinking of him, wondering about him, longing for him. In the morning, we were scheduled to take the early plane and, just as we were about to board at Dallas/Fort Worth, a tall, thin figure strode toward us: Joshua, looking more Texan and princely than ever. We talked for a few moments, I gave Joshua my phone number, then Elizabeth and I boarded the plane bound for Hollywood and for Herbert.

THROUGHOUT the days that followed, Joshua kept calling me, ardently telling me, "I can't live without you. I want to marry you. And I can't see you again unless you divorce your husband and marry me." His argument, given my feelings for Herbert, was compelling. But, before I could succumb to the charms of Mr. Cosden, I still had to contend with the tears of my equally formidable mother, who portentously warned, "You'll never find another Herbert Hutner. Don't make the mistake of divorcing him," with Francesca, who, when I told her I was considering divorcing Herbert, cried and said, "No one ever loved me like Herbert does," and even with Conrad's disapproving comment, "I like Herbert Hutner. He's good, generous, and educated—a real sweetheart."

I knew they were all right. Herbert was a sweetheart. He was kind and generous and a wonderful stepfather to Francesca. I just didn't love him with a grand passion. Whatever my brain and my common sense told me, my heart contradicted. And, from the time that I was twelve and kissed the man who delivered the coal, I had always followed my heart. I couldn't change and I knew I had to marry Joshua.

✳

ONCE I'd made my decision, I still couldn't bring myself to tell Herbert. We went to New York together and throughout the trip, I tried to find the right moment to tell him that our marriage was over, but somehow, the right moment never came. Finally, on the plane back to California, I took the plunge and told Herbert the truth; I wanted a divorce because I planned to marry Joshua Cosden, Jr. Herbert started crying like a little boy and I felt helpless. Soon his tears turned to hysteria and the stewardess intervened, trying to comfort him. I knew that I had hurt Herbert and I told myself that I would probably have to pay. In a way, I think I did; from the moment that Herbert and I divorced, I had nothing but bad luck. My lawyer, Bentley Ryan, gave Herbert the news that, as I had initiated the divorce, I was not going to ask for alimony. And Herbert moved out of my house.

I'VE never expected my life to be problem-free and, in marrying Joshua, I was prepared for problems. From the beginning, I knew that Joshua was suffering from cancer and, around the time that Herbert and I separated, Joshua was rushed to hospital and underwent an operation for the removal of one lung. I was with him throughout the operation. I knew he needed me and I loved him and wanted to be with him.

Then, Eva and I flew to Juarez, Mexico, for my divorce. Immediately afterward, I married Joshua in a romantic ceremony in my house in Bel Air. I wore a white Christian Dior gown and a white veil intertwined with lilies of the valley. I don't think there is anything wrong with a woman who has been married before wearing white. I married George in light gray. Later, I was to marry Michael O'Hara in black velvet. But normally, I get married in white because I don't want anyone else telling me I can't get married in white because of tradition. I hate tradition. If I feel white, I marry in white. White suits me—so I wear it—whether I am marrying for the first time or for the twenty-first. In any case, every time I get married I feel as if it is the first time.

Tony Curtis, one of the wedding guests, my co-star from *Arrivederci, Baby* (remembering the scene in which I played his bride), cracked that he had only just married me himself—two months before! "Zsa Zsa, don't tell him that you are marrying him in the same wedding dress you married me in six months ago." Kathryn Grayson, Gregory Peck and his wife, Veronique, Charlton Heston, and even Conrad Hilton were also guests. So was Jerry Orbach, who wished me luck with the heartfelt words, "Zsa Zsa, now you've got the most wonderful man in the world, from a distinguished Texas family, and I know you are going to be happy with him."

As Joshua and I left on our honeymoon, I hoped and prayed that Jerry was right and that I would finally find happiness at last. But, from the start, our marriage was plagued by bad omens. In Monte Carlo, I suddenly developed severe internal hemorrhaging and checked into the Princess Grace Hospital. In terrible pain, I called Grace, herself, but her butler informed me that Grace—or rather "Her Grace"—could not be disturbed because she was having lunch. She never returned my call and I felt angry and betrayed.

Meanwhile, the doctors decided to operate. After the operation, I woke up with a terrible fever, with Joshua at my bedside. He was hysterical about my fever, blamed the hospital, blamed Monte Carlo, even Europe, for my plight and declared that this would never have happened in America.

We went on to Paris—where I came face-to-face with what would turn out to be one of the biggest conflicts inherent in my new marriage. We went to Maxim's together for dinner—Maxim's where Rubi used to hold court every night, Maxim's the chicest restaurant in the world, Maxim's where every woman is dressed to kill and where wearing three diamond necklaces may not even be enough—and there, fishing chicken out of his soup with his hands and then greedily eating it, was Aristotle Onassis, with Maria Callas (who was chewing away on the bones and was dressed in a babushka). They both looked like peasants who had just come home from a hard day in the fields. I was so impressed. Onassis was a peasant and he ate like a peasant—but I loved him for it. And I loved Maria for it too. In contrast, Joshua was horrified. And although we didn't argue about our different responses to Ari and Maria that night, we both knew that they meant the beginning of a rift.

Joshua was Social Register and cared deeply about his status. I, on the other hand, had never given a fig for titles, status, or snobbery. The only thing that ever impressed me—or ever will impress me—is brains and heart. George used to say that when I arrived in America, I was a princess, but then worked my way down to be an actress. In a way, George had been right—and I was proud of it. I was proud to be an American, proud to be part of the democratic system in which all people were equal. Joshua, on the other hand, was proud to be in the Social Register.

THE Onassis family had always seemed to be a factor in my life. Maria Callas, too, had featured in it. Litza Callas, her mother, went to see my mother and begged, "Mrs. Gabor, give me a job because I am broke." Then she confessed that she was living in a rented room in New Jersey and taking in sewing so that she could survive and that she and Maria had been estranged for ten years.

My mother responded by asking why Maria didn't support her. After a few minutes of embarrassed silence, Mrs. Callas told Mother that her daughter did not support her because years before, one of Maria's lovers had had an affair with her, and that Maria could never forgive her. Unperturbed, my mother replied, "We Hungarians never hold a grudge. The Greeks hold it in. In Hungary, we get mad, smash a glass, and then forget it." When Litza assured my mother that there was no hope of a reconciliation, my mother gave her a job in the shop, before philosophizing, "Don't worry. All of my daughters' lovers also want to sleep with me." Mother is ninety now and she still believes that every man is a little in love with her. She is probably right.

I had met Onassis many times through the years and really liked him. During my time with Rubi, he took me aside during a party in Monte Carlo and appealed to me, "For God's sake, don't go back to America. Whenever you go back there, your Rubirosa goes back too, chasing you, and my wife goes back, chasing him." That was how I found out that Tina, Onassis's wife, had a big crush on Rubi. I knew he wasn't in the least bit interested in her and I liked Tina—so we became friends.

Our paths crossed again, when Tina divorced Ari on account of his affair with Maria and then married my friend

Sunny Blandford—so named because his full name was John George Vanderbilt Henry Spencer-Churchill, the Marquess of Blandford. Sunny's father, Bertie, the Duke of Marlborough, broke the news of the marriage to me with typically British understatement, "Zsa Zsa, Sunny is going to marry Tina Onassis. Which is perfectly all right because now, with all that money, Sunny will be able to repaint Blenheim Palace."

Only one thing troubled Bertie: He was very proud of his handsome blond son and was disturbed by the idea that his future grandchildren's looks might reflect their Greek, rather than their British, heritage. "Both Sunny and Christina have been married before and they both have children. Sunny's are like Botticelli angels—blond and blue-eyed. But Tina's are dark and very Greek, my dear."

That was the first time I learned of the existence of Alexander and Christina Onassis. Later, when Christina was about fourteen, I met her in Monte Carlo. Christina was a bosomy girl and, as Tina and I were such good friends, I suggested to her that she arrange to have Christina's nose and breasts modified by plastic surgery. "I want to," said Tina eagerly, then added resentfully, "but Ari refuses to allow it."

Meanwhile, Tina and Sunny divorced and Tina married Ari's archrival, Stavros Niarchos, because, she confided in me, she had dreamed that her sister, Eugenie (who had been married to Stavros herself), had said, "Go to Niarchos and look after my children."

By now, Ari himself had married Jacqueline Kennedy. But even before Jackie and Ari said their vows in a wedding ceremony held on Ari's private island, I knew that the marriage didn't have much chance of success. First, because I know Greek men well and I know that to a Greek like Ari, the only woman who will ever truly be important to him is the mother of his children. In the view of the average Greek man (and no matter how wealthy Onassis became, he would always remain quintessentially Greek), all women other than the mother of his children are whores.

In marrying Jackie, Ari got what Conrad used to call a package deal. His ex-wife, Tina, had married a titled Englishman. Ari wanted to surpass her by marrying the widow of the President of America. Along with that, he also was in the process of forming his company, Olympic Airways, and knew that, in marrying the President's widow, he would be guaranteed the Senate approval he needed to launch the company. So in marrying Jackie—just as Conrad married me and got me and the Blackstone Hotel—Ari's package deal was Jackie and Olympic Airways.

Jackie's package deal, on the other hand, proved to be Ari and his daughter Christina. At this point, I knew a great deal about Christina, in particular, from a friend of mine, Joe Bolker, a Los Angeles businessman who had once been married to the home-savings-and-loan heiress, Mark Taper's daughter. Joe was a very handsome forty-eight-year-old divorcé who lived in Century City and was a wildly attractive man about town. Between my marriages, we dated and Joe told me that he had just met Christina at the Hotel de Paris, Monte Carlo.

At the time, Christina had been nineteen and, according to Joe, developed a big-time crush on him, calling him at all hours of the night when Joe was back in Los Angeles and Christina was in London. Joe, busy playing the field, wasn't that interested in her, and instead, seemed to have set his heart on seducing me. But, like Frank Sinatra before him, Joe went about it completely the wrong way. At the end of the evening, he practically tore my dress off and I ended up fighting to stave him off. I knew Joe was handsome, I knew he was exactly my type, but I knew I couldn't have sex with him. He was too aggressive.

The next day, Joe called me and announced, "If you don't marry me, I'll marry Christina Onassis instead." Surprised, but not displeased, I countered, "But Joe, aren't you a bit old for her? After all, you are forty-eight and she is nineteen." Over the phone, I could sense that Joe had dismissed my objections and had decided to marry Christina.

I threw a party for the newlyweds at my house in Bel Air and even then, Christina and Joe weren't happy. During their ninety-day marriage, Joe found himself contending with Ari (who couldn't cope with Joe being Jewish) and dealing with his menacing entourage. As for Christina, she made three suicide attempts in the time that they were together. And the Greek tragedy continued. . . .

PERHAPS Joshua and I seeing Maria Callas and Ari at Maxim's on our honeymoon and our contrasting response to them was an omen that heralded what would be the major schism in our marriage: our differing values regarding society and what or who mattered to us. Joshua and I returned from our honeymoon—to be greeted by a letter from the powers-that-be at the Social Register, announcing that

Joshua, as a direct result of having married an actress, had been dropped from the Register. He was devastated. But our problems had only just begun; soon after our return to Bel Air, Joshua came to me with the proposal that I buy him the Four Star TV studio.

"How much does it cost?" I asked, prepared to be open-minded.

"Four million," said Joshua, firmly.

Taking the marital bull by the horns, I replied, equally firmly, "I don't have four million dollars." Joshua's face fell.

IN an attempt to consolidate our new union, I bought a new house for us on St. Pierre Road in Bel Air. The house was Regency style, had been decorated by the ubiquitous Lady Elsie Mendl, and had been originally owned by Mervyn LeRoy, who had directed me in my first film, *Lovely to Look At*. Thrilled and excited about the new house, Joshua and I hired a team of workmen to renovate part of the house. They began work and we followed their progress eagerly, impatient to move into our dream house.

Then, early one Monday morning, I arrived at the house, the first person to get there, unlocked the door, only to find a bird lying dead on the drawing room floor. The poor thing had obviously flown into the house before the workmen left on Friday, had been trapped inside all weekend, and had died of starvation. With tears in my eyes, I picked up the body of the dead bird and buried it in the garden, knowing that now I could never live in the house. Some might say that I carried superstition to the extreme, but I just couldn't live in a house where a bird had died. I just couldn't. So, financial disaster though it was, I sold our dream house.

✱

✱

ANOTHER bird was also to play a large part in my marriage to Joshua—albeit a happier one. On a trip to Dallas, we went to Neiman-Marcus, the great department store, and bought an enormous macaw. We took him home, called him Caesar, and took note of the store's instructions that we must feed Caesar a piece of orange every morning. For a few months, I religiously followed those instructions. Until one day, when—for some unknown reason—I failed to bring Caesar his piece of orange.

A few hours went by while I read a book and didn't look in his direction. Finally, I put down my book and, on my way to the kitchen, passed Caesar's cage. Our eyes met and he fixed me with what, at the time, seemed to be an evil eye (after all, snakes come from birds or vice versa, I can't remember) and, in the clearest voice possible, pronounced the words "Fuck you!"

Totally unnerved and remembering my omission, I fetched the piece of orange for Caesar, careful to avoid his eyes. In silence, he ate it. I breathed a sigh of relief. Prematurely. Because from that moment on, all Caesar would say to me, to Joshua, and to anyone who crossed the threshold of our house, was "Fuck you!" Until Joshua decreed, "The bird must go. We shall send him back to Neiman-Marcus."

We contacted the store, who, on hearing the problem, agreed to reclaim Caesar. His day of departure dawned. Caesar sat perched in his golden cage, surveying the room for the final time, then the butler came to take him back to Dallas. And as Caesar was carried out of the room forever, his very last words were, of course, "Fuck you!"

NOW I was birdless—soon I would be husbandless, yet again, as well. Joshua and I continued to clash over our different attitudes to life and to people and the different values for which we stood. Once, we went to a club and Joshua, for reasons best known to himself, made a disparaging remark about actors. I walked out.

Another time, we went to the Bistro Garden with Kathryn Grayson and some friends. We walked in, Joshua's eyes scanned the room, then he backed out completely, with the words "I can't go in there. Too many Jews. . . ." I was flabbergasted and stuttered, "Are you crazy, Joshua? Most of my friends are Jewish. Didn't you know that?"

Some of those friends eventually met Joshua at a party we threw at my house and he was polite but distant to them. At the end of the evening, we all sat down in front of the television to watch the *Sammy Davis Jr. Show* on which I was a guest star. At the end of the show, Sammy kissed me. Joshua made no comment. Our guests left. Now that we were alone, Joshua looked at me and—with despair in his voice—said, "I'll never be able to go back to Texas now that my wife has been kissed by a darkie."

*

SIX months after our wedding, Joshua and I were divorced. I had gone into the marriage not really knowing him and I left none the wiser. All I had really discerned was that our values clashed, Joshua was prejudiced and I wasn't, and he was more wed to high society than I had ever been or ever wanted to be. We went to Bentley Ryan (my lawyer) together, signed the papers, cried, and then went to Trader Vic's for drinks afterward.

Next, it was back to Juarez for me, where a divorce was waiting, along with a group of Mexicans waving a banner that read WELCOME BACK ZSA ZSA. I laughed. Even though part of me would really have preferred to cry.

*

I was single again. Herbert was remarried to a lovely lady named Julie (who looks a little like me) and was very happy. And Joshua would go on to marry a mason jar heiress and reclaim his place in high society. As for me—I made up my mind to concentrate on my career more than ever.

Montgomery Ward picked me as spokesperson for their auto club, after the University of Chicago had determined that John Wayne and I were the two best known names in show business. I don't know if they ever asked John to participate and he had turned them down, but when they invited me to be their ambassadress, I was delighted to accept. Montgomery Ward hired me for $350,000 a year and featured me in their full-page color advertisements, wearing a chiffon gown and leaning against a Rolls. I toured the country, speaking on their behalf in department stores, opened car races (at which I always had to kiss the winner), and meeting people from all walks of life. I loved it. When I began, Montgomery Ward's auto club had a membership of thirty thousand. When my contract ended, seven years later, membership totaled an incredible eight million.

*

I also ventured into the realms of beauty—getting involved in the manufacture of my own products, based on Hungarian formulas that had been in my family for years. Today, my Zsa Zsa cream is sold all over America and I never go anywhere myself without putting it on first. I don't have a very complicated beauty regimen, in any case.

In the morning, I cleanse my face with cold cream (no particular brand), then I tone with witch hazel. After that, I put my Zsa Zsa cream on to protect and nourish the skin. Next, I put base on. After that, I powder with Mennen body powder (I learned that at MGM), which is white and light. Then I put black eyeliner on top and underneath my eyes. Last of all I do my eyebrows and then put on false eyelashes.

My entire "beauty regimen" takes no more than ten minutes. Movie stars are often accused of spending hours in front of the mirror and being vain because they are beautiful, but that isn't always true. It is those women who are not blessed with beauty who tend to spend more time in front of the mirror. In fact, I have always believed that beauty isn't the most important asset a woman can possess; brains and wit are much more important. Mae West, I think, is a case in point.

She and I met when I broached the possibility of my doing a revival of *Diamond Lil.* Mae was very friendly and greeted me with "Hiya, honey!" but I was momentarily taken aback because, to me, Mae looked like a man and was the ugliest woman I had ever seen.

Trying not to let my feelings register on my face, I started talking about buying the rights. Mae stopped me. "Are you kidding, honey? I'm going to do it myself—in living color!" I was disappointed, but fascinated by Mae. She was incredibly intelligent and from then on I used some of her jokes in my nightclub acts—giving her credit for them, of course.

Sadly, Mae did actually try to revive *Diamond Lil* herself, this time on TV, but at that stage she was far too old and couldn't remember any of the lines. Through the years, I met directors who complained to me about Mae, that she was difficult to work with, that she was a bitch. But I didn't care. To me, Mae West was brilliant because she was witty and had the guts to strip sex of the hypocrisy with which we try to surround it.

MAE West appealed to me because, essentially, she was a great comedian and I have always loved comedians. In a way, I think I am a bit of a comedian myself. I was never trained for comedy, because you have to be a natural comedian—have to be born with it. I even guested for two years on *Laugh-In,* something I adored. Bob Hope is wonderful and he helped me a great deal in my career. Whenever I have worked with him on TV shows, Bob has always sat in the control room, watched me on the monitors, and then advised me on how to improve my performance. One of Bob's major contributions to my career has also been to tell me, "Never try to get a laugh at anyone's expense but your own." In all my acts, my style is always to laugh at myself—even in something like *Nightmare on Elm Street,* in which I had a cameo role. And I nearly died laughing when I saw *Saturday Night Live* after the policeman thing and they did a hysterical parody of me and Leona Helmsley.... No—I never mind laughing at myself and I know Bob Hope's advice to me was right.

However, the new, young comedians of today don't always agree with Bob; when the policeman fiasco exploded in the media, many comedians insulted and attacked me with unnecessary cruelty. Then again, one of the newest and most popular comediennes of them all, Roseanne Barr, touched my heart after the police incident happened, by sending me an enormous bunch of flowers and a card with the sentiment "Fuck them all!"

Roseanne has guts. So does Don Rickles, another great comic genius. Unlike Hope, though, Rickles hasn't always helped my career. Some years ago, Revlon founder Charles Revson wanted to sponsor a television show in which I would star. He took me out to Perino's in Los Angeles to discuss the project and I was really excited about the whole thing. I wore a black Christian Dior gown, diamonds (of course), and a long chinchilla coat. After dinner (which went beautifully and boded well for my series), Charles said he wanted to drop into a club and catch a new comedian whom he wanted to see. The comedian's name was Don Rickles.

We walked into the club, with me on Revson's arm.

Rickles turned the spotlight on us and said, "What the hell is this beautiful Zsa Zsa Gabor doing with that old, ugly, short man?" Revson got up, walked out, never talked to me again, and, of course, I lost the television series. Whenever I see Don Rickles, I always berate him for having ruined my career! Who knows what might have happened to me had Charles Revson and I not gone to that club and seen Don Rickles! That club, by the way, was on La Cienega—the very same street where I was one day to encounter a policeman named Paul Kramer! I don't plan ever to be on La Cienega again. . . .

PAUL KRAMER, as it happens, is not the first policeman with whom I have tangled in my life. In the late sixties, I was on my way to London from Palma, Majorca, and, just before I left for the airport, I found a little mutt in the back streets, who was cold, hungry, and in obvious need of love and tenderness. He was whimpering with unhappiness in a garbage can, and I saw that he had a hole in his head. I knew I had to take him with me.

I had already boarded the plane when the stewardess noticed the little dog. We were bound for London, where quarantine is strict, and she told me that I had to leave the dog behind. Of course, in retrospect, she was a hundred percent right. But at that moment all I could see was the tiny mutt, the little wounded dog who needed me. I refused. They called the police. But—never one to be intimidated by a uniform—I refused. In the end I was escorted off the plane.

Still clutching the mutt, I was taken to the police station and questioned. In the course of the questioning, I was asked if I knew anyone in Palma. Of course I did. George Sanders, my ex-husband, then alive and well and living in Palma. The police—who by then were anxious to get rid of me—wrote down George's name and number, then called him. Whereupon George—my Georgie—said, "Zsa Zsa who? I've never heard of her," and I ended up spending the entire night in jail, with only an American sailor in the next cell as company. My little mutt was taken away from me and I was still distraught, but other than that, my night in jail was not traumatic. Not that time.

I'VE always loved comedians and I've always been able to laugh at myself, which has been my saving grace. One of the greatest comic talents of all times was Noël Coward, my friend. Jimmy Burroughs—who went on to direct *Cheers* and *Taxi*—directed me in one of Noël's most famous comedies, *Blithe Spirit.*

I'd known Noël since the mid-fifties when he came to America to headline in Las Vegas. Before opening night, I threw a party for him in Bel Air. Then, in Vegas, I attended a party for Noël. The swimming pool was filled with roses and four violinists strolled among the three hundred guests, including Greer Garson, Jean Simmons, David Niven, and Jack Benny. All those stars were eclipsed, though, on opening night, when Frank Sinatra, Judy Garland, Bogie, Bacall, Joan Fontaine, Alec Guinness, Van Johnson, Cole Porter, Tallulah Bankhead, Ethel Merman, Jeanette MacDonald, Samuel Goldwyn, Joseph Cotten, George Burns, and Gracie Allen were all in the audience. After the show, I went backstage to congratulate Noël and parted great friends.

I was thrilled to be appearing in one of Noël's greatest successes. The plot centers around a novelist, Charles Condomine, whose wife Elvira (whom I play) is long since dead but who has now returned as a ghost who haunts Charles and his new wife. Charles can see me, but his wife can't—which is the fulcrum of the plot. At one point, Charles's wife pouts, "You only gave me a tiny diamond but look what you gave Elvira—a big diamond." I wanted to insert the line "And I took it with me."

I wrote to Noël asking his permission to make that—and one or two other changes—and he cabled back graciously with the words, " 'Darling, do anything you wish, for I know you could do no wrong. Love, Noël.' " I made the diamond change and it brought down the house. *Blithe Spirit* was such a big success for me that I ended up playing it all over America, to standing room only, in cities like Chicago, where I appeared in the show on three separate occasions.

I also loved playing the part of Ann Stanley in *Forty Carats*—which turned out to be one of the most exciting professional experiences of my life. But I nearly didn't accept the part in the first place because of an amusing comedy of errors. I was in Las Vegas doing my act at the Flamingo when a Mr. Merrick called me and asked if I'd like to take over the lead in *Forty Carats* from actress Julie Harris, who had created the part. My assistant, Carl Parsons, and I knew a Mike Merrick—a publicist—and I made the mistake of thinking the Mr. Merrick was Mike and not David. I readily accepted the part and, then, the moment I put down the phone, immediately regretted it, terrified of replacing the great Julie Harris.

When the contract arrived, I told Merrick that I had thought he was a publicist when he called, and hadn't realized that I was talking to the producer himself and if I had, would have taken more time before accepting. Merrick listened, unmoved. After our telephone call, he took me to arbitration, thus forcing me to appear in the show. To do him credit, though, when critics questioned his wisdom in casting Zsa Zsa Gabor to follow Julie Harris, he replied, "If I can follow Ethel Merman with Pearl Bailey as I did in *Hello, Dolly!* then I can do anything."

On opening night, Jimmy Burroughs and Michael Nouri were in the dressing room with me when I had an acute attack of first-night nerves, agonizing, "I can't go on. How can I ever replace Julie Harris? How can I do it?"

"You have to go on," said Jimmy, shaking me and adding, "Here, take this" and pushing a Librium into my hands. Remembering how Kathryn Grayson's vodka had eradicated my nerves on my first day of filming *Lovely to Look At,* I took the Librium, went onstage, and ended up getting a standing ovation. There were rave reviews the next day and the show was sold out each and every night.

*

*

*

I had a lot of fun in the play—although my fourteen costume changes were not always easy, keeping me and Jimmy extremely occupied. One of my costume changes was so fast that it necessitated my remaining on stage while the curtain was down between scenes. One night, Jimmy raised the curtain too early, revealing me standing center stage, dressed in nothing but sheer black stockings. In my entire career, I'd never had so much applause as at that moment! My Hungarian dresser, Marika, saved the day by running out and wrapping a towel around me, thus hiding my nudity. I carried on with the scene as if nothing untoward had taken place. But to no avail. Every few minutes, the audience burst into giggles, until eventually the whole house was in uproar.

I was paid $2,500 a week to star in the show on Broadway and eventually took it on the road, where Francesca made her acting debut, playing my daughter. We had a wonderful time together, shopping for her clothes in Giorgio Sant' Angelo and ended up spending more on Francesca's outfits than on my own. I didn't mind, but Francesca pointed out, "Mother, the most important thing is not so much how I look as how I act." Exasperated, I replied, "My dear, it is always important how a woman looks!"

*

*

*

MY Broadway success made me very happy. But, as usual, things didn't go perfectly. One night after the show, I went out for dinner with John Lindsay, who was then the Mayor of New York. We went to the restaurant Merv Griffin then owned. When I got back to the Waldorf Towers (where I was staying for the run of the show), the lobby was full of Secret Servicemen, employed to guard President Nixon, who was then in residence. Feeling safe and secure, I followed two elegant gentlemen (both dressed in black tie and white silk scarves) into the elevator. The elevator man pressed the button for my floor and, slowly, the elevator began to rise, bound for the thirty-sixth floor and my suite.

My eyes were fixed on the numbers marking the rise of the elevator and I didn't notice one of the elegant gentlemen pressing the stop button, until the elevator ground to a halt and I came face-to-face with two guns. In a voice brimful of menace, one of the "gentlemen" growled, "If you value your life, you'll give me your diamond ring." Knowing that I wanted to live and not die, I knew that I had no choice so I handed over the $3 million diamond ring, my gift from Herbert. And my diamond earrings ($60,000 from Harry Winston). As an afterthought, eager to save my life, I tremblingly pointed out, "You didn't ask for this, but take it too"—handing over my blue turquoise and diamond ring in the hope that this would mollify the thieves.

Then they ordered the terrified elevator man to take the elevator down to the lobby. As the elevator door opened and I saw the battalion of watchful Secret Servicemen milling about in the lobby, I wanted to scream, but didn't, aware that the guns the "gentlemen" were brandishing very definitely were not toys but were one hundred percent real and totally functional.

Afraid to follow the gunmen, the elevator man took me back up to the thirty-sixth floor and my suite, where I called the police. Within ten minutes, they came to my rescue—after liberally helping themselves to Scotch from my liquor cabinet. Then they took me to the 51st Street Precinct. Although I was still in shock, I tried not to show it, smiling pleasantly at a group of nice-looking ladies sitting with me in the waiting room. Eventually, we struck up a conversation, embarking on the kind of small talk more prevalent at the royal garden party in Buckingham Palace than at a police precinct.

A policeman interrupted our chat, began to take my statement, then, with a perplexed look, asked me, "How do you know those hookers?" Very taken aback, I explained that the ladies, dressed in their impeccable Ralph Lauren outfits, hadn't looked like hookers to me. But even if they were, I had nothing against hookers, believing as I do that prostitution is a very respectable profession and that hookers are often far more honest than the average wife. Bemused, the policeman continued taking my statement.

When I woke up the next day, I had a terrible headache and called the drugstore to ask the pharmacist to send up some aspirin. Sympathetically, he inquired as to why I had a headache. I related the story of the previous day's robbery, expecting profuse condolences. Instead, the pharmacist brokenly informed me, "My poor little mother recently was walking along Sixth Avenue and was brutally beaten by muggers who wanted to steal her handbag. She only had two dollars and fifty cents in that bag—but my mother died for it." Chastened, I offered my condolences and silently counted my blessings.

Despite the aspirins, my headache continued to plague me, so I canceled the matinee. Later, David Merrick was to dock my pay for that matinee. Not only that, but when I told him about the robbery, he merely pointed to a stack of newspapers—all bearing headlines about the robbery and noting the coincidence that I was appearing in a play named *Forty Carats* and that my ring, which had been stolen, also was around forty carats—and enthused, "Such great publicity for the play!" oblivious of both me and my reaction, adding, "Isn't it wonderful?" "Wonderful!" I said angrily, "I just lost over three million dollars!"

Although he owned the Waldorf Towers himself, Conrad (who was then still alive) advised me to sue the hotel on the basis that more security guards should have been on duty. The police never solved the crime, the jewelry was never found, and as the hotel was insured, I took Conrad's advice. During the trial, the attorneys for the insurance company asked who had given me the various rings and I answered that although Herbert gave me the $3 million ring, Rubi had given me the other one. The defense attorney then proceeded to mention Rubi repeatedly, giving the impression of—I am still not quite sure what—and, to my surprise, the court ruled against me.

I was also involved in another controversy, one that greatly saddened me, when the show was playing in Philadelphia. One night, during the performance, I heard some noises coming from the front row. In the interval, I found out that the noises had come from a group of spastic children in wheelchairs and that the theater owner had moved them to the back of the auditorium. I had nothing to do with it.

But the next day, when the theater opened, a group of retarded children picketed it in protest. Then the theater owner called me up and begged me, "Please tell the press you requested that the children sit at the back of the auditorium, otherwise the pickets will close the theater." I refused, telling him that I would not lie. His response was to fire me, breaking our contract. Eventually, Equity examined my case, ruled on my behalf, and I was awarded $60,000.

ANOTHER, less harrowing controversy related to the show erupted in Dallas not long ago when I was there touring and after the performance, couldn't find a restaurant and ended up at Taco Bell. I ordered coffee and was served it in a white styrofoam cup. I hate styrofoam cups so I said I wouldn't drink out of it. For some crazy reason, all the newspapers picked up the story and the upshot was that Taco Bell presented me with my very own china cup marked *Zsa Zsa Gabor: Taco Bell.*

Away from the stage, I was still being pursued by a number of would-be husbands and lovers. There was the A&P heir, multimillionaire Huntington Hartford—whom I found interesting but ultimately too eccentric for any deep involvement. Before that, even before my marriage to Herbert, there was the Duke of Marlborough—Bertie, as he was known. He was six foot four, but lived in such an aristocratic ivory tower that he didn't even know how to put toothpaste onto a toothbrush. But he wasn't stupid. Far from it.

Years later, his daughter, Sarah, told me that Bertie had dropped a penny in White's—the prestigious club to which he belonged. According to Sarah, Bertie got down on all fours and, in full view of the club's members, tried to find his penny. Finally, one of them couldn't help asking him why he was bothering, impatiently telling him, "Bertie, it is *only* a penny!" Bertie continued his search, pausing only to answer gruffly, "Yes, but many pennies make a pound."

Bertie invited me to dinner at one of London's chicest clubs—Annabel's. As we drove there, he informed me that, as it was the season, he was planning to order grouse for dinner. When we were seated, he motioned the waiter to come over and ordered the grouse. Once the waiter had left for the kitchen, as an afterthought, Bertie turned to me and said, "My dear, have you ever had grouse?" Exuding sophistication from every pore, I answered, "Of course, quite often."

Actually, the truth was that I didn't even know what a grouse was. In fact, to me it sounded like a man in a bad mood. But I didn't want to reveal my ignorance. The grouse appeared and I bit into it and quickly discovered how much I hated it. In the meantime, Bertie was chatting to some friends. Then he started eating the grouse. Suddenly, he put his fork down, called over the waiter, and said, "Waiter, this grouse is ripe." I made it into the powder room just in time, vowing that never again, as long as I lived, would I ever even look at a menu featuring grouse.

Bertie had always shared my passion for horses—which made us soulmates. In London, I owned a black Arabian stallion—a very rare horse because Arabian stallions are normally white. At first, I had called him Kemal Atatürk, until a representative from the Turkish embassy turned up at my Wilton Crescent house and pronounced, "Miss Gabor, you cannot call any horse, even the best horse in the world, after Atatürk, because he is sacred to us." So, out of respect, I changed the horse's name to Harem. One day, Bertie called me, greeting me with the words, "My dear, I hear that you have a black Arabian stallion. I would so much like to see the animal." I understood Bertie's request and agreed to have Harem transported to Bertie's home—Blenheim Palace.

A few days later, he called again, inviting me to bring Francesca to Blenheim with me. Sensing the subtext—that neither Bertie nor his stable hands could manage Harem—I accepted. I wanted to help him—but I was also delighted to be going to Blenheim, one of my favorite places in the world—a soaring, rhapsodic structure set in the English countryside (complete with solid gold fountain)—a symbol of England and all for which it stood. Not that America and Americans were unconnected with Blenheim; Consuelo Vanderbilt, Bertie's mother, an American, naturally, had lived there and had poured millions of dollars into the palace.

When Francesca and I arrived, we had lunch with Bertie and, over our potted shrimp, he confessed, "Nobody here has even dared to mount your fantastic horse. He is too vigorous and my stable boys are too old. They simply cannot master him." I laughed and promised that I would attempt to rectify things. After lunch, Bertie escorted us to the stables, which were painted purple and decorated with big brass buckles—courtesy of the Vanderbilt millions. I thought to myself that many of the finest homes in America were not as elegant as the Blenheim stables.

When I saw Harem, he seemed to recognize me. I went

back to the house and changed, eager to ride him again. Then I came back and mounted the horse. As expected, he was nervous and jittery. After all, I told myself, the poor animal had not been exercised for five days. We went out on the Blenheim trails and I led the way, followed by Bertie and Francesca and other guests.

For a while, the ride was calm and pleasant, but it changed drastically when the trail took us to a green area in front of the palace. To behold that immense, impressive building looming up out of the middle of a vast expanse of green lawn is, indeed, a startling sight. And apparently, Harem was seeing it for the first time. He began to buck and kick. I am a good rider, but not a rodeo cowgirl. Thinking quickly, I decided that my best alternative would be to jump off. I dropped the reins and threw myself off the bucking horse, hoping to scramble to my feet immediately and out of Harem's path. But as I was falling, I lunged out at a nearby tree, hoping to break my fall, and landed on my hand. I got up, aware that my hand was hurting me.

Meanwhile, Harem was galloping off across the meadow, his head held high, his nostrils flaring, his mane fluttering, his tail streaming behind him like a silken flag. Bertie was furious. "Stop," he yelled, "My croquet lawn! The horse is destroying my croquet lawn!"

I was livid and screamed back, "For all you know, I may have broken my neck, but all you care about is your silly croquet lawn."

Back at the palace, Bertie recovered and, remembering his manners (especially now that Harem was safe and sound back in the stables), showed me to the bathroom. And what a bathroom it was! A veritable palace within a palace, the walls covered in pictures of Winston Churchill as a baby (including one of him sitting on a potty) and a photo of the

Queen of England as a baby, posed naked on a bear rug. Before leaving me to change, Bertie, in his low-key British way, said slowly, "This is the duchess's bathroom. And if you want to, you can live in this house forever." The Duke of Marlborough was offering me the chance to become his duchess—the Duchess of Marlborough. I knew I didn't love him so I refused, but the Duke of Marlborough's proposal still remains the most unusual one I have ever had in my entire life.

I left Blenheim, still Zsa Zsa Gabor, but with the added inconvenience of a hand that now was excruciatingly painful. I ended up in St. George's Hospital in London, where X rays indicated that—during my fall from Harem—one of my knuckles had been dislocated. After getting a morphine shot to kill the pain, I went home to suffer in silence. Only I didn't do that but, instead, followed one of my cardinal rules: when in trouble, take a bath and wash your hair. I did. And as I was rinsing the soap out, heard a click. My knuckle had clicked back into place; my doctor was stupefied but my hair-washing cure had worked.

ANOTHER Englishman who wanted to marry me was Winston Churchill's son. But after spending some time with him, I discovered that he drank too much and it was clear that he was not for me. I did feel sorry for him, though, especially after he longingly said, "Wait until my father dies! Then I will show them who I am!" Our relationship ended one morning when he came to call on me when I was in my bath and, acting on her own initiative, my perky English maid sent him away. When I demanded an explanation, she replied pertly, "I wouldn't want him. And if I wouldn't want him, why would you?"

I turned my romantic sights back to America again, but still didn't find the man of my dreams. Often, I encountered a great deal of disillusionment. I had always admired Henry

Fonda. One day, I went to visit Tyrone Power's ex-wife, Linda Christian, who had invited Pamela Mason and me to have dinner with her at her house in the Hollywood Hills. We were just in the middle of eating our takeaway Chinese meal, when the door opened and Henry Fonda appeared, dressed in tennis clothes.

At that point, Linda, Pamela, and I had been joined by two other women, whose names I can't remember. And Henry looked at us all, then asked, "Who is going to sleep with me first?" For a moment, I was reminded of Elizabeth Taylor and of the story George Sanders had told me about her in London. But this was different. This time I was present. And this time, the person who had expressed the sentiment was none other than Henry Fonda—my idol, an American icon.

Before I could examine my feelings, Henry was upstairs, along with one of the other two girls. Leaving me to turn to Linda and indignantly say, "Linda, how could you do this to me?" Meaning that I suspected Linda of setting the whole thing up. "Don't be so snobbish and old-fashioned," snapped Linda in return. "Don't you want to sleep with Henry?" I didn't reply. I was in shock. Pamela and I left immediately.

Although I was highly disillusioned by Henry, I still empathized with him sometime during the Vietnam War years, when we met at a party and I asked him about Jane—then involved with the Viet Cong. As he fought back the tears, Henry's sole response was "When I'm alone, I cry a lot."

*

*

*

I had seen other macho men cry—not just Henry Fonda. At John Huston's 1972 wedding to heiress Cici Shane, the director had tears in his eyes all through the ceremony. I had remained friends with John through the years and in the future was to appear at a tribute to him at the Beverly Hills Hilton, along with Michael Caine, and say, "John, you made me rich and famous. I thank you for my career, though you were nasty and mean to me. My only regret in life is that I didn't sleep with you. I would have if I hadn't been married." At this, John's marriage to Cici, I still had doubts about the match succeeding, perhaps rather tactlessly telling Cici's mother that "Your daughter is in such trouble with John. He is a wonderful but difficult man." I don't think Mrs. Shane appreciated my comments, but when the marriage shattered, I was proved to be right. Poor Cici came to me crying, "I could kill myself! John took my Mexican maid and left home with her." I needed no reminder that both men and marriage are difficult propositions.

*

STILL, men and marriage continued to seek me out. At one point, hearing that I was single again, the Texas billionaire H. L. Hunt sent a private plane for me. Startled, I was even more stunned when the pilot informed me that Mr. Hunt had asked him to deliver a message to me. I waited expectantly. And I was not disappointed. The message was simple: "I want to marry you." I was mystified. I had never, to my knowledge, ever met Mr. Hunt. I sent back a polite refusal. And I never regretted it. Everything I knew about him led me to believe that Hunt was an extremely boring man. And I've always believed that nothing can compensate for being bored. Not even one hundred million dollars.

ANOTHER wonderful man who wanted to marry me for years was J. Paul Getty, at that time one of the richest men in the world. I'd always known that Getty was interested in meeting me. During my days in England shooting *Moulin Rouge,* Jimmy Woolf told me that Jean Paul Getty was dying to meet me (so, apparently, was millionaire Charles Clore), but I was far too much in love with George at the time to care about meeting Getty. But now, years later, Getty invited me to take part in the benefit for Bangladesh at the Grosvenor House in London, and I flew to England for the benefit. The benefit went well; I wore a white gown with diamonds and rubies. Getty came onstage with me. Also in the audience was Margaret, Duchess of Argyll, a great beauty who was one of Getty's closest companions. I don't think the Duchess was highly delighted by my advent in Getty's life, nor by the amount of time we began to spend together.

My relationship with Getty had begun when one of his drivers met me and my wonderful assistant, Carl Parsons, at Heathrow and drove us straight to Paul's Sutton Place home, a seventy-two-room palace just twenty-three miles from London, in Guildford, Surrey.

The first thing I noticed about Getty was his magnetic blue eyes. Though bent with age, he was still dapper and well groomed. Years of work in the oil fields (later he would proudly tell me, "I'm still a wildcatter at heart") had given him a sinewy, lean body of surprising strength and agility.

Henry the Eighth had owned Sutton Place and I wasn't thrilled when Paul told me that I had been allocated Anne Boleyn's room. Remembering that Anne had been executed for infidelity, I tossed and turned all night, while dreaming that I was being dragged into a courtyard and prepared for execution.

Over breakfast (the classic English meal) I told Getty about my nightmare and he responded thoughtfully, "The ghost of Francis may have visited you." He went on to explain that in 1521, King Henry had given Sutton Place to his courtier Sir Richard Weston, but had then discovered Weston's son, Francis, was having an affair with Anne Boleyn. Whereupon he ordered Francis's execution. I shuddered involuntarily at the thought of both Francis and Anne—so young and lovely—meeting with such a barbaric death.

Paul invited me to accompany him on his morning walk. Followed by Paul's twelve German shepherds, we strolled through the formal gardens of Sutton Place, chatting about animals and about antiques—both of which Paul loved. Then we visited the grave of his favorite German shepherd, Shaun. We sat on a bench, surrounded by flowers, and Paul told me that his only childhood friend had been his dog Jip. Reminded of Budapest and Lady and sensing a kindred spirit, I showed Getty pictures of my own dogs, my Shih-Tzus. Paul admired them so much that next time I was in London, I went to Harrods, bought him a Shih-Tzu of his own, and had it delivered by Rolls-Royce to Paul at Sutton Place.

Paul named the dog "Mandy of Sutton Place." Mandy was the luckiest dog in the world, pampered by the wealthiest man on the planet. Once, when Paul and I were having cocktails with his son George in Sutton Place's yellow and gold living room, Mandy proceeded to pee on his Aubusson rug. Horrified and feeling slightly responsible, as I had originally introduced Mandy to Sutton Place, I shouted, "Don't do that!" Whereupon Paul held up his hand like a king about to make a proclamation and declared, "Mandy of Sutton Place can do no wrong."

I grew to love my strolls with Paul among the yew trees of Sutton Place. They were shaped like giant tulips and Paul lovingly pointed to them and said, "That tree has lived much longer than I ever will. It is already over two thousand years old." Animals abounded at Sutton Place: two white snow leopards that were kept in a cage (each with a full-time trainer), a lion named Nero, and a whole stableful of horses. One day, as we approached the animals, we saw a famous duchess striking poses in front of the cages.

When she saw us coming, she took off her scarf and danced around. "Look at that woman," said Paul, derisively, "she must be nuts." It seemed that the Duchess was one of many women set on marrying the great Paul Getty. At one luncheon he gave, the guests included a French princess and a German countess, both of whom longed to become Mrs. J. Paul Getty.

I, however, had no such aims. Nevertheless, it was rumored all over London (even on the BBC) that Paul and I were engaged to be married. We were, indeed, extremely close and both of us considered marriage. I was never aware of Paul's age when I was with him. It has always seemed to me that age is irrelevant; it is interests that count. Paul was vitally interested in every human being, every animal, and everything that he ever encountered. He was vital and alive and I liked him. So much so that I couldn't bear the idea of the heartbreak I would suffer if he predeceased me.

While the future lay in the balance, I learned more and more about Getty. I learned that his favorite pastimes were going to Annabel's, studying art at the British Museum, watching Greta Garbo in *Queen Christina*—over and over. We had a great deal in common and had gone nightclubbing in the same places without ever having met until now. But like me, Paul wasn't really a nightclub person but preferred to spend hours absorbed in a book.

His favorite author was a man named G. A. Henty. Observing him reading many of Henty's book's, I finally asked him why he liked this particular writer. He explained, "I've been reading these adventure stories since I was a boy. They tell you everything you need to know to make money: Work, save, and learn." Down the line, he added some of his own philosophy: "Be a nonconformist. Avoid the accumulative mentality. Never let money idle."

After Paul's death, unkind writers labeled him as a miser, focusing primarily on the pay telephone that he was said to have had installed in Sutton Place. But I never ever saw it. I did receive calls at Paul's house, though. Once, the maid came in and whispered to me that a gentleman named Conrad Hilton was calling. With a scowl, Paul demanded, "Why is that Texas hotel man calling you?" I didn't answer and, instead, picked up the phone. Only to hear Conrad blast, "What the hell are you doing in London with that Texas oil man?" I suppressed a giggle and changed the subject.

One morning, I was in my suite (as it happens, coming to grips with one of the works of Mr. Henty), when the intercom crackled and I heard Paul's voice asking me, "Please come downstairs. I want to tell you something very important." For a moment, my heart stood still. I was terrified that Paul was about to propose to me formally, to ask for my hand in marriage and that I'd have to make a decision—a decision that had already been half made. I would refuse Getty's offer of marriage because I was too attached to him, too petrified that I'd love, then lose him.

With trepidation, I approached Paul, who was sitting in the drawing room, his head resting between his hands. But I soon discovered that my fears were all for nothing. Paul had sent for me because he wanted to give me the tragic news that his son George had committed suicide. As I looked at him, he seemed to age before my very eyes. Suddenly, Jean Paul Getty, the richest man in the world, had given up on life.

GETTY died in June 1976 and the Duke of Bedford eulogized him as "the kindest and most generous of friends." I agreed. I had never asked anything from Getty and I had never wanted anything from him either. A short while after his death, I was working at a Boston theater when an old man in a homburg appeared at the stage door and, with the hurried words, "Jean Paul Getty wanted you to have this," handed me a jewel case, and disappeared as mysteriously as he had come. I opened the jewel case to find a breathtakingly beautiful pair of diamond earrings—a souvenir of J. Paul Getty, the man I had admired, but would never marry. As my wonderful friend Carl Parsons put it, "Zsa Zsa, you are the only woman in existence who—for twenty years—turned down Paul Getty—the richest man in the world."

INSTEAD of opting for Getty, and gathering a multitude of diamonds while I could, I fell for—and married—a man who definitely was not poor but whose financial status was a million miles removed from that of J. Paul Getty. Jack Ryan was a genius. A Yale graduate and an electronics engineer, Jack helped develop the government Hawk and Sparrow 111 missile systems and invented the prototype of the transistor radio. For eighteen years, he was with Mattel Inc., where he invented the Barbie doll and also Chatty Cathy.

He was my neighbor in Bel Air and lived in an eighteen-bedroom estate where he threw lavish parties packed with unusual elements: fortune-tellers, jugglers, handwriting analysts, calypso musicians, go-go dancers, minstrels, and harpsichordists. His parties were also excruciatingly noisy. So noisy that on many a night I was forced to call the Bel Air Patrol and complain about the racket. One day, Jack would joke, "I had to marry Zsa Zsa to shut her up."

I wasn't looking for romance at the time. I had been making a Bob Hope special in Las Vegas (for which I wore the most beautiful beige-colored chiffon dress, covered in rhinestone, very clingy, and trimmed with marabou) and flew back to L.A. one afternoon at five. As I walked into my house, the telephone rang. One of my girlfriends was calling to invite me to a party. As I had nothing much to do (and my Vegas makeup and hairdo were still intact) I agreed to go.

We arrived at the party and I instantly realized that I'd never in my entire life been to a party like it. It was thrown by financier Bernie Cornfeld at his fortresslike house (which had once been owned by actor George Hamilton), and the guests included a liberal cross section of call girls and call boys. I left early. But not before I took the opportunity of getting to know my noisy neighbor. Jack was intelligent and fascinating and on this, the first time we had ever really talked, I was thoroughly beguiled by him.

The next day, he called and invited me to lunch at his house, a vast mansion complete with fifty-three telephones (each with an individual ring that resembled the call of a particular bird) and eighteen bedrooms. Jack was really big style and the next day he sent over a team of workmen to my house with instructions that they build a top story for the house. Perplexed, I telephoned Jack and asked what he was doing. With absolute certainty, Jack replied, "Your house needs another floor." The cost of that floor would be $1 million and the "floor" would end up housing what I now call "The Moulin Rouge"—as it is a replica of the Moulin Rouge itself.

I wasn't one hundred percent convinced that Jack Ryan was the right man for me. He was wild and Irish and unconventional—a genius with a shadow side that sometimes dominated his moods and upset his equilibrium. Part of me knew that life with Paul Getty would have been far more tranquil. In the end, I even introduced Jack to Getty. When I did, I felt sorry for Paul, basically a shy man, because when I introduced Jack to him, he blushed and stammered, "You got the girl I wanted to marry." At that moment, Getty was right. Jack had "got" me. But not for long.

One evening, during a party at his house, Jack proposed to me in true Ryan theatrical style, falling to his knees in front of me in full view of a hundred guests (including my beloved friend Prince Johannes Thurn und Taxis, who has just recently died) and asked me to marry him. His proposal was irresistible and, in a way, so was he. On hearing of our engagement, the press quipped that Jack had married his very own Barbie doll (in fact Jack did have plans to make a Barbie doll who was a Zsa Zsa look-alike—a not too startling thought, as years before Saks and Bonwit Teller had featured mannequins who looked just like me). Jack and I married on October 6, 1976, in a ceremony (catered courtesy of Conrad) in the Las Vegas Hilton. Jack had bought my $12,000 engagement ring from Van Cleef & Arpels and I wore a white accordion-pleated chiffon gown designed by Bob Mackie. I was now Mrs. Jack Ryan and I felt wonderful.

WE went to Tokyo on our honeymoon, as Jack had business with a Japanese toy manufacturer. On the second day Jack had to go to a business meeting. He informed me that I would be shown the delights of the city by *my* own guide—a handsome, young, and very charming Japanese man. Stunned, I had no time to protest. The next thing I knew, Jack had left me alone with my guide, who, even now, had whisked me away to some unknown destination in his limousine. I felt nauseated. Unaware, the guide took me to lunch at an elegant Tokyo restaurant, feasting on caviar, wild duck followed by champagne and pastries. I didn't say a word or eat a thing. Oblivious, my guide washed down his lunch with brandy, then turned to me and, without further ado, announced, "Now we go to bed."

I looked at him in horror as the truth began to dawn on me. Reading my expression, the guide went on to elaborate, "Miss Gabor, your husband has paid me to go to bed with you. I don't understood." I understood very well. George had wanted me to have a liaison with Guido, but George had loved me, had proved his love to me, and his suggestion was just a momentary aberration. But Jack Ryan, on the other hand, Jack my knight in shining armor, the inhabitant of a fairy-tale castle, Jack, my new husband (it now appeared) was a full-blown seventies-style swinger into wife-swapping and sundry sexual pursuits as a way of life. I demanded that my "guide" take me back to the hotel, where I lay in bed, watching the ceiling fan rotate in the steamy afternoon air and contemplating my future and our marriage.

I knew Jack had had many girlfriends. But that never disturbed me. Many girlfriends are never a threat. They are just the product of a man's insecurity. Men who run around with a lot of girls are insecure because they know they can't satisfy one woman. It takes a real man to satisfy a woman on a regular basis. Or to live a happy and fulfilled life with one woman. When we got back to Bel Air, I discovered that, far from building a life with me, with one woman, Jack had every intention of continuing his swinging life-style—a life-style that I had never dreamed existed.

I had expected Jack to sell his house and move in with me. But he had other plans. For a start, he wouldn't have dreamed of leaving his tree house. Jack's tree house was, indeed, a masterpiece. He had built it himself in big style—it seated twelve for dinner and was lit by a crystal chandelier. I decided that I ought to enter into the tree house spirit and suggested we throw a homecoming party for ourselves in the tree house. Jack was delighted by the idea, ever gregarious and friendly.

But when it came to planning the dinner, it transpired that Jack had already delegated all the arrangements to his secretary, a lady named Linda—whom he'd hired when she was only sixteen. True, the party did turn out to be magnificent, with the tree house garlanded in lace and crystal and gold. But I had nothing to do with any of it. My party, which I had suggested, became the sole property of Linda.

It seemed that Jack's life was so well arranged that he had no room whatsoever for me in it at all. We did have fun together, though, because Jack really was a very bright and witty man. Eva and I starred in *Arsenic and Old Lace* in Chicago and, one night, when we played the scene in which we hide a dead body in a window seat, I opened the seat—to find Jack hidden in it. I nearly died myself, laughing.

But despite Jack's wicked sense of humor, the problems still remained. He never gave up his house, nor his ex-wife and two mistresses who all lived there with him. He did live with me some of the time, but whenever we had the slightest problems, Jack was prone to announce, "Okay, I'll go down the road to my mistresses." I just couldn't cope. Not with Jack, not with Linda, not with the tree house, and definitely not with the mistresses. To top that, Jack's weird menagerie also included twelve UCLA students whom he had dubbed "Ryan's Boys." There was also the matter of Jack's dungeon, a torture chamber painted a sinister black and decorated with black fox fur. All in all, Jack's sex life would have made the average *Penthouse* reader blanch with shock. And as for me—I wanted no part whatsoever in any of it.

JACK RYAN and I divorced after just seven months of marriage. But we have remained friends throughout the years. He is now married to a charming Polish lawyer and he and his wife often come for dinner with us. Sometimes he goes up to the Moulin Rouge (which was never completely finished, as we got divorced) and says, "Didn't I do a wonderful job?" Which, of course, he did. Jack Ryan is a wonderful man. He just wasn't husband material.

But despite the unconventional, stormy quality of our

marriage, being Mrs. Jack Ryan had somehow given me a new taste for matrimony. I like being married—as long as it is to the right man. I can't live alone. I love to learn from my husbands. Then again, I do my best not to be too dependent on them—because no woman should depend totally on a man.

My beliefs were reinforced when I married my seventh husband, Michael O'Hara. We met after my trusted attorney, Bentley Ryan, died and my divorce from Jack Ryan was handed over to Michael—a top lawyer—to handle. At first, we met over the telephone, as I was appearing in *Blithe Spirit* in Boston and we couldn't discuss the divorce details in person. Then, when everything was finalized, I flew to Las Vegas to sign the divorce papers and Michael, as my attorney, was present during the signing.

The moment I set eyes on Michael, I was enthralled by him; he is six foot four with green eyes and tanned skin. Beautiful, sexy, and the epitome of masculinity. I suggested we go out to have dinner. Then we got married. Right there in Las Vegas. In the same chapel where I had married Jack, only seven months before. As I walked in, again the blushing bride, brimful of hope and promise, the chapel owner blinked as if to say, "I saw you here not long ago." I was beginning to feel like Bluebeard.

I almost feel like characterizing my marriage to Michael O'Hara by just writing his name and leaving a blank page. But that wouldn't be fair. I did have some happy times with Michael. And I adored his tiny daughter Melina, who was about five when we first met. But basically, I should have listened to the words of my friend Merle Oberon, who cautioned, "Be careful. I wouldn't marry a lawyer because it can only cost you."

My marriage to Michael O'Hara did, indeed, cost me. Emotionally, that is. We were married for five years and, at first, things were wonderful. But then I discovered that, despite his extremely Irish-sounding name, Michael was not a fun-loving Irishman in the Jack Ryan mold. In fact, he was Yugoslav—related to the Karageorgevics—the Yugoslav royal family. Yugoslavia, of course, is close to Greece and to Turkey, the lands of Atatürk. Naturally, Michael O'Hara was not Atatürk, but he still managed to radiate a godlike enough quality to capture my imagination.

I was wildly attracted to Michael, but problems destroyed our marriage—most of them personal to Michael. A major factor, though, was his moodiness. I don't really mind moody men at all. A moody man is a challenge. In fact, I find it boring if a man is always the same. Then again, moody men are difficult to handle. When a man is in a bad mood, I try not to say anything but just cook him his favorite food-and place it in front of him. If that doesn't work—I just suffer.

I did suffer during my marriage to Michael. I suffered because I loved him, because he loved me, and because, ultimately, everything changed. I am still not sure what really happened. Only that Michael and I don't—to this day—ever exchange a word. And that he is the only ex-husband who is not still my friend.

YET again, I was single and still not sure if I'd ever find the man of my dreams. Along the way, though, I did meet plenty of men who are the men of other women's dreams. There was Elvis Presley. I was playing at the Flamingo in Las Vegas when I got a message that Elvis (who was also appearing there) wanted to meet me.

My assistant, Betsy (a beautiful, tall girl from Ohio who is wonderful and has been indispensable to me for many years), was with me and I scornfully said to her, "Elvis! That sleazy little singer! Who the hell wants to see him! Not me!" I had no idea that Betsy was a passionate Presley fan—but I soon found out when she begged me, "Please, Miss Gabor. Please accept. I must see Elvis."

So there I was, in Elvis's dressing room, backstage, waiting for him, feeling disinterested. I knew nothing about Elvis. Nor did I want to. Then the door of the dressing room was flung open—and there stood one of the most gorgeous, sexy men I have ever seen in my life. He wasn't a cowboy or a tough guy, but a cross between a gentleman and a big black sexy snake. We talked for a moment, then Elvis was called away.

Before he left, he drew me to one side, bent down from what seemed an enormous height, and whispered seductively, "When can I see you again?" I was madly attracted to Elvis, but at the time I was in love with someone else, so I was torn. To me, Elvis radiated sexuality. But, because I really was in love at the time, I said no. In this lifetime, at least, Elvis Presley and I were not meant to be.

*

I also met and made friends with the Beatles. We met when I was appearing at a charity event, "Night of a Thousand Stars," in London. My act ended with me introducing the Beatles. At the time, I had no idea who they were. But backstage, we made friends as I enjoyed their irreverent sense of humor. I invited them for cocktails at my hotel (the London Hilton, of course) and we had a lot of fun there together. I wasn't involved with any of them romantically, but I admired their verve and spirit. My favorite, for some reason, was George Harrison, the quiet one. Perhaps because we are so different.

*

I had another encounter—a less pleasing one—with a rock-related lady, Britt Ekland, who once lived with rock star Rod Stewart. I first knew of Britt through her then husband, Peter Sellers. Peter, a very sexy man, liked young girls and always was after Francesca, but never got anywhere with her.

Then, when I was married to Michael, we were both invited to a dinner party at a best-selling novelist's Hollywood Hills house, thrown by his wife. The dinner table was elegant, the guests chic, but when we sat down to eat, I was confused by the fact that next to every place setting was a fragile porcelain bowl filled with sugar, and couldn't quite work out what sugar had to do with the dinner party.

Bewildered, I hesitatingly asked Michael why we were having sugar for dinner. Taken aback, Michael whispered, "Darling, that isn't sugar. It is cocaine." I hid my surprise and continued with dinner. After dinner, we were all led up to the hostess's bedroom where—in the middle of the room—a stark-naked, incredibly beautiful Britt Ekland sat motionless in a Victorian bathtub filled with a substance that I now knew was *not* sugar.

I was in New York at a party with Carl Parsons, when a young man said enthusiastically, "All I want is to be photographed with Zsa Zsa Gabor." I obliged, then asked Carl who the young man was. "His name," said Carl, "is Mick Jagger." Mick turned out to be sweet and nice and flirted with me. I thought he was wonderful. But then, I've always had a tremendous weakness for all types of Englishmen.

O**NE** of my other favorite Englishmen is the current Duke of Wellington. We first met when I was in England for an event for the World Wildlife Fund—Prince Philip's charity. Before dinner, at the Duke's house, someone informed me that the Duke of Wellington had said he would only attend the dinner if he could sit next to Zsa Zsa Gabor. So naturally, he did. I was wearing an Oscar de la Renta gown of pale lavender and turquoise blue and the Duke flirted with me, eating asparagus off my plate. He had to make speeches that night and nearly deafened me by banging his gavel so hard on the table next to me.

We were served Beef Wellington and, pushing it away, I said, "I am not going to eat it." I explained to the Duke that I felt it was inappropriate to eat the flesh of an animal when we were all here to support an organization dedicated to preserving wildlife. The Duke smiled, then picked up a piece of asparagus from his own plate, and fed it to me with his fingers.

Watching us, Christina Ford, another guest, not knowing who he was, bitchily remarked to Carl, "Can you imagine how rude that Zsa Zsa Gabor is? In the Duke of Wellington's own house she refuses to eat Beef Wellington!"

"You don't have to worry about that," replied Carl curtly, "she's sitting next to him and he hasn't taken his eyes off her décolletage. The very last thing the Duke of Wellington cares about is what Zsa Zsa is eating."

Carl seems to have been right, for the following day, the Duke sent me an enormous bouquet of white lilies and pink roses (I much prefer pink roses to red ones), along with an elegant love note. I went to Asprey, bought him a silver gavel, and had it engraved with the words *Next time you hit a gavel, remember not to deafen a girl.*

A few years passed. Then, about two years ago, the Duke and Duchess of Wellington came to attend a polo match at the Palm Beach Polo Club where I have a house. I was asked to present one of the trophies—as was the Duke. I was delighted to see him again and introduced Frederick, my husband, to him. In an extremely friendly way, the Duke demanded, "How long are you going to stay here in Palm Beach?" And I replied, "We are leaving tomorrow." And the Duchess of Wellington tartly retorted, "Good!"

*

*

I'VE never been that riveted by royalty—only by intelligence and achievement. Throughout my life, I've never been intimidated or impressed by someone because they have a title. But, now and again, I sometimes look back and wonder what might have been. . . .

It all started in London. I was there to film the exteriors for *Moulin Rouge,* was married to George and really missed him. But I kept myself extremely busy—or rather John Huston did—with filming and coaching. My coach was the venerable Constance Collier—who also became my friend and invited me all over London. Soon, the British press began to follow us and my picture was plastered all over the papers, the accompanying stories saying that I was in London, working with Constance. Apart from being a great actress and a wonderful coach, Constance was also an extremely well-connected lady. In her living room, she had displayed a large photograph of Queen Mary holding the little Princess Elizabeth in her arms, inscribed with the words *Isn't my granddaughter beautiful?* And although Constance was never one to brag about her royal connections, that particular picture spoke volumes.

I continued going to Constance for lessons. Then one day, on a typically gloomy, damp London morning, I arrived to find her slightly agitated. Her voice shaking with excitement, Constance said, "Zsa Zsa, you won't believe it. Someone called from Buckingham Palace to say that Prince Philip would like to meet you and wanted to arrange a meeting." Momentarily dazzled by the glamorous aura of British royalty, I enthusiastically replied, "I'd love to meet Prince Philip and Queen Elizabeth." Constance didn't answer. I waited. Slowly, almost as if she were overwhelmed, Constance patiently explained, "You don't understand. Zsa Zsa, the Prince wants to meet you. Alone."

For a moment, I felt close to fainting. To me, Prince Philip and Queen Elizabeth had always been the most fairy tale of all couples. The two most beautiful people in the world. I still didn't know what to say or what to think. Constance stood, waiting. I didn't know what to say. So I stalled, laughed, and tried to change the subject by doing the ultra-British thing of commenting on the weather.

But I knew I had to come to a decision. After all, I was married to George and I loved George. And Prince Philip was married to a woman whom I admired and respected. I knew there was no future, no sense in starting something that was destined to end in disaster and in pain. At last, I gave Constance an answer: "Tell Buckingham Palace that Miss Gabor is very honored by the Prince's request but that, at present, she is involved in filming."

According to Constance Collier, Prince Philip's representative called three more times, asking to see me. And each time, she gave the same answer. No.

DURING that stay in London, I also met Lord Mountbatten of Burma, a handsome and distinguished man, a war hero who, until his death, was Prince Charles's favorite uncle. I met Mountbatten at a big London premiere. I was wearing a low-cut dress and Dickie, as he was called, had terrific eyes for me and couldn't stop staring at me.

The next day, a message came requesting a meeting. I had been bowled over by Dickie and so we did meet. He kissed me and wanted to make love to me. I might well have succumbed, but for the telephone, which rang, heralding a call from John Huston demanding my presence on the set. So Lord Mountbatten and I never did consummate our relationship.

AS the years went by, I was glad that—so far as the British royal family was concerned—I had done nothing for which I could ever reproach myself. Prince Philip and I did finally meet, face-to-face, when I went to London for the World Wildlife Fund. I traveled with a party of Americans, including socialite Mercedes Kellogg—who later divorced her husband, Ambassador Kellogg, and married Sid Bass, one of the wealthiest men in America. I spent some time with Mercedes and—although she claims to be a high-born Iranian—found her pushy and lacking in social manners.

I had already raised $23,000 of jewelry for the fund and was happy to have been of help. The climax of our stay was a cocktail party held in London. Mercedes, Ambassador Kellogg, and I were all staying at Leeds Castle, quite far from London, and our car was late picking us up. As a result, we arrived just as Prince Philip was leaving the party. I said, "Hello, Prince Philip," and he just ignored me. I was livid and said to the Duchess of Argyll, "How dare he be so rude when I gave so much money for his World Wildlife Fund!" Afterward, though, when I had cooled down, I couldn't help remembering London all those years ago and the calls received by Constance Collier.

P**RINCE PHILIP** and I saw each other again in Windsor, where he was playing polo in front of the Queen and the Queen Mother. I enjoyed his polo but was amused to observe that whenever he didn't manage to hit the ball, Prince Philip uttered an extremely unprincely "Fuck it!" Whereupon Queen Elizabeth looked highly shocked but the Queen Mother appeared to love it.

I didn't meet the Queen herself that time in Windsor. But when the Queen and Prince Philip came to California on a three-day visit, through my friendship with Nancy and Ronald Reagan, I participated in various events during the visit. On the first day, Nancy Reagan gave a big party for the Queen and Prince Philip at the 20th Century Fox studios and phoned me, her voice full of panic, saying, "Zsa Zsa, for God's sake, you've got to help me." So, although I had a terrible cold, I dressed myself in a black Jean Louis dress and dragged myself to the party.

Finally, I was introduced to the Queen. She was dressed in a white organza dress embroidered with oranges (in honor of California) and I thought she was really lovely; she has the most beautiful skin in the world and the most beautiful blue eyes. I said respectfully that I was very glad to meet her. Then (not being a royalist and unable to curb my innate Hungarian desire for justice), chidingly reminded Prince Philip of our last meeting, telling him, "You really offended me in London, you just shoved me aside." The Prince smiled disarmingly and said, "But Zsa Zsa, I didn't realize it was you."

The ice between us was broken, he was sweet and friendly and we started chatting animatedly about animals. Suddenly, in an impatient voice, the Queen interrupted with "What are you two jabbering about?" Remembering London and Philip's calls, I ended the conversation, feeling almost guilty.

The next day, Nancy telephoned me sounding miserable and said, "What shall I do? The Queen and Prince Philip are coming to my little ranch and it is raining." Nancy had recently visited Buckingham Palace and seemed to be feeling a certain amount of discomfort. I don't know what happened during her lunch with the Queen, but I do know that on the same day when I was voted Woman of the Year of the City of Hope, the Queen had attended. It was raining hard, we could hardly walk, but the Queen still looked serene, protected by a blue umbrella.

On the third and final day of her California visit, the Queen invited the Reagans on to the royal yacht *Britannia*. Afterward, Nancy confided, "I've never seen so much jewelry in my life! The Queen wore all her diamonds and I felt like a poor relative!"

I first met Nancy and Ronald Reagan when I was campaigning for President Nixon's second term. I always admired and supported Nixon and, even after Watergate, still do. In fact, *during* Watergate, I went on the *Merv Griffin Show*, then being taped at Caesar's Palace in Las Vegas, and proclaimed, "Nixon was one of the greatest presidents of modern times. He opened Russia and China for us. Why don't you give the guy a break?" And although the audience booed me—I didn't care. I believe that loyalty is one of the most important qualities a human being can possess and, looking back, am proud that I have always remained loyal to Richard Nixon.

I campaigned for him with all my heart. I toured the country with Jimmy Stewart and John Wayne—all three of us campaigning so rigorously that by the time we got to Dallas, Texas, I had finally lost my voice. Whereupon John Wayne, with a twinkle in his eye, declared, "Thank God. Now maybe I'll get a chance to talk."

One time, I was with the Reagans and Nelson Rockefeller during the campaign and the audience started chanting, "We want Zsa Zsa for President!" At which Rockefeller quipped, "Well, now we have elected the President, who is going to be Vice-President?"

After his election, President Nixon sometimes called me. Once, he spent half an hour on the telephone quizzing me on Hungary and Turkey. He seemed especially interested in Burhan's perspective on Turkey and keenly questioned me on confidential state matters Burhan had discussed with me. At the time of my conversation with President Nixon, I had some houseguests. When I hung up the phone, a houseguest nosily asked why I had been on the phone so long. Weighing up the question for a second and then opting for the truth, I came out with the implausible-sounding statement "The President wanted my advice." The houseguest nearly passed out in shock.

SOON I was to make an even closer friend in the Republican Party. President Nixon invited me to attend a state dinner in San Francisco. Proud to be the only actress honored with an invitation, I accepted and flew up for the evening. Nixon was on the dais and I was seated between a German prince (I can't remember which one) and a short man whose name I didn't quite catch when we were introduced. Over dinner, I soon discovered that the short man had a quick, incisive mind and I began to relax and enjoy the conversation.

Inquisitive as always, I asked him, "How much money do you think the President makes?

"He makes exactly $200,000 a year," answered my neighbor.

Scornfully, I said, "I make more than *that*!"

"Yes," said the man, suppressing his laughter, "but think about the fringe benefits."

I immediately revised my impression of him; he was brilliant.

After dinner, I mingled with the other guests and Nixon came over to me, his face radiating curiosity. Drawing me away from the crowds, he inquired, "Well, Zsa Zsa, and how do you like Henry Kissinger?"

"Henry Kissinger?" I replied, puzzled as to why the Secretary of State's name had suddenly been mentioned. "I don't know what I think of him, because we have never met."

The President smiled and said, "But you just spent the entire evening talking to him!"

"*That* was Kissinger?" I asked in wonder.

"Yes. And you looked as if you were going to talk to him all night."

Contrary to the President's expectations, Henry and I did not talk all night. Not, at least, on that night.

THE very next day, President Nixon called and asked me what I thought of Kissinger and then ruminated, "Can Henry really be as smart as I think he is?" I was perplexed, not quite knowing what to say. But everything was clarified when Pat Nixon called, suggesting that I date Henry. I was touched to discover that even though they were the most powerful couple on earth, President and Mrs. Nixon still had time to do a little matchmaking.

Henry and I did go out. He took me to the Bistro Gardens in Beverly Hills and then took me home. I wasn't married at the time, so I didn't protest when he asked if he could come in for a drink. We started talking, then things got more personal, with Henry showing signs of making an amorous approach to me. I don't know what would have happened, had his beeper not suddenly cut into the silence and broken the moment. Nixon wanted him immediately at San Clemente.

Without any hesitation, Henry jumped into his black sedan and roared down my driveway, bound for presidential service—only to get stuck between my electronic gates, then in the process of some kind of malfunction. I was watching his exit on my remote security television, ran down to the gate, and helped Henry out of the car. We managed to pull the gates away from the car, then stood back and examined the damage. The car was badly dented. So, in a way, was Henry. I was surprised, having characterized him as a man who was not particularly enthralled by material things and expected he would have a devil-may-care attitude to a dent in his car. I soon understood his reaction, though, when he declared, "Oh my God, this is President Nixon's car!"

Later, I sent Henry flowers (I like sending men flowers and giving them presents) and ordered a French bouquet in a basket to be delivered to him in Washington. When Henry called to thank me, he said laughingly, "Zsa Zsa, my whole staff looks at me differently since I got flowers from you."

My next contact with Mr. Kissinger came a short while later when I was in Boston, touring in *Blithe Spirit* and Henry made a date with me to fly down and take me out. But on opening night, he called and canceled. A trifle piqued, I asked why. And Henry gave me the reason—a reason that even I (who really like to get what I want when I want it) couldn't quibble with: "I can't fly down because we are invading Cambodia tomorrow. It is a big secret, you are the first person outside the White House who knows about it."

I was flattered that Henry trusted me, disappointed that our meeting had been canceled, but told myself that there would be many other opportunities for Henry and me to see each other. However, it turned out that, for once, my optimism had been misplaced. For as I later explained to my favorite matchmakers—the Nixons—when I was invited to dine with them at "21" in New York, "Henry and I can never seem to arrange to meet. We are both so busy and if it isn't Cambodia, it's something else."

The Nixons were disappointed but sympathetic, Henry went on to get involved with Jill St. John and Liv Ullmann and I resigned myself to the fact that destiny obviously did not intend for Mr. Henry Kissinger and me to have a romance—no matter how much it might please the First Lady and the President of the United States.

I wasn't just loyal to the Nixon administration. I was also a friend and supporter of President Ford's administration as well. On one occasion (when I was not married) I was invited by President and Mrs. Ford for a formal White House dinner. I was seated at the same table as Princess Diane Von Fürstenberg—the fashion designer.

White House protocol dictates that none of the guests begin to eat until the President himself has started eating. On this particular evening, President Ford did not pounce on his food the instant it was served but continued a conversation he had been in the midst of having when the food was served. With an impatience that I considered to be less than admirable, Diane Von Fürstenberg pouted, "Tell the President to start eating because I'm hungry."

During dinner, I sat on the left of the President and the wife of the President of Ireland sat on his right. When Baked Alaska was served for dessert, the President turned to me and said, "Zsa Zsa, move a little away from me because if I drop the dessert into your lap the whole world will hear about it!"

After dinner, I danced with the President and he whispered to me, "If I weren't married the two women I'd want to go to bed with are you and Ann-Margret." I don't know if President Ford had just invented that sentiment to flatter me (although by including Ann-Margret, he didn't really display a dazzling grasp of diplomacy). But I do know that after our umpteenth dance together, Betty Ford (whom I like and admire) intervened, by chidingly saying, "I want to remind you, Mr. President, that there are other guests in the White House, not only Zsa Zsa." The President took the hint and that was the end of our dance. The next day, the *New York Post* splashed a picture of me and the President on the front page with the caption, "Zsa Zsa Gabor and guess who!"

I'VE always been on very good terms with the Reagans and, during their administration, socialized with them a number of times. I visited Nancy and the President in the White House many times. I went to parties at the White House when Nancy gave concerts in which Marvin Hamlisch played his songs and he and Nancy sang them to the President. It was all very romantic.

Nancy is a good person—tough—but to me, Nancy is the most elegant woman in the world. She is divine—a perfectionist who almost succeeds in being perfect. She is a woman who has blinkers on—who is brilliant, determined, sets her heart on something and invariably gets exactly what she wants. She really is the force behind Mr. Reagan—without Nancy, he would never have become president. I like Nancy a great deal but would hate to have her as my enemy. When Donald Regan wrote his tell-all book—I went on the Larry King show and defended Nancy Reagan's belief in astrology (which had, as a result of the book, been criticized) and said, "There is nothing wrong in believing in astrology. Since the beginning of time, great men have been influenced by astrology." I respect and love both the Reagans very much. He is a charming man. He has always been very influenced by President Nixon and during his presidency called him for advice at least twice a month.

NANCY and I share the same hairdresser, Julius, who is half Swedish, half Italian, and a brilliantly creative hairdresser. Nancy used to take Julius everywhere with her. Even when she and President Reagan went to see the Pope. Julius also was in the entourage when the Reagans went to London to see the Queen and, I believe, actually had breakfast with the Queen and Mrs. Reagan in Buckingham Palace.

Both Nancy and I depend on Julius and sometimes poor Julius is torn between the two of us. When I was in New York and doing the David Letterman show, the phone kept ringing in my suite at the Waldorf with calls from Mrs. Reagan's staff imploring, "We need Julius!"

Julius does make himself indispensable. He not only attends to hair but is also a wonderful escort. We attended the opening of *La Cage aux Folles* together in New York. I was wearing a new Bob Mackie dress, very embroidered, and in the middle of the performance, the zipper broke. Within minutes, Julius had taken me backstage to Gene Barry's dressing room and sewed me back into my dress.

Then, last year, I was given the Best Actress Award at the San Sebastian Film Festival, walked down the aisle of the auditorium to collect it, got my heel caught in a rung, and broke my ankle. It turned out that I had torn three ligaments and I had to have a wheelchair. I spent months in a cast and when I flew to Montreal to make a TV show, Julius came with me and pushed me everywhere in a wheelchair. As I said, Julius is indispensable to both of us—to Nancy and to me and to all the ladies in L.A. who love him.

*

*

IN 1988, I rode in an International Horse Show in Washington—riding Silver Fox, my Tennessee walking horse who is the love of my life (more on him later—he is one of the most important elements in my entire existence), and Nancy was there. After the show, she asked me to stand next to her in the receiving line. Afterward, the press unkindly said that I pushed my way next to her—but that is ridiculous. No one can push their way next to the President or the First Lady. I was there because Nancy asked me to be. In the course of the day, Nancy asked, "Zsa Zsa, how can you ride a horse that wild?" Proudly, I told her, "Because I love him so. And, after all, what a glamorous death it would be to die on a white stallion!"

I do like Ronnie and Nancy enormously and I was so touched when, during the police debacle, I was at a dinner with them both and Ronnie held my hand and tried to comfort me.

*

SINCE I first came to America I've been on good terms with a succession of presidents and, for the past thirty years, have been welcome at White House social functions in every administration. With one exception: the Kennedy administration.

It all began in the years between my divorce from Conrad and my marriage to George. One night, in New York at the Stork Club, I met a glamorous up-and-coming young congressman whose name was Jack Kennedy. Jack gravitated toward me naturally that night because I was a blonde and Jack was mesmerized by blondes. He asked me out and I accepted. Later, Jack, who was an intelligent dreamer, blurted out that when he told his friends that he was dating Zsa Zsa Gabor, they had warned him, "Don't get involved with her, Jack. She is a gold digger."

Stung by the unfair criticism, I asked Jack what he had replied. In a voice ringing with conviction, he said, "I told them that if Zsa Zsa were a gold digger, she would own half of Fort Knox by now." Jack had a natural sense of justice, which, to me, was one of the most attractive qualities he possessed.

Jack and I began dating. Throughout our time together, I noticed a number of things about Jack. First, that when people talked to him, he gave the impression of listening but simultaneously had the air of being off in another world. He was never completely in the here and now and always seemed to be thinking about something else.

Jack was also very restless. We would go to the theater together, but after the first act, Jack got bored and insisted we leave and go to "21." When we got there, he only ordered vanilla ice cream and toyed with it while I ate a normal dinner. Perhaps Jack's lack of appetite was due to the fact that his pockets were always packed with Hershey bars and caramel candy, which he told me he loved because the sugar helped him maintain his energy.

Jack definitely did have energy. Sexual energy. Lots of it. Out of bed, Jack radiated sexuality and an insatiable desire to conquer every woman with whom he came into contact. Especially if she was a blonde. Like me. And hundreds of others. From the start, I was aware that Jack was extremely active in terms of his sexual exploits. Which really put me off, because I have always found that a man who sleeps around usually is not a good lover.

Whether Jack Kennedy was or was not a good lover will remain a mystery to me because although we dated for six months, Jack and I never made love. It may seem incredible that Jack Kennedy—who was insatiable, charming, and a consummate seducer, never got beyond what Americans call "first base" with Zsa Zsa Gabor, who loved men of power, charm, and sex appeal. But that is the truth. I was already in love with George. Jack was far too promiscuous for my taste so I never capitulated. And, in a strange way, Jack appeared to like me for it—to like me because he couldn't have me. So nothing came of my relationship with Jack. Instead, I went on to marry George and to become a movie star.

IN 1953, I flew back from London after making *Moulin Rouge* and on the plane sat next to a young photojournalist named Jacqueline Bouvier, who had also just come back from London where she had been covering the coronation of Princess Elizabeth. During the entire seven-hour flight, Jacqueline and I chattered away and she mentioned she was having a romance with some senator. We had a good time together.

Then the plane landed at Idlewild and we walked toward the customs hall together and straight into none other than Jack Kennedy himself. Jack swept me off my feet, kissed me, and said, "It's so good to see you! I love you!" Next to me, Jacqueline stood waiting, so I turned to introduce her to Jack, then stopped myself. Coming out of my jet-lag haze, I put two and two together: The young senator with whom Jacqueline had been involved was Jack Kennedy.

In the meantime, Jack had dashed ahead, picked up my luggage, and was rushing me through customs. In five minutes flat I had unwittingly upstaged Jacqueline, let her know that I had been romantically involved with Jack, and the end result was that Jacqueline and I never spoke again. Nor did I receive a single invitation to the White House during the Kennedy administration.

Not an official one, that is. I got a glimmering of what was about to happen when my former friend "Chaps" DeLessups Morrison, goodwill ambassador to South America, attended a meeting with President Kennedy. In the midst of the meeting, a Marine discreetly handed Chaps a note from the President. Perplexed, but honored (assuming that the note concerned the current meeting), Chap opened the President's communication and read the following words: "Is it true that Zsa Zsa Gabor is so good in the hay?"

When Chap told me what had happened, he didn't tell me his response. Which didn't matter, because I had already mulled over the note and knew exactly what it meant. Even though he was President of America, Jack Kennedy still wanted me.

Soon after, the call came—from a woman close to the President—a woman whom I can't name here, but who was renowned as the woman who made certain arrangements for him. I was asked to come to see the President because "He is dying to see you." And I was told that he would send Air Force One for me. For a second, I was tempted. But not very. So I did not accept the President's invitation.

No—I didn't want to be the other woman in anyone's life—not even the President of the United States—because I've always preferred being a wife and not a mistress. I think that nowadays, I am able to be alone, but I never will be because I always have a string of men waiting to marry me. I love being married and I've never had any trouble in finding men to marry me. In fact, they have always found me.

When I'm interviewed by journalists who ask how a woman can get a man to marry her, I always joke that the best way is to have a big bosom and a small brain. But really, I only mean half of that—the bosom half. I think that although men find thin model girl types very attractive out of bed—because when they walk into a room with a model on their arm every other man is envious—in bed it is quite another story. If a woman wants to be attractive to a man, she should have a little flesh on her body and not just be skin and bones. All the men I ever met in my life, when they look at those models' pictures exclaimed, "My God, how could I ever make love to that?" Rubi used to describe them as "unfuckable."

As for the first part of the statement—although I have often wisecracked that the only place men want depth in a woman is in her décolletage, the truth is that a woman does have to have a brain in order to catch a husband. Now, all of this may sound very unliberated, but even the most liberated feminists still seem to want husbands. Anyway, the way to do it is to be smart—but in an unconventional way. A woman has to judge when it is dumb to be smart and when it is smart to play dumb with the particular man she plans to marry.

If I had to give a woman just two pieces of advice on how to persuade a man to marry her, I would first say this: Remember that what a man really wants is complete worship and adoration for himself and for everything he does. He knows he's perfect but he likes to hear it from you. Believe me.

The second thing is this: A man wants to marry a woman who can be his pal. George used to say that he couldn't have a better companion on a trip than Zsa Zsa. And I think it is vital for a man to feel this—to feel that you are his companion, his pal, his friend, that you are always on his side, by his side, no matter how adventurous the adventure, no matter how tough the times—that you are with him and for him no matter what.

All in all—I love being married. I love the companionship, I love cooking for a man (simple things like chicken soup and my special Dracula's goulash from Hungary), and spending all my time with a man. Of course I love being in love—but it is marriage that really fulfills me. But not in every case. Take the Duke of Alba, for example, the man whom I call husband number eight and a half.

FELIPE DE ALBA and I met at a polo match in Palm Beach and I found him handsome, gallant, and chic. The years passed and the only time I ever thought of Felipe was when the columns reported on his romances with Estée Lauder and the ex-Mrs. Revson. Then, after my divorce from Michael O'Hara, I spent some time in Palm Beach (because I adore polo, have a house at the Palm Beach Polo Club, and also because my wonderful friend and adopted godmother Liz Whitney lived there for part of the year). One day, as I was walking along Worth Avenue (one of the chicest shopping streets in the world), a Rolls-Royce pulled up next to me. At first I didn't recognize the man driving the Rolls, but then he pulled down the window, leaned out, and I saw it was Felipe de Alba.

We chatted for a moment, then went our separate ways. But although Palm Beach is undeniably supersophisticated, in many ways it is still a small town where one just can't avoid meeting the same people over and over. And so it was that Felipe and I kept running into each other at polo matches and parties. Now and again, he would escort me home. I always say that the Rolls is my favorite car because it is the most comfortable car in which to make love—but Felipe and I definitely didn't take advantage of the plush leather backseat (or front seat, for that matter) of his Rolls. He may have been tall, handsome, and eligible, but still emotionally bruised after my divorce from Michael, I didn't intend to encourage another serious suitor. Especially one who didn't seem to have any occupation other than being the boyfriend of wealthy or famous women.

Felipe didn't appear to have much money of his own—and although that never stopped me from being attracted to any man (witness my marriage to George), there was something about Felipe that I didn't quite trust. I am not normally the kind of woman whom anyone can influence. However, there have been one or two exceptions. First—Pamela Mason, James's wife, whom I had always called my guru and who convinced me not to remarry George. Then, of course, my mother, who made me what I am today. And, finally, Liz Whitney, who told me, "Zsa Zsa, Felipe de Alba is just like you; he was educated in Switzerland and speaks six languages fluently. He's a gentleman and you should marry him." Naturally, I didn't instantly rush into Felipe's arms and swear eternal matrimony, but I did respect and admire Liz, so her opinion did play a part in the ridiculous scenario that subsequently unfolded.

*

AT that time, Eva was married to Frank Jameson, vice-president of North American Rockwell, and we were all getting on extremely well. I love Eva, always did, and always will, my whole life. But Eva has always resented that I became an actress. Bundy (my friend the Hungarian writer) once perceptively said, "All her life, Eva wanted to become an actress. Then—overnight—you became a big star." Bundy was right. Since Eva was five, she has prepared to be a star and she really is a very good actress. Whereas I really wanted to be a vet. So when I became an actress by accident, my career came between us.

As a result, our relationship is sometimes a little bit strained because of jealousy and because Eva has never approved of the things I do. I am too wild for Eva, she is very conventional and we have different friends. But although we do fight, I really admire Eva. In a way, we are almost like twins although Eva is two years younger than I am.

I think she was wonderful in *Green Acres*. I also have liked the men she married. After she divorced Dr. Eric

Drimmer, I was responsible for finding her second husband. One day, I was having a sable coat fitted in Beverly Hills when the furrier pointed out a gorgeous Marine and told me that the Marine had asked to meet me. "I can't," I replied. "Because I am Mrs. Conrad Hilton. But I have a sister . . ." I introduced the Marine (whose name was Charles Isaacs) to Eva and they fell in love and got engaged.

I gave the wedding for them in Conrad's house. The only problem was that Conrad walked out on the whole thing, declaring, "I am not staying in my house while my sister-in-law marries a Jew," and left town. I gave the wedding anyway and picked a simple black dress with ermine muff and ermine hat to wear. But just before the ceremony, Eva asked me not to wear the hat and the muff in case I upstaged her. So when we sent Mother the pictures (she was still in Europe at the time) she sent back a letter complaining, "Eva looked gorgeous but Zsa Zsa looked like a poor refugee."

Charles and Eva eventually divorced, and she married Frank Jameson. But Charles still loved Eva and used to have breakfast with George and me because he said I made him happy because I reminded him so much of Eva. Then he died and I went to the funeral. Eva did not as she was filming so she was lucky that I did, because everyone thought I was her. People often do and call me Eva and her Zsa Zsa—which neither of us really appreciates.

So Eva was married to Frank at this time and I flew down to their yacht, *Laura,* then berthed in Puerto Vallarta. John Huston was there too and so was Felipe de Alba. One thing led to another and before I knew it, I was dressed in a salmon-colored velvet floor-length Oscar de la Renta, a twenty-four-piece mariachi band was playing romantic music, and I married Felipe de Alba. It was momentary craziness and everyone knew it. Later, when I called John Huston and told him, "The marriage only lasted a day," he laughed cynically and said, "I didn't give it that long."

Nor, it seemed, did Eva's husband, Frank. According to the law of the sea, a marriage can be performed by a ship's captain and will be legal, provided that when the ceremony is performed the boat is 12.3 miles out to sea. On that day, the seas were particularly rough—so rough that everyone on the boat had to hold on to ropes, chairs, and railings as their Dom Pérignon splashed out of their champagne glasses. As a result, when we were only eight miles out to sea, Frank Jameson, Eva's husband, fully aware that the marriage would be invalid, told his captain, Peter, to perform the marriage then and there, privately telling Eva, "Perfect. Now the marriage will be exactly as legal as Zsa Zsa wants it to be." Although he was my brother-in-law and not my brother, Frank must have been clever enough to sense my reckless mood and make sure that the flighty step I was about to take was not irrevocable. In short, my marriage to Felipe de Alba was not in the least bit legal. Aside from the mileage technicality, there was also the matter of my divorce from Michael O'Hara. We hadn't yet received the final divorce decree from the state so, in effect, we were still legally married.

In the midst of all the hysteria surrounding my marriage to Felipe, the fact that it wasn't really legal was simmering in the back of my mind as we flew back to California. Felipe and I still hadn't consummated anything, nor had we even really kissed properly, and by the time we landed I had no plans to take things any further. But when we arrived home in Bel Air, a big party was under way celebrating my eighth marriage—the press had been alerted and it just didn't seem the right time to announce that this, my so-called eighth marriage, was really the marriage that never was and never should have been. A few days later, Michael O'Hara obligingly arranged everything. Michael took Felipe to the airport and said good-bye for me.

I never really mind what people say about me—I am far too unconventional and far too dedicated to being true to myself to let other people's disdain or nastiness upset me for long. I know who I am and what I want in life and I don't let anyone's jealousy or bitchiness rattle me for long. But it never ceases to surprise me when strangers with no motive other than jealousy suddenly attack me for no reason.

That seems to have happened with Aileen Mehle—who writes a social column under the byline of "Suzy." My private opinion of Suzy is best summed up by what happened at a party in Estoril thrown by Antenor Patino, the tin king of Bolivia whom I knew from my days with Rubi. It was the most beautiful party in the world, with the dazzling turquoise and coral decor costing Patino an incredible $3 million. I went with Prince Johannes Thurn und Taxis as my escort and we spent part of the evening chatting to Antenor (whose granddaughter was wearing an amazing emerald cross cut out of one entire stone). In the course of our conversation, he pointed to a blonde swathed in pink feathers and wearing sequined false eyelashes and asked, "Tell me, who is that extraordinary-looking American woman?" I told him. Then, when I got back to New York, I read Suzy's column and, to my amusement, discovered that when she had written about the party, she said, "My good friend Antenor Patino"—when Antenor didn't even know who she was.

But back to the Zsa Zsa and Suzy story. From as long ago as I can remember, Suzy has attacked me in her column. I never understood why, until, by chance, I mentioned it to my then boyfriend, Bob Straley, who owned the Athletic Club in Palm Beach. Bob, with an exasperated sigh, explained, "I used to date Suzy but you are a younger and more beautiful version of her and I think she is jealous that I am dating you." Now that the situation had been clarified, the very next time Suzy attacked me in her column, I went on a talk show and countered, "Suzy is only jealous of me because I date her boyfriend."

The next day, Suzy out-vipered herself in her column, bitching, "That Hungarian goulash is too fat." Suzy had launched our feud in earnest and, no matter what I did, I have never been able to make peace with her. On Princess Grace's last trip to America before she died, we met again at a party attended by Suzy. Grace knew about the feud and she came over to me and said (in a sad voice, because Grace, at the time, was very sad), "For God's sake, Zsa Zsa, life is too short. Why don't you make up with Suzy?" So I went over to her and said, "You know, Suzy, I don't really want to fight with you," and held out my hand. Suzy turned and walked away.

*

PEOPLE can be harsh and unfair and dealing with them is often traumatic. Which is one of the many reasons why animals are my entire life. The truth is that I love children and animals more than I love grown people—they are innocent, not jealous, and they show their feelings. I feel secure with animals. I know that if I give them love, I will get it back. With people, you never know. They pretend to love you and then you leave the room and they badmouth you. Animals make me feel secure because they will always love you truly. Animals are honest. They never lie and they love you for what you are, forever. If you earn the love of a man, he can turn on you just as fast. But once you earn an animal's love, he will never turn on you.

To me, every animal is beautiful—it is only human beings who distort themselves by dressing badly. And animals possess a pure and wonderful judgment—a sensitivity that is infallible. Animals know who is a good person and who is a bad person. My dogs help me in deciding who to hire as help, who to trust and who not to trust. When I am interviewing someone for a job, I let the dogs in and if the dogs go to him or her, I know that I am dealing with a good person.

I was born loving and caring for animals. First there was Lady, my German shepherd, my childhood companion. Then there was Mishka, my Scottie dog, whose death in an Ankara street accident was partly instrumental in my leaving Turkey. Then there was Çanum (a Turkish name meaning "my soul"), a little mutt I bought in a Turkish market and gave to my mother. Mother loved Çanum and he was part of the family in Budapest.

Then, when the Russian Communists marched into Budapest during the Second World War, my mother was asleep and Çanum's barking alerted her, waking her. In those years, there was a law that any civilian found with a gun would themselves be shot. And my mother had a gun, hidden in the house. But because Çanum's barking had warned her that the Russians were coming, my mother hid the gun and was completely composed when the Communists entered the house.

Instructing her to get dressed and to leave with them, the leader of the Communists was completely taken aback when my mother imperiously replied, "Young man, I am not going out on the streets of Budapest without my bra or my sable coat." The man allowed her to dress and also agreed to her demand that she find my father first. They did and she and my father were then taken to the police station—from where they phoned Magda, who appealed to the Portuguese ambassador, who arranged for their release. The Portuguese ambassador saved my parents' lives. But so did Çanum by warning my mother by barking. My mother spirited the little dog out of war-torn Europe and took him with her to America.

I love Shih-Tzus. Currently I have four: Zoltan Gabor, Genghis Khan II, Macho Man, and Pasha Effendi. But I will never forget the first Shih-Tzu I ever had, Genghis Khan. I never think about death (I feel as if have lived two or three times before) but when I do die, I hope I will come back as Genghis Khan, my dog. Nobody ever lived a life like he did. He was like the boss of my entire existence. British quarantine laws don't allow dogs into the country—so I forswore all trips to the United Kingdom (except to appear in a play that ran for six months) on account of Genghis Khan because I didn't want to leave him behind. I was so much in love with him that he had his own stationery, his own Christmas cards, and his own birthday card with his picture on it. He was a person to me and when he died of cancer, I was absolutely shattered. I was so hurt that I couldn't even cry. Before his death I had taken him to UCLA every day for six months to get chemotherapy from his doctor, Dr. Gebhard.

I don't just love Shih-Tzus. I love *all* dogs and I am involved in Mercy Crusade in L.A. (a charity set up to save dogs and cats) and Love Unlimited in Palm Beach (a charity that raises money to train and nurture drug-sniffing dogs). But, starting with Fatushka (the horse I used to ride in Ankara) and then Harem, I have also always adored horses. The love of my life right now is my horse, Silver Fox. He gives me more pleasure than any of my husbands ever have. If someone would give me a million dollars for Silver Fox, I wouldn't take it. To me, animals are my family. I could be starving, but I would never sell an animal.

Silver Fox, a white gelding, came into my life—as have many things—as a result of a combination of fate and coincidence. I was in the middle of having a massage when my masseuse, Nancy Spector, appealed to me saying, "Miss Gabor, I desperately need help. A friend of mine needs $5,000 or he will die. He has had a heart attack, has no insurance, and needs the $5,000 for an operation that could save his life. He will sell you his horse for $5,000." That did not seem so much to pay to save a human life, so I agreed.

A few days later, Nancy called me up, told me the man had had his operation and was doing well, and then asked me if I wanted to arrange to get the horse. I arranged for my trainer to pick him up and he said, his voice palpitating with excitement, "Miss Gabor, this horse isn't just any horse. He is Silver Fox!" None the wiser, but realizing that my trainer seemed to be on the verge of ecstasy, I asked, "Who the hell is Silver Fox?" And his answer completely stunned me. "Silver Fox is the world undefeated champion Tennessee walker." I couldn't wait to see the horse. And I fell in love with him. In fact, when the British version of *This Is Your Life* came to California to tape the show, the star of the evening was Silver Fox, who was led onto the stage at the end.

Until Silver Fox, I had only ridden Arabian and English horses and had never in my entire life sat on a Tennessee walker. I ordered a red saddle from my favorite London saddlemaker. But when it arrived, it didn't fit Silver Fox properly and when I tried to mount him, I promptly fell off.

Then I was invited to go to Arizona to ride Silver Fox in one of the biggest American horse shows—The A to Z Horse Show. This time, I had a flat saddle, but I was still scared to death of riding Silver Fox. One of my girlfriends was on hand and gave me a puff of her cigarette (I don't normally smoke or drink), which I didn't realize was marijuana. Suddenly, I wasn't scared anymore. The last thing I heard as Silver Fox trotted into the arena, with me on his back, were the instructions, "Remember to tell Silver Fox to canter." In the midst of the excitement of the show, I got all confused, told myself that cantor is a Jewish priest, and so spent the entire show telling Silver Fox to "rabbi." Miraculously, he understood and we left the arena with the championship ribbon, covered in glory.

Since then, Silver Fox has given me nothing but happiness. In 1984, I was invited to open the Olympics in Los Angeles on Silver Fox. When we rode into the arena at the Santa Anita racetrack, the audience of about thirty thousand yelled, "Silver Fox." Not "Zsa Zsa" but "Silver Fox." My horse Silver Fox was more famous than I am. And I was delighted and proud.

Today, Silver Fox lives on my ranch outside of Los Angeles and I try and go there to ride him almost every day. We are invited to show all over America and usually we walk away with one of the top awards. When I ride him I am happier than at any other time. When I am with Silver Fox, I forget the world.

*

*

*

AFTER my *folie* with the Duke of Alba, I was involved for a time with King Rechad, who wanted to marry me. I toyed with the idea and (although Rechad, who spoke Hungarian, still wanted to marry me even after I had become engaged to Frederick, my present husband) finally I decided against it. My mother, after having sagely pronounced, "Zsa Zsa, you can't start your life with a Turk and end up with a Tunisian," was delighted.

Married or not, I still concentrated on my career, making personal appearances and starring in films like *Up the Front* (with British comedian Frankie Howerd). Although the days of *Bachelor's Haven*—the program that made me a star—are long gone, I work all the time in television—whether it is on a show for Australia (where the audience is very friendly and down-to-earth), a show for England (where the public loves risqué jokes), or an American network TV show.

Johnny Carson and I go back a long way—in every sense of the word. Before Carson took over the *Tonight* show, I appeared many times when Steve Allen and then Jack Paar hosted the program. I remember when Johnny took over, thinking how brilliant he was and believing him when he confidently predicted, "I'm going to have this show forever. They'll have to carry me out on a stretcher."

When I was married to Herbert, I appeared on the show with Marlon Brando. The show was still live in those days, I wore a low-cut pink Oscar de la Renta evening gown rather like a powder puff, and, of course, my diamond earrings and diamond necklace. Marlon was on before me and, watching with Herbert from the green room, I noticed that throughout the whole show, he sipped water incessantly. Then it was my turn. I joined Marlon (now into his umpteenth glass of water) on the set. We started bantering about this and that. Then Marlon leaned forward and leered, "I don't know why Zsa Zsa has to talk so much. With those boobs she really doesn't have to say anything."

Marlon's first comment was fairly acceptable to the American TV audience. His next comment, though, definitely was not. After finishing yet another glass of water, Marlon announced, "Do you know what I want to do with that girl, Johnny? I want to fuck her." Then, turning his attention to me, Brando went on, "Zsa Zsa, a man can only do one thing with you: throw you down and fuck you!"

Pandemonium! For although Brando's expletives had been bleeped three times, his facial expression was such that his meaning was obvious. In the green room, Herbert was electrified, amazingly flattered that his wife should attract the amorous attention of a great star like Brando. But although Herbert was not the least bit perturbed by Marlon's on-camera come-on to me, Mother, watching at home, definitely was.

She phoned me the next day from New York—telling me off as if I were still twelve and had just finished kissing the coal man—reprimanding, "Zsa Zsa, how could you be on television with a truck driver like him!" I tried to pacify her, to explain to Mother that Marlon Brando is one of this century's greatest actors, a legend and a superstar, but Mother refused to be placated. In the end, in exasperation, I blurted out the truth, "Mother, I loved every moment of it."

Fade out (as they say in Hollywood). Two or three years after Marlon and I first met on Johnny's program, I went to my Beverly Hills dentist. In the parking lot, I noticed Marlon, ogling me, his eyes fixed on what he had described as my boobs. Laughingly, I said, "Marlon, look a little higher. This is Zsa Zsa!" A trifle embarrassed, Marlon smiled, then I went off to the dentist, feeling a small amount of regret. I really did—and do—like Marlon Brando and wish I had had an affair with him. The only problem was that I didn't really know whether or not Marlon really was attracted to me. You see, the water he was drinking during our Carson show appearance was, in fact, vodka. I will never agree to make love to a man unless he asks me to when he is sober. And unfortunately, Marlon Brando never did.

I found Marlon Brando attractive. I also greatly admire Australian personality Barry Humphries, who stars in a British television show called *The Dame Edna Experience.* In the show, Barry dresses as a female character he has created, named Dame Edna Everage, who has become one of the most beloved characters in British show business. The format of the show is classic talk show with a twist, in that the interviewer—Dame Edna—is really a man. Barry invited me to London to guest on the show. He rehearsed as a man and was wonderful and sexy. But in the studio, Barry, now transformed into Dame Edna, made a very plausible woman. I was on with feminist Germaine Greer and I admired her very much. Germaine is intelligent and knows what life is all about.

When Barry came to California, I gave a party for him. I am also extremely attracted to his fellow countryman—Paul Hogan of *Crocodile Dundee* fame. In fact, whenever I am on Australian television (I have family over there and I really love Australia), I always make sure to say, "Paul Hogan, wherever you are, I love you!"

I also find Sylvester Stallone attractive because he seems to me to be wild and intelligent—all at the same time, which is an interesting combination. On the other hand, I am not crazy about Warren Beatty. I met him years ago at Chasen's, when Jimmy Woolf introduced us. Warren propositioned me but, although I found him beautiful and full of life, he was far too obvious for me.

As I said before, propositions and love affairs don't excite me nearly as much as marriage and being a wife. Which is why I married my ninth and last husband, Prince Frederick von Anhalt. Our marriage is colorful, volatile, and completely unconventional. And our relationship didn't begin any differently. About seven years ago, a German photographer made an appointment to fly to Bel Air and shoot a layout of me for one of the German magazines. But before he left Germany, he accepted one more assignment—to photograph Prince Frederick von Anhalt. This particular photographer, it seems, was drawn to the controversial and the unconventional because, in his own way, Frederick is as unconventional and controversial as I am.

Put simply, Frederick's story is this: Born in Germany, he was a good friend of Crown Prince Carl Franz von Anhalt. When the Crown Prince died tragically in a car accident about ten years ago, his mother (the Kaiser's daughter-in-law, Princess Marie Auguste von Anhalt) the Princess asked Frederick if she could adopt him as her son. Frederick's mother—who had four sons and felt sorry for the old lady—agreed. But his father never forgave Frederick for giving up his own name. And the Princess's nephew and two nieces caused a lot of trouble over Frederick's adoption. But despite everything, Frederick was now the adopted heir to the throne of Germany (had there been a throne). And in his own country, he was as controversial as I sometimes am in mine.

Anyway, before leaving for California to take pictures of me, the German photographer decided to take pictures of Frederick. When he walked into Frederick's house, he found it filled with pictures of me—Zsa Zsa. Intrigued, he asked if Frederick knew me. And Frederick, his voice exuding certainty, replied, "No, but I am going to marry her." Amazed at the coincidence, the photographer told Frederick that he was just about to fly to California to photograph me.

Frederick offered the photographer $5,000 if he would agree to introduce him to me and the photographer said yes. When they got to California, the photographer phoned me and I asked him to meet me at a horse show where I was showing Silver Fox. The next day, he arrived with Frederick in tow. At first, I didn't take much notice of him. As I've said before, I am not in the least bit impressed by or interested in titles. But when I saw him playing with my dogs, watched their response to him, watched them wag their tails and love him, I was suddenly very interested in and impressed by Frederick.

As I watched him giving my horse champagne, holding the paper cup so that the horse could drink from it, I think I fell instantly in love with Frederick, with the man I didn't know and whom I knew nothing about. I invited him and the photographer to join me at a party Julius was giving later that day at Los Angeles's chic Le Restaurant. Frederick, who is a reserve naval officer, arrived wearing his formal naval uniform. I thought he looked marvelous. Then one of the guests, an American film producer, on hearing Frederick's German accent, stormed, "Don't put that Nazi next to me!"

I went white with anger. Tony Quayle once said to me that he was betting that I would never accept Cornelius Vanderbilt Whitney's marriage proposal (he had just asked to marry me) because I always married underdogs. At the time, I remember considering Tony's statement; Burhan had been somewhat of an underdog—a Turkish diplomat, yet a rebel. So had Conrad—a Texan hotelier, initially, at the time of our marriage, looked down on by the East Coast establishment. George had been a Hollywood star, but a rebel and an underdog who refused to conform to the system.

Tony had been partly right. I have always sprung to the defense of the underdog and fought on the side of what I believed to be right and fair. The film producer's unfair attack on Frederick only served to make me warm to Frederick even more.

THE next day—and every day afterward—Frederick spent $500 sending me ninety-six roses mixed with orchids. And after that, he seemed to pop up unexpectedly all the time, always nice, sweet, and friendly to me. I went to Munich to take part in *Circus of the Stars* and Frederick and I met there again. Soon, I began to consider him a good and valued friend. Then, one of my female friends jolted me out of my complacency, saying, "Don't you see, this man is madly in love with you?" I began to reevaluate Frederick and the grand gestures he kept making in my direction.

He had rented a Rolls-Royce because he thought it would impress me. He had always lived in the best hotels. And he was always sending me the best flowers and the most eloquent love letters written on the most intricately engraved stationery. He was always around and we spent a great deal of time together.

We also fought a great deal as well. And we also made up a great deal. We started traveling together but we still hadn't made love. The truth is that—strange though it may seem—both Frederick and I are truly shy.

In 1983, he came to Philadelphia with me, where I was appearing in *Forty Carats*. There, I got very upset during one of the rehearsals and asked him to come back to the hotel with me. Once we got there, Frederick came to my room with me. I lay on the bed feeling terribly depressed. Seeing

Frederick about to leave, I motioned for him to stay, indicating that I wanted him to lie on the bed with me. Frederick reacted by saying, "I hope this means you are finally making advances to me and we are going to make love at last."

He was wrong. I never make advances to a man (other than telling George that I was in love with him—which is a verbal rather than a physical advance and, in any case, took place at a cocktail party and not in a bedroom). And I wasn't making advances to Frederick. Nor did I plan to make love to him that night. Which was just as well, because soon after he received the sad news that his adoptive mother—the Crown Princess of Germany—had died. He was now the Crown Prince of Germany. Frederick went pale with anguish and left for Germany immediately. He had been a devoted son to her.

We were apart for a few months while Frederick was in Germany dealing with his adoptive mother's estate. Naturally, the other side of the von Anhalt family was livid that the title had fallen to an outsider—as they considered Frederick—discounting the years of happiness he had given his adoptive mother. And when Frederick wrote to me proposing marriage, one of the other von Anhalts—Eddie—warned me not to marry Frederick, dropping the bombshell that he had already been married four times.

But I loved Frederick and I wanted him and—always the positive thinker—told myself that the other women had probably married Frederick only because they were after his title. When Frederick finally came back to America, there were more revelations in store for me. Telling me that he wanted to begin our life together with totally honesty and communication, he confessed that during the six months he was away from America he had had a love affair with seventeen-year-old girl, Andrea Molnar, who was Miss Hungary. Frederick went on to tell me that Andrea hadn't spoken

German and he hadn't spoken Hungarian—and that he was not in love with her and had kept telling her that he was planning to marry me. Her parents, he added, owned a restaurant on Lake Balaton. I knew I had nothing to complain about really, as Frederick and I had not yet made love. Frederick was reliable, nice, friendly, kind, loved animals, and was a great companion. For a moment, I was struck with the irony: The man I wanted to marry had just had an affair with a woman who came from the same part of Hungary that I had so loved as a child. In the midst of my shock, the artistry and symmetry of the situation still didn't escape me.

But there was more to come. Telling me, "Zsa Zsa—there is going to be a real scandal," Frederick confessed to me that Andrea had just committed suicide. He was upset about her death, but didn't blame himself because he had never promised to marry her. And now the story was about to be blazed all over front pages of newspapers throughout the world, with Frederick portrayed as the villain of the piece. I knew I had two choices: to abandon Frederick or to stand by him. I've always believed in loyalty, I knew it was high time I settled down again because I would never find another man like Frederick. So I decided to forget the past—all of it—and to marry him.

FREDERICK and I got married on August 14, 1986, in a beautiful ceremony at my house in Bel Air. Until then, I had always secretly considered George to be my only true husband. But that changed when I married Frederick. I married him for life, for always. And I don't think that will change because, despite our fights (one of the worst ones was when he was ten minutes late picking me up before the Rose Ball and I was so furious that one of my dogs sensed it and bit Frederick), we are good companions.

Frederick was with me in Mexico when I made the film *Dr. Frankenstein's Wife*. On our honeymoon I had to go to East Germany to make the film *Johann Strauss*. The costumes were beautiful but the director was belligerent and kept yelling at the cast in German, treating them in a way Hollywood actors would never tolerate, insulting them and telling them that only Austrians (he was Austrian and looked just like Kurt Waldheim) know how to make movies. In exasperation, I told him, "Mr. Antel [that was his name], if you treated the actors like this in Hollywood, they would walk out on you." But he didn't take any notice. I was the only actor who could really understand him and, one day, got fed up with the whole thing, announced that I couldn't speak a word of German. From then on, the director was compelled to communicate with me via an interpreter. And he was livid.

During filming in Germany, Frederick and I stayed in one of Hitler's favorite hotels—The Elephant Hotel in Gotha. When we arrived, the manager proudly told me, "Miss Gabor, this will be the biggest honor of your entire life; we are giving you Hitler's suite to sleep in." "Fuck you!" I exploded. "*Sieg Heil*," replied the manager, because he hadn't understood a word that I was saying. Anyway, Frederick and I slept in Hitler's bed, as there were no other rooms available and we had no choice. In the morning, an old bedbug crawled out of the mattress that must have been living there since the time of Hitler.

WE went to New York together and stayed at the Plaza. Ivana and Donald Trump heard we were in town and, although Donald and I had never met, he telephoned me and we ended up chatting for nearly an hour. He was very sweet and told me how he loves European girls, how much he likes my kind of woman, and I could tell he was trying to flirt with me but didn't quite know how. He was nice and I had the feeling that he was wonderful. Above all, he wanted to know all about Conrad and said that he admired him so much and had always wanted to be another Conrad Hilton.

After my conversation with Donald, flowers, caviar, and champagne were sent up to our room, courtesy of him and Ivana. Frederick and I were in town for a business meeting at "21" and before leaving we went to see Ivana, whom I had never met before. I was wearing a sable coat, a black silk dress, and diamonds. Ivana wore a black suit with black fur on the hem. The skirt was terribly short and her legs, in pale stockings (if a woman doesn't have good legs, she should never wear a black skirt with pale stockings as that only emphasizes her legs), looked skinny. Her hair was bleached a yellow peroxide (nothing looks cheaper when a woman is very pale, as Ivana is) and was far too backcombed.

Aside from her appearance, Ivana's manners also made a terrible impression on me. I had bought her flowers; she took them and then proceeded to give four of her managers (then in the office) a long sequence of orders. She didn't like the tablecloths so they must be changed. Certain rooms needed new lamps. And so on. I felt that this display was Ivana's attempt to impress me—the ex-wife of Conrad Hilton, who at seventeen had been the owner of the Plaza—with her power. But it had quite the reverse result. When Conrad owned the Plaza, he never showed off but always underplayed his success. That definitely was not Ivana's style. She never stopped talking in a shrill voice that was so grating that it made you want to scream. She had airs and graces, but no manners. Neither Frederick nor I was in the least bit impressed. In some ways, though, I felt slightly sorry for Ivana.

I think that when her marriage went on the rocks and Donald offered her the option of an open marriage, in my opinion, she should have grabbed it. Ivana should have let him play around, should have given him a long leash so that he could have had his fun with the Marla Mapleses, et al., and then come home to her in the end. If Ivana hadn't turned down Donald's original financial offer, she could have sustained his friendship when they were divorced. After all, my husbands (with the exception of Michael O'Hara) all remained my friends even though we were divorced. And, as a result, Conrad's financial advice was invaluable, George nurtured me with his interest and his love, and Herbert Hutner to this day remains a valuable friend.

But back to Frederick (whom I hope will never become one of my ex-husbands). We also have appeared on many talk shows together—although Frederick never says a quarter of what I do. He isn't a very talkative man—which is probably for the best because if he were like me neither of us would ever get to talk. This way, I talk and Frederick either switches off or puts up with it and listens.

For the first two or three years of our marriage we still fought constantly. In despair, I appealed to Mother for help but Mother, being Mother and ever practical, shrugged her shoulders and said, "The whole day you fight like Gypsies. Then at night you make up. What are you complaining about!" I knew that Mother, as always, had a point. Grandmother used to say the same thing about her marriage to Father—and they had three of us!

THERE is, of course, an age difference between Frederick and me. Mother always says that after a certain age a woman should marry a man who is younger than she is—otherwise she will end up nursing an old man. Yes—there is an age difference between me and Frederick, but what exactly that age difference is completely escapes me. Some people are dyslexic and can't read. I am dysageic. I have no concept whatsoever of age, numbers, or of getting old. I believe that the minute a woman starts to be afraid of getting old, that is when she will start to *get* old. I never think about it. If anything, I think of myself as being the same age as when I was twenty-one. I think of myself as being twenty-one. As far as I am concerned, age does not exist. I know twenty-year-old girls who are older than me. I believe that time doesn't age people. People age themselves. I just don't think about age at all. If I see a gorgeous man I want, he can be a hundred and I am not deterred. To me he is gorgeous, no matter what his age. And as for me, even when I do get to hundred, no one will know it. Nor will I. I forgot my age. It isn't an issue for me, nor has it ever been an issue in my marriage to Frederick.

Frederick owns a champagne business in France (which doesn't help me, as I hardly ever drink) and he is sometimes away from me. During those times, I miss him and long for him to be back with me. But when we are together, we don't really go out much. In a way, my social life with Frederick is not much different from my social life with George. Frederick and I are not late-night people (we think small talk is a waste of time). We are always the first to leave every party and although some hosts think we are rude, we still do it. Both of us believe in being true to ourselves—which sometimes causes conflict. I love dancing but Frederick hates it—and there is nothing that I can do to change his mind. Frederick is a tough guy and I respect that in him. I need a tough man to dominate me, otherwise I'll end up walking all over him and having contempt for him because he lets me. We think alike and we really do love each other, so I truly believe that our marriage will last forever, with God's help!

FREDERICK and I may well have lived happily ever after—had it not been for my encounter with a certain Beverly Hills policeman named Paul Kramer, which has cast a shadow over our lives that is only now beginning to lift.

What happened to me with the policeman could happen to anyone. I don't think that because I am a star I am above the law and am invulnerable. If I do something wrong and, as a result, someone treats me badly, I am intelligent enough and educated enough to say that I am wrong. I don't think that because I am Zsa Zsa I can do anything I want. Quite the reverse.

What happened between me and the policeman was a terrible misunderstanding. A malevolent chance must have put me on that part of La Cienega on that particular day in June. That morning, I was happy and put on a beautiful new black dress with red and purple roses on it (that I had bought in Rome where Frederick and I had just been, as I had made a TV show there for the Ryan Company in French, German, Hungarian, and English). The dress had a big black rose on it and I also wore a diamond brooch. I drove myself in the Rolls to Le Dôme, where I had luncheon with a girlfriend. After the luncheon, I drove along La Cienega, thinking about how beautiful the day was, when out of the blue, this policeman roared up to the car (rather like a bat out of hell) and demanded that I stop.

Surprised, I looked up at him and saw that he was a Tom Selleck look-alike. I find Tom Selleck very attractive—he is just the kind of macho, dominant type of man I love. And the policeman was just like Selleck so I smiled at him. He scowled back at me and growled, "Your license plate is expired." Amazed, I told him that it couldn't have. Car registration for British cars like the Rolls-Royce is very expensive in California and I hadn't forgotten the $1,000 license fee that I had paid in January. I told the policeman, adding that if I had made a mistake, I would be glad to pay a fine but would he please let me go, as I was late for a doctor's appointment.

Instead, he radioed to his headquarters and it seemed to be taking forever. Finally, I asked again if I could leave.

His response was short and simple: "Fuck off."

In England (where I spend a lot of time) "Fuck off" is another, less elegant way of saying, "Please leave." So I left. But as I started to drive away, the policeman stopped me and started to yank me out of my car, yelling, "You fuck, get out of the car."

"Officer, you're hurting me." In response, he said, "Who the fuck do you think you are?" Then, as if to answer his own question, he said, "Now I'm going to break your fucking arm."

It was a nightmare. I was petrified. I knew he had a gun in his holster and I could feel his hatred directed at me. For a moment, it flashed through my mind that this man, this macho peasant, was about to shoot me. And I said to myself,

Is it possible, Zsa Zsa Gabor, that after everything you have been through—Turkey, Baghdad, Hungary—this Beverly Hills policeman is going to kill you?

I was afraid for my life. Only once before—in Hungary—had I been in conflict with the law, with a big Hungarian guard on the border who refused to let me take the only legacy my father had left me, a painting, out of the country. But this man—this Paul Kramer—this representative of America, the country of democracy that I had grown to love so much—frightened me far more than that Hungarian Communist. For the Communist was intelligent. He knew that I was right and that no matter how powerful his position, no matter how forceful his might and his gun, I was in the right. Paul Kramer, however, did not, at that moment, seem interested in the concept of right.

He was hurting my wrist tremendously. More important still, perhaps, he was damaging my dignity—which I have always prized dearly. At that point—Kramer says—I attempted the slap—a slap that would echo around the world. I did, indeed, make some kind of a defiant gesture, but in my terrified state, I was never sure what exactly that gesture was. I only know that Mr. Kramer is about six foot four, I am five foot five, he had a gun, I was unarmed. The possibility that I could have mustered up the courage and had the ability to slap him is, in my opinion, extremely remote.

The next thing I knew, Kramer pulled my hands behind my back and bent me over the trunk of the car. He slapped handcuffs on me and while I was bent over the car, I felt him kick me on my thigh. Then Kramer made me crouch down on the sidewalk in the sun. I was in handcuffs, my skirt had ridden up my thighs, my diamond brooch was on the ground, and I was surrounded by crowds of onlookers, sweating in the sweltering California heat. I was so hot I thought I'd have a heart attack and told him so. He said to me, "I hope you get a fucking heart attack; then I'll call the fucking paramedics." Imagine! A woman in the crowd cried, "What are you doing to my little Zsa Zsa?" but Kramer did not respond.

I kept screaming for help, while Kramer pulled everything out of the car. Three policemen arrived on the scene but none of them helped me. Finally, another officer pushed me into a squad car and out of Kramer's range. At the police station, I was greeted by a policewoman who told me, "I'm not taking your jewelry. I don't want to be responsible for that." I don't know if my Kramer-created reputation had preceded me and she was trying to provoke me. In any event, all I did was agree.

At the police station a Mexican policeman fingerprinted me (and said, "*Bonita Señora,* this can only happen in Beverly Hills to a beautiful lady like you") and took what he described as a "mug shot." By now, away from Mr. Kramer, the events were beginning to sink in and when the picture was taken, I was even able to crack a joke that I didn't care much for the lighting. Eventually my wonderful doctor, Deborah Judelson, picked me up and took me home.

MY case received worldwide publicity and so did my seventy-two-hour prison sentence. Some people have said that I milked the case for publicity but that isn't true. I didn't ask Paul Kramer to stop me. I didn't ask him to handcuff me, insult me, and then have me dragged to the police station. I would have much rather spent the day as planned and gone on to my ranch and ridden Silver Fox. I may not be seventeen anymore—nor am I as old as my enemies insinuate—but either way, I could have thought of less taxing and more enjoyable things to do than being arrested in broad daylight in the middle of Beverly Hills and being hauled away like some bank robber to the police station.

I have never needed publicity nor have I ever sought it. As I said before—publicity has always sought me. The judge—much against my will—allowed TV cameras and lights in the courtroom. He wanted the lights, the cameras—not me. I have had quite enough cameras and lights in my life and if I needed any more, I wouldn't go to the trouble, expense, and heartache of enduring a court case in order to attract them. I would just make another movie or appear on another talk show.

THE Kramer incident has brought me nothing but disaster. First, emotionally. My mother was so upset about the case that she fell and broke her hip—a dangerous thing at her age. Frederick was crushed by the whole case. And I was deeply disappointed in American justice. By now, I consider myself as being far more American than Hungarian. I live in America only because I love it. I don't need to live in America, because I speak many languages and could work all over the world. I live in America because I have always believed America was the land of the free and the land of laughter. All those years ago, in Nazi Europe, we all dreamed of America as being the land of justice and the land of freedom. And I was hurt and disillusioned that, in my case, I felt there had been no justice.

I hated every minute of the trial and all the events that preceded it. In fact, if a producer had sent me a script involving a scene in which a big, bullying, macho policeman raged at me, called me names, cursed and handcuffed me, I would probably have turned it down as being too distasteful.

I spent the weekend of July 27, 1990, in jail after having paid the princely sum of $85 a night for the privilege of being incarcerated in the El Segundo City Jail—a seventeen-bed facility outside of L.A. My jail sentence lasted exactly seventy-two hours and, looking back, those hours were among the most frightening of my entire life. I tried, as always, to be positive even when the authorities asked me to wear a red shirt with the words *Trustee* on the front and *Trustee Big* on the back. I took with me a little white leather bag that I bought for $1,200 in London—packing it with a nightgown, T-shirts, and a large mirror.

Frederick and my lawyer, Harrison Bull, accompanied me to the jail and when we arrived I realized that we had made a terrible mistake in deciding that I should serve my sentence over a weekend and not during the week. All the head jailers were away and I was left to the tender mercies of the second-string jailers—jailers who, I told myself, would probably want to prove their power by being tough with Zsa Zsa Gabor.

When I first was taken down to my eight- by ten-foot cell, Harrison came with me. Which was just as well. I (who have had appalling claustrophobia since the robbery at the Waldorf) took one look at the cell and cried, "I can't stand it, Harrison, I'll die here, I simply can't stand it." Luckily, my pleas did not fall on deaf ears (otherwise I don't know what would have happened) and I was moved to a bigger cell. My heart sank when the heavy door clanged shut, leaving me imprisoned inside the cell. The cell was furnished with four beds, a stainless steel table, four small stools (made for small asses), a stainless steel toilet, and a tiny sink with a faucet I never managed to learn to operate. Instead, I washed my face and body with Evian water—which Frederick had brought for me but which the jailers eventually confiscated. I wasn't allowed a television.

I did have *Town and Country* magazine with me, as well

as a bottle of perfume. So I sprayed the cell with the scent and then settled down to try and read the magazine. But I just couldn't concentrate. Soon dinner arrived—a black hamburger, some soggy mashed potatoes, green beans and carrots (that didn't seem to have been cooked at all), and apple sauce—all scrambled together. I was hungry so I forced the food down. Then—desperately thirsty—I tried to open the faucet, failed, asked one of my jailers for water (she was scornful about my inability to work the faucet), and I ended up waiting four hours for something to drink. Finally, I was given Sanka and hot water. I shrank at the sight of the jailer's gun (which she had in her pocket)—remembering Paul Kramer and the sensation that my very last moments on earth were nigh and I was about to die at the hands of a Beverly Hills policeman.

AT night, huddled on my hard bed (which I had tried to soften by piling two mattresses on top of one another) covered in what appeared to be a horse-hair blanket, I heard the screaming of the man in the cell next door, yelling, "Let me out of here, let me out of here," banging on my door, shouting obscenities. I don't know what happened to that particular man—but I did discover that another man was once found dead in that very same cell next door to me. I must say, though, that one of the policewomen was kind to me and—because she realized how petrified I was—gave me a cup of mint tea to calm me down. Before I finally fell asleep—shivering, as it was freezing in my cell—I thanked God for the sweatshirt my friend Fred Hayman had sent me. Eventually I fell asleep wearing a flannel nightgown, the sweatshirt, and a pair of socks. So much for glamor!

THE next morning, after my first day of prison, I washed myself as best as I could, then smothered my face with my Zsa Zsa cream (which I had smuggled in and hidden under the mattress). No Kleenex were available, so I removed the cream with hard brown toilet paper. Next I was taken to an office to file. To me filing normally means having a manicure—but not this time. I worked from ten to four—with a break when Francesca and Frederick visited. Mother called from Palm Springs and nearly broke my heart by crying. None of her family had ever been in jail and she was so unnerved by the entire episode that she had a bad accident and broke her hip. Eva also called me but didn't visit me. In the meantime, I filed away—after Francesca had written the alphabet down for me on a yellow pad. I didn't mind filing that much, though. I wasn't quite sure what exactly I was filing—it seemed to be something to do with government applications. But I found part of it interesting—especially details of airlines who had applied for permission to fly.

The restaurant Polo Loco sent over chicken, rice, and coleslaw for me, and my jailers unwound and shared the food with me. That was the first and last time that I ate a proper meal during my stay in jail.

THE second night was punctuated by yet more screaming and the cries of two drunken women who had been taken into custody. By the next morning there appeared to have been a change in the regime and a shift in policy; when Francesca and Frederick came to see me I was forced to talk to them from a telephone inside a glass booth. I wasn't allowed close to them or to touch them—as if I had murdered someone or something. Back in my cell the bars were locked and my meals were passed to me between the bars—as if I were violent. I was not a murderer or a drug dealer—yet I was being treated as if I were one. And I had always believed that American women were treated with courtesy and revered and not thrown into jail for minor offenses.

Some of my jailers were nice to me—one gave me a neck massage—but others treated me with gratuitous cruelty, taking my makeup from me and not allowing me to accept the cold cuts and a towel a friend had bought for me. But however the jailers had treated me, nothing would have obliterated my biggest fear—that one of them was a friend of Paul Kramer's and might want to win points with him by staging an "accident" for me. On my very last night in jail, I didn't sleep a wink for fear that someone would kill me and I would never again reawaken.

On the day of my release—aware that the world press was outside, wanting to record the ravages a jail sentence had wrought on me—I improvised my makeup (using a lead pencil) and (because I wasn't allowed electric rollers) put on my cowboy hat to disguise my messed-up hair and walked out into the sunshine to face the press.

As far as I am concerned, my jail sentence was given far too much publicity. I have alternately been painted as a wild, tempestuous Hungarian (which I am) and a petulant Paprika Princess who doesn't give a damn about anyone else but herself (which I am not). Yes, jail was terrifying. I've always had claustrophobia—even more since the robbery at the Waldorf when I was held up in a small elevator by two armed bandits—and to me, being incarcerated in a prison cell surpassed my very worst nightmare. I was petrified far more than I had ever imagined I could be when the man next door to my cell started screaming and yelling.

Prison was, indeed, a terrifying experience. Suddenly,

I was stripped of my clothes, my makeup, and, more important, of my dignity. I was afraid of being shot, afraid of being raped, afraid of being abused. But through it all, I always knew that I would survive. Being in prison was terrible for me, but, no matter how terrible, I knew in my heart that it was only temporary. That soon I'd be free. That outside Frederick and Francesca were waiting for me. That I'd soon be home in Bel Air, swimming in my pool and playing with my dogs. So how could I not survive? And how could I not, ultimately, laugh at myself and the whole experience?

All my life, I have been a positive thinker, in the dark years of the war when I was separated from my parents, in the frightening times when Conrad had me committed, when my house burned and my dog Ranger died, and in the sad times when George killed himself, I have always been able to survive by telling myself that no matter how bad things are, they will one day be better. And that out of every event—no matter how tragic—one can always find a way to survive and even, perhaps, to be a little bit happy.

The policeman fiasco was no different. I was, indeed, able to wrest some happiness out of all the laughable drama and unpleasantness of the whole thing. That happiness wasn't just happiness that I received—but happiness I was able to give.

AT first, the judge sentenced me to some sort of a psychiatric evaluation. Years ago, I went to a psychiatrist during one of my depressions. I went to his office and paid for ten sessions at $150 a time. Then I walked into the room. The psychiatrist looked at his watch. I looked at my watch. He sat down. I sat down. I never said a word. Nor did he. He didn't ask me a thing and I didn't say a thing. Nine sessions went by in the same vein. Then, on the tenth, the psychiatrist started talking to me. And what he said was this: "I am thinking of getting a divorce and I'd love to have your advice." That was the end of my experience with psychiatrists.

MY sentence included 150 hours of community service at a shelter for homeless mothers and children in Los Angeles. When one is sentenced, that sentence is supposed to represent punishment, but the judge obviously knew nothing whatsoever about me (other than diamonds and "dahlinks"), otherwise he would have known that helping poor women and children would not be a punishment to me. Nor is doing charity work. I have worked for charity throughout my entire career and have over seventy awards from charitable organizations ranging from the Shriners' Hospital for Crippled Children to the City of Hope to the United Jewish Welfare Fund, the United Cerebral Palsy and the Veterans of Foreign Wars of the United States national convention, whose National Ladies Auxiliary presented me with their Patriotic Builder Award.

Just because I am a movie star, it doesn't mean that I am impervious to those in need. I may be a movie star, but I am also down-to-earth. I do the gardening myself at five in the morning, make food for my dogs, sometimes order clothes from mail-order catalogues, and don't have any airs and graces. I never think about myself as being a star. And I did not need a judge to force me to do charitable work—I have always done it of my own volition.

When I got to the shelter, I was greeted by a little African American boy who lisped, "We never saw a movie star before." But he soon stopped looking at me as if I were a creature from outer space, when I started playing with him and he realized that I was just another person who wanted to make him happy.

I liked the women at the shelter and discovered that many of them were there because they had had problems with men. We talked a great deal and I did my best to convey the message (which I believe in) that a man is never the answer. The answer is only within oneself. I tried to tell them never to despair. To believe that all problems—if they involve a husband, a lover, money, weight, appearance—everything—can be solved if you don't give up hope. I tried to teach them to believe in themselves and in the possibilities of life. I didn't talk to those women in the voice of a movie star, but as one human being to another. I hope that I helped them. After it was over I gave a fundraiser for them at the Beverly Hilton and raised $160,000 for the shelter.

*

*

*

MY work with the homeless made me happy and, I hope, made them happy too. Only the judge didn't seem to be happy. Accusing me of having manipulated the head of the shelter into letting me work fewer hours (which was not true), he decided to sentence me to 160 more hours of community service. I burned at the injustice, not at the sentence.

Before deciding where I was to serve my new sentence, I was interviewed by a social worker. Many people believe that I began working with underprivileged people only because I was sentenced by the court to do so. But that isn't the case. Throughout my career, I have worked for cancer, for crippled and retarded children. So I asked the social worker whether I could spend my sentence working with retarded children. The social worker replied that she strongly recommended that I not work with retarded children because she thought I would be frightened and upset by them. Again, like the judge, she didn't know me. I am frightened by the thought of getting sick, I am frightened by spiders, snakes, and stupid people. But I have never been frightened by poverty (because you can always work) and I have never yet been afraid of people who are ill or helpless.

I had come into contact with retarded children once in Chicago and I loved them. But they broke my heart because they are so love-starved and they can't say what they want, and even if they do, no one has time for them. I told the social worker that I wanted to work for retarded children because they are so helpless and misunderstood and need love so badly. I told her that I wanted to help them with patience and love. In the end, she was convinced and assigned me to a wonderful school—Macbride School—in West Los Angeles.

At the center I saw children who had been raped, abused, drugged, infected with AIDS, unable to walk, talk, or to find anyone to love them. One little boy told me, "I know who you are. You are Jar Jar" and I nearly burst into tears afterward on hearing the story of his tragic past from one of the staff. Another little girl, Annie, was blind and dying of cancer. Some children were in wheelchairs. Others came to me, hugged me, reaching out for love. The judge had forbidden me to bring any presents—a ruling that makes my blood burn—why should he deprive children who have suffered so much? Why is punishing Zsa Zsa Gabor more important than giving abused and sick children presents to make them a littler happier? I could find no answers, only questions that didn't really make sense.

Many of the children were scared. At first, they sat far away from me, then, as I began to teach them a little French song ("Dîtes moi, pourquoi la vie est belle" from *South Pacific*), they began to move closer to me, to hug and kiss me, and to try and pronounce the name "Zsa Zsa." The children were so full of love and of need that I wanted to hug them all and never let them go. Yet I felt helpless myself, because many of them were terminally ill and had no hope of anything. But I did all I could, loved them and cherished every moment I was able to spend with them. I will always love that school and visit my little helpless friends who are so close to my heart.

TODAY, my life is more exciting and fulfilled than ever. I still visit the children at the Macbride School and will always be involved with them. My mother is still an enormously important part of my life. I telephone her almost every day and she calls me with advice. Now and again, though, I also give her advice. It has always been that way. I remember filming in London and Mother calling me on the set and asking, "Zsa Zsa, I am going to the April in Paris ball and I don't know if I should wear my green chiffon gown and emeralds—or the green chiffon gown with rubies." I told her, "Wear the green chiffon dress with the rubies because that is more sexy."

I don't know whether my mother took my advice but I am glad she is still around to ask it and to have lunch with Eva, Magda, and me on Sundays at her favorite restaurant in Palm Springs. We are still so proud of her—even though she does her best to keep us all on our toes and tries to make us compete with each other. For example, I phone up excitedly and say, "Mother, I have got a wonderful new part in a movie." And instead of just saying, "Great," Mother's answer will invariably be something like "Great. But did you hear that Eva got a part in . . . ?" Mother doesn't react that way because she doesn't love us, but because she believes that competing with one another will only make us better. That is how she has made us world famous.

We all compete for Mother's love and admire her tremendously. Mother has terrific allure. If she serves hamburger, she serves it as if it were caviar. She is very, very big style. And she doesn't know the meaning of the word *defeat.* For example, not only did she recently break her hip, but Edmund de Szigethy, her husband for over thirty years, suddenly died in a car accident around the same time. Edmund loved Mother with a grand passion. They met in 1956 when she went to visit a Hungarian refugee camp in New Jersey. When Edmund left the camp, he had only $100, spent every penny on buying a hundred red roses for Mother, and had been devoted to her ever since. So Mother suffered a tragic loss when Edmund died, but she still has remained bright, cheerful, and endearingly vain.

AND as for Eva—since her divorce from Frank Jameson, she has been happily involved with Merv Griffin and has a marvelous life with him. I like Merv a great deal, did hundreds of shows with him, and am glad that Eva is now so happy. We all see each other in Palm Springs, when we go to Mother, and we often get together in California, where we both live.

Eva and I are very different but are still close. She did disappoint me, though, after the police incident when she didn't come to court once. All my friends came to support me, but not Eva. She just said, "Mrs. Kirk Douglas and I just had lunch and we agreed that if you hadn't talked so much, this stupid thing would never have happened." She may have been right, but I didn't need to hear that at that particular time. But I forgave her because I love Eva and she loves me and if anything happened to me she would die and if anything happened to her I would die. And we both feel the same way about Magda, whom we love very very much.

Francesca lives close by to me, and, as I wrote before, is writing her own autobiography. She is very talented in everything she does, is a talented comedienne and horsewoman, and I am very very proud of her. We see each other often and at special events (like the party I threw for Macho Man's birthday recently, complete with party hats and a doggie cake) Francesca takes marvelous pictures to commemorate the occasion. She is an extremely good photographer and has made a career of it.

As for my own career: As I am writing this, I have just completed my eighth Las Vegas appearance, at Las Vegas World. I played to standing room only every night, outsold even Sinatra and Julio Iglesias on New Year's Eve and even though a live show is usually stressful and nerve-racking, loved every minute of it.

Next I am going to Europe for another, even more exciting reason. Frederick has now claimed his inheritance and we are now the proud inhabitants of Ballenstedt Castle, in Ballenstedt, of the Hunting Castle and Roehrkopf Castle. All those castles are in East Germany and used to be the homes of Frederick's adopted mother, Princess Marie Auguste von Anhalt. After the war, the Princess had fled East Germany and the castles were confiscated by the government. But now, with the end of the Berlin Wall and the advent of a free Europe, Frederick was able to move into the castles—as is his right as the Prince von Anhalt.

We plan to turn a fourth castle—Moosykau Castle—into a museum and display the family's collection of over two hundred paintings and antiques for the public to enjoy. We will hold charity events there for the benefit of the East German people. And as Ballenstedt Castle (dating back to 1170) stands on 50,000 acres, Frederick is planning to turn the castle into a hotel amid a park with a lake and a theater. And most important of all, the castle will have a park in which animals can wander, wild and free.

FREDERICK is so thrilled about the castles and using them for the benefit of the people—that he celebrated by buying me a bracelet that used to belong to Catherine the Great of Russia and has also commissioned a $350,000 diamond and emerald tiara specially for me.

The tiara and the castle all belong to the Princess von Anhalt. However, to myself, I still remain Zsa Zsa Gabor, with my feet planted very firmly on the ground. I may be a princess, but my life really hasn't changed. I get up at five every morning, swim (in the nude) for half an hour, then fix a breakfast of chicken, rice, and vitamins (which I cook myself) for my dogs. Next, Frederick and I have coffee (I drink at least twenty cups of coffee a day—I know I shouldn't but I've been doing it all my life and can't break the habit).

Then I have a bubble bath and go through my makeup routine (which I wrote about before). I wash my hair every other day and have a manicure when I need it—usually with flesh-toned or clear polish. Then I have a breakfast of toast, grapefruit, and another cup of coffee. Often, I cook lunch for both of us. We eat a great deal of chicken and turkey. I like steamed vegetables and fish and omelets that I make myself out of egg white. I am very rarely tempted by desserts as I don't have a sweet tooth.

Generally Frederick and I prefer to eat at home. Our happiest times are spent at home together, talking about the day and playing with our animals or riding on the ranch. I love the fresh clean air out there and the beauty of the natural world. I particularly love flowers. In fact, Francesca always says that in one of my past lives I must have been a florist. I adore arranging flowers—my favorites are long-stemmed pink roses and white lilacs.

But back to our routine: Neither of us likes going to bed late and I often go to sleep before ten. Despite all the coffee I drink (even late at night—I sleep with coffee by my bed in case I wake up and want some) I still sleep well without pills. I hate pills of any description—all I take is vitamin C and an aspirin per day to prevent heart attacks (perhaps that is what saved me from Mr. Kramer). I sleep four hours a night, but I catnap during the day and seem to be able to sleep whenever and wherever I want. When I sleep, I do dream, but I am not sure whether I dream in Hungarian or English.

All in all, Frederick and I prefer the quiet life to all the Hollywood hoopla. Frederick and I sometimes do enjoy going for lunch to the Friars Club (they roasted me after the policeman incident) where the atmosphere is friendly and casual. Basically, I am casual myself, except when I am performing and I have to live up to what the world expects of Zsa Zsa.

WHEN I have to be Zsa Zsa for a professional engagement, I first consult the diary I keep, which lists what I wore to each show (so that I don't duplicate the same dress on the same show). Most of my clothes are designer clothes, but on a recent *Geraldo* show I wore a mail-order dress that looked fantastic. One of my favorite designers is Oscar de la Renta. His clothes flatter me. So does the color white. I also like wearing low-cut dresses, as they are sexy. I love wearing diamond earrings, because they make the eyes sparkle, but I am not afraid to mix real diamonds with fun fake jewelry.

Whatever I am doing, be it formal or casual, I always wear perfume, sometimes two or three different perfumes at once. Often, when I apply perfume, I think back to my childhood and remember how Mother used to be angry because Father had used some of her French perfume and I laugh nostalgically, half wishing for the years to come back, for my childhood to return and reclaim me. To wake up and find myself in Budapest, with my dog Lady, with my parents, engulfed in their love. Instead, here I am, a lifetime away, in another country, thousands of miles away from the home of my birth. No longer Sari, but Zsa Zsa. No longer Hungarian, but American. No longer a little girl who kissed the man who delivered the coal, but a movie star and a princess.

Sometimes I look back and I wonder how the whole thing happened. How I became who I have become. How I managed to live so many lifetimes, to love and be loved by so many men, to survive so many adventures. Yet still be myself. Yet still be Zsa Zsa. Once upon a time, when I was twelve years old, once upon a time, in the days that will never come back again, I was, indeed, a little girl who kissed the coalman and whose mother said, "This child will come to no good." When I look back on it all, I hope and pray that I have proved my mother wrong. In my heart, I believe I have. Not because I am a movie star and a princess, but because I have tried to live my life—this one lifetime—with love.